Let Her Finish
Voices from the Data Platform

Authors:
Melody Zacharias
Rie Irish
Cathrine Wilhelmsen
Jen McCown
Kathi Kellenberger
Meagan Longoria
Mindy Curnutt

PUBLISHED BY
MVPDays Publishing
http://www.mvpdays.com

Copyright © 2017 by MVPDays Publishing
All rights reserved. No part of this lab manual may be reproduced or transmitted in any form or by any means without the prior written permission of the publisher.
ISBN: 978-1973811763

Warning and Disclaimer

Every effort has been made to make this book as complete and as accurate as possible, but no warranty of fitness is implied. The information provided is on an "as is" basis. The authors and the publisher shall have neither liability nor responsibility to any person or entity with respect to any loss or damages arising from the information contained in this book.

Feedback Information

We'd like to hear from you! If you have any comments about how we could improve the quality of this book, please don't hesitate to contact us by visiting www.mvpdays.com or sending an email to feedback@mvpdays.com.

Foreword

By: Kevin Klein

The fact that gender relations have progressed to the point in our society where we coin new terms for specific types of bad behavior is telling. Take, for example, the term "mansplaining". This occurs when a man explains condescendingly to someone (especially a woman) about something he has incomplete knowledge of, with the mistaken assumption that he knows more about it than the person to whom he is talking. For example, at a dinner party, a man with a career in sales tries to explain the nuances of a particular accounting deduction he heard about from a friend without ever allowing the woman he's speaking with to mention that she is a Certified Public Accountant and a partner in an auditing firm. It is real and it happens, a lot. Every woman I know, from high school age upwards, can point out at least a half-dozen times this has happened to her – in the last week!

Yet if you look up this word not on https://www.merriam-webster.com but on https://www.urbandictionary.com, you will have to go THREE FULL PAGES deep into the search to find valid definitions that are not explicitly anti-Feminist or fully misogynist. Clearly, women have given name to a real issue that many men have when communicating with women. Clearly, some men are overreacting to the invention and use of this term. The entire dynamic of a word like "mansplaining" is emblematic of a deeper struggle woman in modern Western society face and goes to the heart of the matter for those of us who are actively encouraging and support women in technology.

Looking back over my own three-decade career in IT, I have seen such offensive behaviors repeatedly and occasionally much worse. I consider myself lucky that my first professional IT boss-employee relationship was horrible. The experiences that came out of that relationship greatly enriched my understanding of bad behavior and opened my eyes to how commonplace it was. I had an abysmal boss in that first professional job, a real bully. He was a chauvinist and a bigot to anyone he perceived as less powerful than he was. He was straight out of central casting for someone trying to create a workplace training film on how not to behave.

In contrast, the next four bosses I reported to were all women. Each of those relationships and the jobs I was performing were an order of magnitude more enjoyable and productive. But what was so different about them? The first images that I recall in my relationships with Liz, Pat, Beverly, and Joanne was that whenever I brought them a problem or issue, they listened until I was finished speaking. (Goes directly to the title of this book, doesn't it?)

By: Kevin Klein

Often, they would pause for a moment or summarize with a paraphrase of what I had said to them. Then, the discussion would begin. Sometimes the resolution was what I hoped for. Sometimes it was a resolution I didn't want, for example, putting in a lot more hours to fix a problem in the code. But even now, remembering those meetings engenders a warm and positive feeling for me because I knew that I was welcomed and heard. In the same way, I noticed it was extremely important to everyone, not just women, that they are allowed to fully express what's on their mind. Interrupt the dialog and you don't just limit the information flowing between two people, you might even damage the relationship.

In contrast, most men I know have brains which are devoted primarily to perceiving and solving problems, first and foremost, while taking the human being into account secondarily. Men intrinsically derive their self-worth from their ability to fix that which is broken. This way of interpreting the world works fairly well for IT professions, since so much of what we do is about discerning the signal from all of the noise and, more often than not, has a troubleshooting and problem-solving component. Conversations even when they are about solving a problem are, only in part, a simple exchange of information. They are also a validation of a relationship and a confirmation of the fibers of a social fabric that binds teams together in many invisible ways.

A second experience I want to recount goes back to the founding of PASS. Our first president was Pam Smith, VP of Systems Integration at Morgan Stanley. Pam was another outstanding model of strong leadership, providing an example that I wanted to emulate. In those early and tenuous days of the organization, Pam consistently put in long hours on behalf of PASS and held frequent meetings with the founding sponsors to keep the organization solvent and functional. One of the things that she said that has stayed with me all of these years was "For communications, men tend to report information while women tend towards rapport. Both sides need to move closer to the other's expectation to have a successful exchange of ideas".

In a way, Pam was mapping a wider code of acceptable conduct for the PASS board of directors. I think that this sort of deliberate attention to communication styles and not a reliance on unspoken rules was one of the keys to success in those early days. People, by their very nature, default to their internal communication styles. She would also use other techniques, such as explicitly restating the rules of communication. For example, she'd sometime say something along lines of "Hear me out until I get my thoughts out. I'm not sure yet that I even have problem that needs solving". This sort of reset helped the problem-solvers from jumping in prematurely and led the conversation to a satisfying resolution.

Men are so frequently working in male-dominated IT shops that I think they're blind to their own conduct and unaware of their assumptions and biases. In polls on the topic, the most common kind of damaging behavior is simple rudeness, exemplified by men interrupting a woman speaker or language/content that makes women feel unwelcome. But let's go further into the data. I think the most telling statistic that demonstrates men are ignorant of their own damaging behavior is the growing body of data showing that women are much more likely than men to exit the IT industry early or at natural break points, such as after maternity leave, not return to IT. So while the high

By: Kevin Klein

barriers to entry are something we should all combat, it seems even more compelling to overcome the behaviors that are causing women in technology careers to walk away.

With that thought in mind, this volume is another step by the PASS Women in Technology (WIT) leadership to move the conversation forward. Creating institutions that are both durable and responsive to their constituents, such as this professional association, requires deliberate construction and active maintenance. I'm thrilled to see the WIT leadership work so hard to put out what I hope is the first of many such volumes. It provides a safe and welcoming avenue for women to give voice to their thoughts on our technical discipline.

Kevin Kline

Founding board member and PASS President, 2004-2008

Acknowledgements

Acknowledgements

The writing of this book was a collaborative effort taken up by seven very talented IT professionals. All too often, books like this get derailed due to some, but usually most, of the authors getting bogged down by work, life, family, health, or some other unexpected ordeal. So, it needs to be acknowledged that these authors can be relied upon to complete the things they commit to.

Despite their collective talent, this book would not have been possible without the expert advice and guidance from MVPDays Publishing. This book was their idea, and they have guided its progress from the beginning. Dave has provided excellent advice and just the right amount of cajoling to keep us all on track.

Finally, the third leg of this structure is our sponsor. SentryOne has provided the light at the end of the tunnel that gives us all hope that the many hours spent after work (and family), is not all in vain. The avenues for distribution that they are providing was necessary for all of us to justify our efforts.

Thank you to all for your contributions to this book. Without any one of you, this book would not have been possible.

About the Authors

Melody Zacharias – MVP: Data Platform

Melody wears so many hats it is a wonder how she finds time for it all. In addition to finding a little quiet time for her morning coffee, she is an insightful mentor, a sought-after speaker for technology events, a Microsoft MVP, a PASS chapter leader for the Southern Interior of British Columbia, the Regional Mentor for PASS Canada, a PASS Outstanding Volunteer a very successful entrepreneur, and a highly talented IT professional with an international reputation for completing both large and small projects on time.

She is able to do all of these things because she loves what she does. She brings enthusiasm to all that she does and it shows.

You can follow her blog at: sqlmelody.com

You can learn more about the IT services she provides at ClearsightSolutions.ca

You can follow her infrequent Twitter posts at: @SQLMelody

Cathrine Wilhelmsen – MVP: Data Platform

Cathrine loves teaching and sharing knowledge. She works as a consultant, technical architect and developer, focusing on Data Warehouse and Business Intelligence projects. Her core skills are ETL, SSIS, Biml and T-SQL development, but she enjoys everything from programming to data visualization. Outside of work she's active in the SQL Server and PASS communities as a Microsoft Data Platform MVP, BimlHero Certified Expert, speaker, blogger, organizer and chronic volunteer.

Jen McCown – MCM: SQL Server

Jen McCown is CEO of MinionWare, LLC; a Microsoft Certified Master for SQL Server; and an independent consultant. She is Senior Editor at MidnightDBA.com, where she creates training videos, the DBAs at Midnight webshow, blogs, reviews, and podcasts. Jen is a member, volunteer, and speaker in PASS, and the PASS Women in Technology virtual chapter.

Kathi Kellenberger – MVP: Data Platform

Kathi Kellenberger is an independent database consultant and Data Platform MVP. She is the author, co-author, or tech editor of 15 SQL Server books. She loves traveling around the country speaking at SQL and developer events including PASS Summit. Kathi is the co-leader of the Women in Tech Virtual Group at PASS. When she is not busy with work, she loves to spend time with family and friends, sing, and climb the stairs in tall buildings.

Rie Irish – MVP: Data Platform

Rie Irish is a single Mom raising her beautiful, strong-willed daughter in North Georgia. She is currently the Director of Database Management for a payment security firm in Atlanta. Over the last 20 years, she has been a SQL Server DBA in many industries including the non-profit sector, big pharma, federal contracting, eDiscovery and payment processing. She is very involved with the Atlanta MDF User Group, helps plan SQL Saturday Atlanta and is co-leader of the PASS Women in Technology Virtual Group. She is a frequent speaker at SQL Saturdays, tech events and women's conferences. She is a Microsoft MVP in the Data Platform , an Idera Ace and a PASS Outstanding Volunteer.

About the Authors

Mindy Curnutt – MVP:Data Platform

Mindy Curnutt is a 3X Microsoft MVP, Trimble Distinguished Engineer and Idera ACE. She has been actively involved in the SQL Server Community for over a decade, presenting at her local North Texas SQL Server User Group, SQLPASS Summits, as well as numerous SQLSaturdays across North America. For two years, she was a Team Lead for the SQLPASS Summit Abstract Review Process and since 2015 has served as one of the 3 SQLPASS Summit Program Managers. She was a SME for a couple of the SQL 2012 and 2014 Microsoft SQL Server Certification Exams and helped to author the MS Press Book "SQL Server 2014 - Step by Step". She is currently working on a 2nd MS Press book, this time as a named co-author. She mentors others, helping to educate and promote scalable and sustainable SQL Server architecture and design. She is passionate about Data Security, Accessibility, Usability, Scalability and Performance.

You can follow Mindy at her blog, mindycurnutt.com and on Twitter where she's known as @sqlgirl

Meagan Longoria – MVP:Data Platform

Meagan Longoria is a Solution Architect with BlueGranite who lives in Denver, Colorado. She is a Microsoft Data Platform MVP who spends a lot of time thinking about how to use Biml, DAX, and data visualization techniques to make data useful for people. Meagan has over ten years of experience with business intelligence, data warehousing, and reporting. She has presented at PASS Summit, IT/Dev Connections, the Kansas City Developer Conference, and many SQL Saturdays and user group meetings across North America. Meagan is a board member of the Denver SQL Server User Group and an active member of the Mile Hi Power BI User Group.

You can visit her blog at DataSavvy.me or follow her on Twitter at @MMarie.

Editors

Cristal Kawula – MVP

Cristal Kawula is the co-founder of MVPDays Community Roadshow and #MVPHour live Twitter Chat. She was also a member of the Technical Advisory board for a Silicon Valley startup and is the President of TriCon Elite Consulting. Cristal is also a Microsoft MVP, and only the 2nd Woman in the world to receive the prestigious Veeam Vanguard award.

BLOG: http://www.checkyourlogs.net

Twitter: @supercristal1

About the Authors

Dave Kawula - MVP

Dave is a Microsoft Most Valuable Professional (MVP) with over 20 years of experience in the IT industry. His background includes data communications networks within multi-server environments, and he has led architecture teams for virtualization, System Center, Exchange, Active Directory, and Internet gateways. Very active within the Microsoft technical and consulting teams, Dave has provided deep-dive technical knowledge and subject matter expertise on various System Center and operating system topics.

Dave is well-known in the community as an evangelist for Microsoft, 1E, and Veeam technologies. Locating Dave is easy as he speaks at several conferences and sessions each year, including TechEd, Ignite, MVP Days Community Roadshow, and VeeamOn.

As the founder and Managing Principal Consultant at TriCon Elite Consulting, Dave is a leading technology expert for both local customers and large international enterprises, providing optimal guidance and methodologies to achieve and maintain an efficient infrastructure.

BLOG: www.checkyourlogs.net

Twitter: @DaveKawula

Melody Zacharias – MVP

Melody wears so many hats it is a wonder how she finds time for it all. In addition to finding a little quiet time for her morning coffee, she is an insightful mentor, a sought-after speaker for technology events, a Microsoft MVP, a PASS chapter leader for the Southern Interior of British Columbia, the Regional Mentor for PASS Canada, a PASS Outstanding Volunteer a very successful entrepreneur, and a highly talented IT professional with an international reputation for completing both large and small projects on time.

She is able to do all of these things because she loves what she does. She brings enthusiasm to all that she does and it shows.

You can follow her blog at: sqlmelody.com

You can learn more about the IT services she provides at ClearsightSolutions.ca

You can follow her infrequent Twitter posts at: @SQLMelody

Contents

Foreword iii
By: Kevin Klein iii
Acknowledgements vi
About the Authors vii
    Melody Zacharias – MVP: Data Platform vii
    Cathrine Wilhelmsen – MVP: Data Platform viii
    Jen McCown – MCM: SQL Server viii
    Kathi Kellenberger – MVP: Data Platform ix
    Rie Irish – MVP: Data Platform ix
    Mindy Curnutt – MVP:Data Platform x
    Meagan Longoria – MVP:Data Platform xi
    Editors xii
    Cristal Kawula – MVP xii
    Dave Kawula - MVP xiii
    Melody Zacharias – MVP xiv
Contents xv
Chapter 1 20
Azure Data Catalog 20
    What is it? 20
    Getting Started 21
    Register a data Source in Azure Data Catalog 23
    Accessing your Catalog 27
    The dashboard 28
    Tool Bar 31
    Asset Tiles 34
    Details Panel Information pane 37
    Information panel Tabs 40
    Search function Basics 44

Contents

Advanced Search functionality	46
Saved search	47
Tagging	50
Glossary Tags	51
Glossary and tagging	56

Chapter 2 59

Biml for Beginners: Script and Automate SQL Server Integration Services (SSIS) Development 59

Traditional SSIS Development	59
Pain Point 1: Many SSIS Packages	60
Pain Point 2: Frequent Source Changes	60
Pain Point 3: Slow Graphical User Interface	61
Pain Point 4: SSIS .dtsx File Format	61
Have you ever experienced this?	61
What is Biml?	62
Why use Biml?	62
Will Biml solve all your pain points?	63
Solution 1: Many SSIS Packages	63
Solution 2: Frequent Source Changes	63
Solution 3: Slow Graphical User Interface	63
Solution 4: SSIS .dtsx File Format	64
What do you need to start using Biml?	64
BimlExpress	64
BimlOnline	64
BimlStudio	64
How does Biml work?	65
Biml Syntax	65
Biml Syntax Example	66
Biml Syntax Example: Root Element	66
Biml Syntax Example: Collections of Elements	66
Biml Syntax Example: Elements	66
Biml Syntax Example: Attributes	67
Biml Syntax Example: Full vs. Shorthand Syntax	67
Creating your first Biml Project	67
Install BimlExpress	68
Create New SSIS project	70
Add New Biml File	71
Edit the Biml File	72
Check Biml for Errors	73
Generate SSIS Packages	76
Source and Destination Databases	78

Biml Code	80
Biml Code: Connections	81
Biml Code: Packages with Variables	81
Biml Code: Control Flow	83
Biml Code: Data Flow	84
Generated SSIS Package	85
The Magic is in the BimlScript	87
BimlScript Syntax	87
BimlScript Code Blocks	87
BimlScript Syntax Example	88
BimlScript Syntax Example: Import Database Metadata	88
BimlScript Syntax Example: Looping over Tables	89
BimlScript Syntax Example: Replace Static Values with Expressions	89
Preview Expanded Biml	90
Creating all Truncate and Load SSIS Packages	94
Summary	97
What are the next steps?	97
It is your turn to experience this	97

Chapter 3 99

Care and Feeding of a SQL Server 99

Backups	100
Databases and their transaction logs	100
Backup Types	101
How to back up a database	102
Full vs Simple Recovery Model	103
Restoring backups	105
Review	107
Integrity Checks	107
Taking Integrity Checks	108
Recovering from Corruption	109
Review	110
Index Maintenance	111
Prevent Index Fragmentation	113
Defragment Indexes	113
REORGANIZE vs REBUILD	114
Detect Fragmentation	115
Generate and Run Statements	117
Procedure dbo.SimpleIndexMaintenance	118
Review	119
Disk Management	120
Disk Space Information via PowerShell	121
Saving the Data to SQL Server	122

Upgrade Your Solution	123
Review	123
Alerting	124
First: Set up Mail	125
Backup Alerts	125
Integrity Check Alerts	128
Index Maintenance Alerts	130
Disk Management Alerts	131
Review	132
Chapter Review	133

Chapter 4 134

Indexing for Beginners 134

Introduction	134
Dictionaries, Novels, and Textbooks	134
Heaps	136
Clustered Indexes	136
Nonclustered Indexes	143
Covering Indexes	147
Sargability	148
Filtered Indexes	152
Unique Indexes	152
Joining Tables	153
Missing Index Hints	154
Summary	155

Chapter 5 156

Data Visualization in Power BI 156

What Is Data Visualization?	156
Preparation Before We Put Anything on the Report Page	160
Choosing the Right Chart Type	163
Smart Use of Color	168
Alternatives to the Standard Power BI Report	171
Considerations for Users' Preferred Consumption Methods	172
Use What You Got	174
Data Visualization is Iterative	183
Get Creative	189

Chapter 6 192

Creating a Disaster Recovery Plan 192
    Define what's important... before a disaster. 193
    Who are my stakeholders? 193
    What are my critical systems? 194
    RPO & RTO 195
    Document your Physical Structure/Facilities 196
    Define & Document Technology 197
    Define Suppliers, Delivery Services, Contract Technicians 198
    Building a Backup Strategy 199
    Building a Recovery Strategy 200
    Establishing Responsibilities 201
    Build your plan 202
    Test your plan 203
    Define disaster 204
    Publish your plan 206
    Building it out 207
    Plan complete. Get yourself a drink. 209

Chapter 7 210

Using Extended Events to figure out why an Application is slow 210
    Extended Event Session Setup 211
    Long Running Queries 214
    Occasional Slowness 214
    Specific Application Area Slowness 215
    Statements within a Batch 216
    Thousands of Paper Cuts 218
    Common Causes of "Thousands of Paper Cuts" Syndrome 219
    Application Pauses / Latency 224
    Summary 229
    Analogies and Nuggets 230

Sponsors 232

Sentry One 232
    About Us 232

Chapter 1

Azure Data Catalog

By: Melody Zacharias - Microsoft MVP Data Platform

Not to be confused with a "catalogue" which is some form of ancient paper based device, a "catalog" is a collection of metadata. It is a directory of information that describes where a data set, file or database entity is located. Additional information about the data may also be included such as the producer, content, quality, condition, and any other characteristic that may be pertinent. It is a tool that allows an analyst to find the data they need. There may be solutions hidden in your data. A data catalog, at the least, will tell you where to look.

What is it?

In any organization, data is collected and stored across different departments, multiple databases, and in a variety of formats. In banking, for example, the customer information that a bank manager sees isn't the same as what the Finance Department sees. In fact, the bank manager is likely not even aware that a separate and unique data source about their clients even exists. Registering these sources in a catalog allows people to become aware of the existence of data they may find useful.

Suppose you are at the library and you want to hold in your hands a map with information about Hole-in-the-Wall Falls in Oregon. You could look at numerous maps and not find anything. The first map you pick up may be a highway map. If the catalog you are looking at has the map descriptions, it will save you a lot of searching. The catalog may describe the map you are looking for as a topographical map showing hydrology for the state of Oregon, with the map being located at a specific library. Now, instead of travelling from library to library looking through a variety of maps of Oregon, you can focus your attention on tracking down this single map with the information you need. This is what Microsoft did with the Azure Data Catalog, they produced a simplified way to collect meta data and crowd source additional information to annotate it.

Microsoft's Azure Data Catalog ("ADC") is a fully managed service. With ADC, when you register a data source, you can point to the source of that data and ADC will automatically extract the structural metadata. The source of the data does not have to be in the cloud, nor does it have to be moved to the cloud even though the solution is cloud based. Only the meta data collected is stored in ADC.

Once a data source is registered, the information can be used by anyone with access to ADC. Those users can then annotate it with tags, documents, and more to enrich the metadata. ADC allows for crowd sourcing of metadata in order to provide a catalog rich in details. Tags can include, for example, descriptions of how the registered data can be used to find what otherwise might be obscure or unique solutions.

The source of the data is registered in ADC, however, a user cannot connect directly to that data source through the catalog. If the user has access to the underlying data source, then they can view a subset of the data. If they do not have access to the underlaying data, they will not see any data. If the data is such that it shouldn't be freely shared throughout an organization, ADC will allow the registrant to restrict access by defining ownership of the data and authorization requirements for access.

Organizations produce data at an enormous rate. Storage for that data is likely to run the full gamut of places from an individual computer to the cloud, with locations anywhere on the planet. This exponential growth of data and data sources makes a data catalog a very useful enterprise tool for making that data useful and accessible to everyone within the organization. Through the use of ADC, you can actually find that needle in the haystack.

Getting Started

It is my intention to walk you through an introduction to ADC. I will try not to make any assumptions about what you do or do not already know. At times, you may feel I'm putting in too much detail because what I'm saying is obvious to you. At other times, you may be thanking me for including the minutia. This section on ADC is the "101" course and therefore is written for the uninitiated. If you are ahead of the curve, please bear with me as I slowly walk everyone through ADC.

To create a Data Catalog all you need to do is sign up here: https://azure.microsoft.com/en-ca/services/data-catalog/

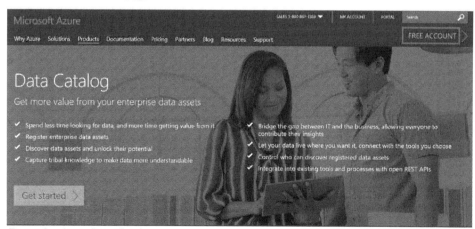

Figure 1 – Azure Data Catalog

The nice thing about this Get started page is that it allows you to get an Azure account as well as start with your Data Catalog, all from one page. If you don't already have your free Azure account, click the *FREE ACCOUNT* button in the top right to sign up.

Once you have your Azure account, choose *Get Started* and sign in (if you have not already). One of the keys to remember with Data Catalog is that the Azure account you use must be a corporate or student account and you must be the owner or co-owner of the subscription. I will get into more details on this when we get to administration of ADC.

Once you click Get started, you only need to tweak a few settings to complete the creation of your first Data Catalog.

You will need to create a name for your Catalog. Here I have called mine DemoCatalog. If you are signed in, the Subscription will auto fill for you. You only need to change it if you have multiple subscriptions and would like to use a different one. The Catalog Location is also defaulted but you should ensure it is pointed to the location nearest to you, and change it if it isn't.

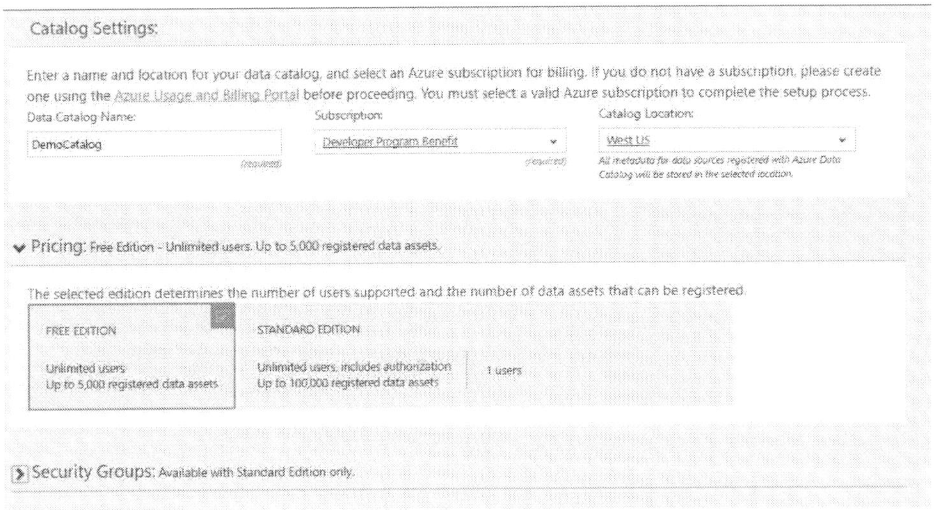

Figure 2 – Catalog Settings

Figure 3 – Creating your first Catalog

You will notice that here I have chosen the Free Edition option. I will cover the functions available in the Standard Edition towards the end of this chapter.

My User name and Administrator designation automatically default to the account I am logged in with. Once you have made your choices and click **Create Catalog** it will only take a few minutes to process and you will have created your first Data Catalog!

Register a data Source in Azure Data Catalog

Having a data catalog with zero data in it is like having a book with all blank pages – meaningless. To give it some meaning and a place to build from, the first thing that ADC will want you to do is to register your first data source. The registration app needs to be resident on your computer, so, ADC will start by asking you to install the app. This allows the registration app easy access to both on premise and cloud data sources

From the ADC home screen, choose Publish from the menu in the top right and then choose Launch Application. You can choose to create a manual Entry, an option if you do not want to download the application. This is a much longer method and will require you to enter much of the detail the application will collect for you. It limits the bulk load abilities as well so only use it if you have a specific requirement.

ADC will prompt you to download the registration application program to your local drive. You will see the following install screen which you are all familiar with:

Chapter 1   Azure Data Catalog

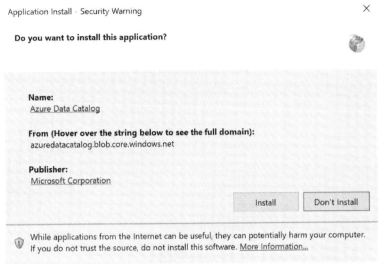

Figure 4 – Installing Azure Data Catalog

Note: How long it takes to download will depend on your connection, but since the file is only around 100MB, it shouldn't take very long.

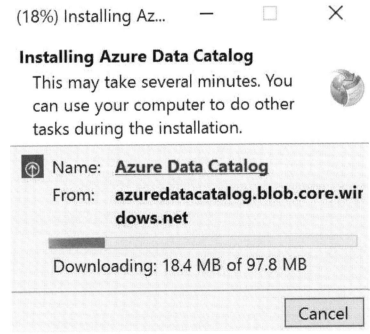

Figure 5 – Installing the Azure Data Catalog

Chapter 1   **Azure Data** Catalog

Accept the license and you now have a handy app that will walk you through to process of registering your data sources. The next time you want to register another data source you can launch the app from your start menu. When the application starts it automatically checks to see if a newer version of the registration tool is available and will ask you if you would like to use the new version.

Sign in through your new app to begin. Remember to use the same account you used to create your Data Catalog.
For the following example, I chose a SQL Warehouse as my first data source.
Enter the details of the Connection.

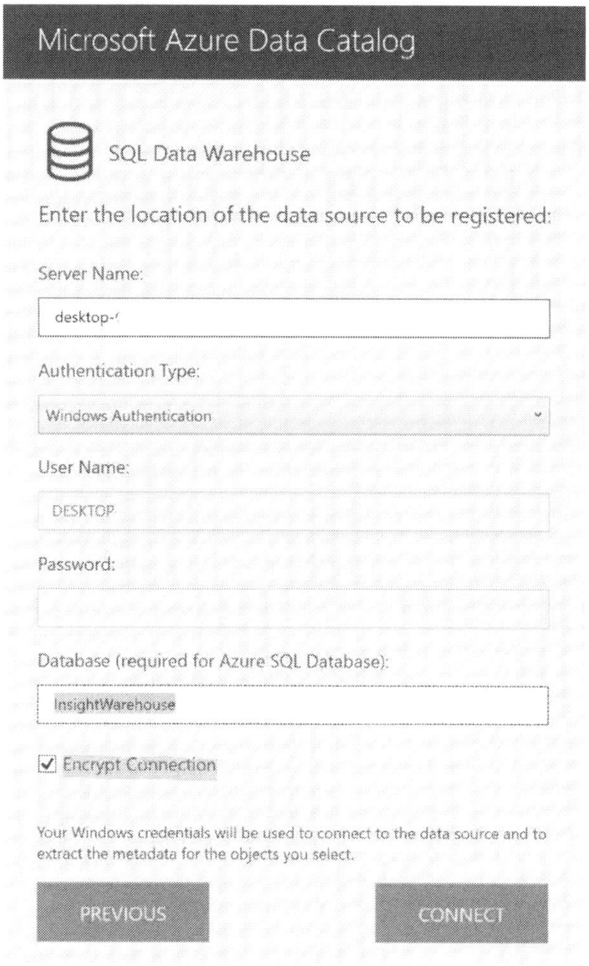

Figure 6 – Configuring your first Azure Data Catalog

Chapter 1   Azure Data Catalog

Here you select the objects you want to register. The metadata for the objects will be registered in the Catalog. For Sources that support previews you can choose to include a 20-record snapshot of the objects data. I recommend including that; if it is available. I have highlighted the Encrypt Connection to remind you to use this option. It is not on by default. Best practices dictate that you encrypt your stored data and communications. There is no reason not to encrypt the connection and there is no harm in using the encryption.

Note: Just because you include the data for preview it can only be seen by users that already have access to the underlying data. Even if you include the data for the preview it does not guarantee a user can see it. It is still all security based

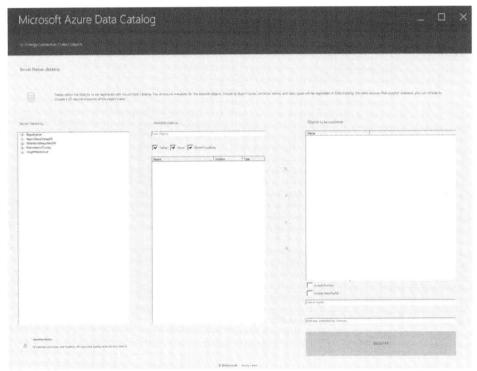

Figure 7 – Azure Data Catalog Configuration

Select the Database from the far left and then you can choose the objects. The ">>" arrow will move all objects displayed to the "objects to be registered" column. I like to include preview and profile to get the most out of my data.
"Preview" allows you to preview a sample of the data if you have permission to view the underlying data. The profile will gather as much detail about each object as is available. I find this feature will fill in as much detail as it can find about my source and limits the amount of typing I must do later.
Note: Just above the *REGISTER* button you can add tags separated by commas. This allows you to start documenting as you load. Keep in mind however; every comment you enter goes against

all objects being registered. Ensure the comment is relevant to all objects before you choose this option and enter it.

As soon as you choose *REGISTER*, the service begins. Once your objects are registered, you can choose to register more objects by simply going back to the Register Page with the button on the bottom of the page, and selecting more objects.

Accessing your Catalog

Once you have registered a source of data for your Data Catalog, the next step is to gain administrative access to that data via the cloud based ADC Application. From the Data Registration screen, you can jump directly into the ADC portal by clicking the View Portal button here:

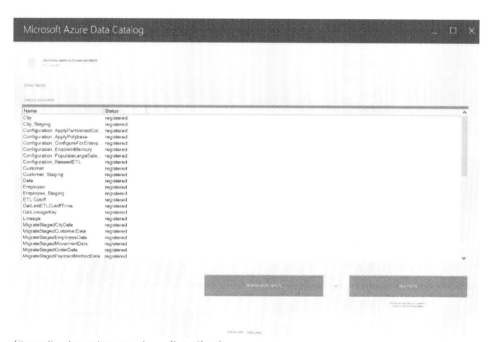

Figure 8 – Accessing your Azure Data Catalog

There are more ways to access your catalog, but this is the quickest and easiest when you are already in the Registration screen. To access your catalog from a regular web browser type http:\\azuredatacatalog.com. If you are not logged in it will prompt you for your login credentials. If you are already logged in it will take you directly to the home screen. The home screen, also called the dashboard is discussed next.

The dashboard

At this stage, you should be looking at an ADC portal for your own Catalog. To get to the dashboard, choose the home button. This screen is also the default screen you see when you go to azuredatacatalog.com when you are logged in.

The dashboard looks like this:

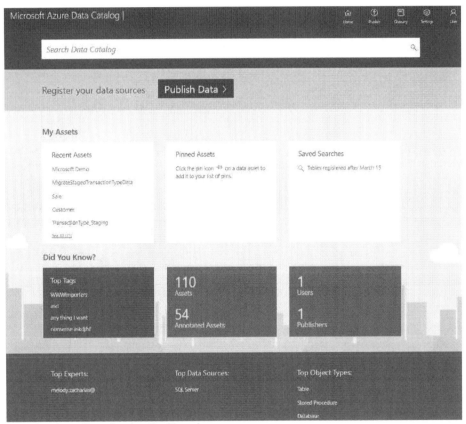

Figure 9 – Azure Data Catalog Dashboard

This is a cleanly designed dashboard with a few basic metrics about the meta data you have registered in the Catalog. Now for a tour of the items you see in your dashboard.

The first item located at the top of the dashboard is the *Publish Data* button.

Chapter 1   **Azure Data** Catalog

Figure 10 – Publish your data sources

This button conveniently takes you back to the **Publish Your data now!** Screen, which will allow you to launch the application again or create a manual entry. This takes you to the same screen that clicking on the publish menu item does.

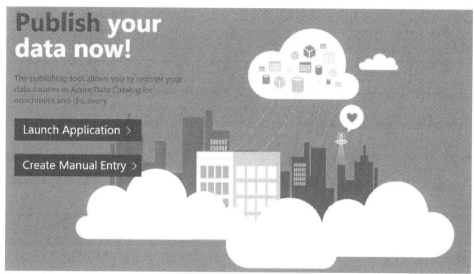
Figure 11 – Publish your data now splash screen

Either button, allows you to complete another round of registration for an additional data source. (Now you refer to "either button", but I still don't know what screen, and you have changed from the first sentence "this button" to "either button" but you have only introduced one button?) Each asset you have whether it is a database or ftp site must be registered individually. At the writing of this book, here are some of the many types of assets that can be registered.

Figure 12 – Azure Data Catalog Data Sources

Below this are some Key Performance Indicators (KPIs) about your data. The idea behind these metrics is to give you, at a glance, an overview of your entire Catalog as it currently exists. As you add more data and make changes and annotations to the data, these metrics will change.

Figure 13 – Azure Data Catalog KPI's

The middle of the dashboard covers the metrics of the assets in the catalog; who is using them, and how they are using them. The Top Tags highlight what is being made note of in the catalog; this tells you the top ways people are annotating the meta data. It also shows any searches you have saved, and what has been recently added.

Chapter 1 **Azure Data** Catalog

Figure 14 – Azure Data Catalog Dashboard Metrics

The final piece of the dashboard displays which assets have the greatest usage. On the left, you can see who is doing the most annotations in the Top Experts category. In the center, the Top Data Sources tells you the types of data sources most represented in the catalog. Finally, on the right, the Top Object Types tells you which object types you have the most of based on registered sources.

One of my favorite features of the ADC dashboard is the search bar.

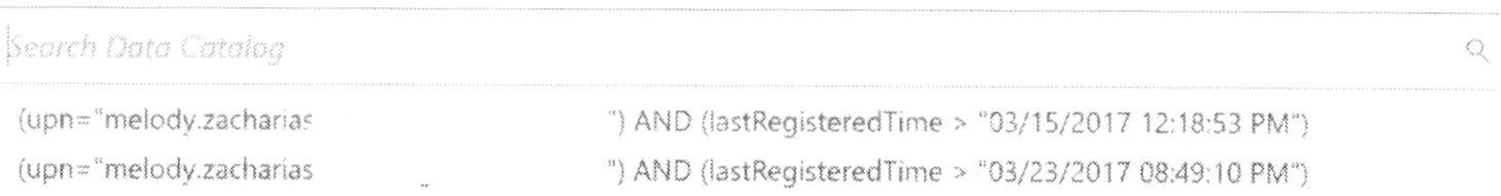

Figure 15 – Azure Data Catalog search bar

This image does not do it justice. What makes the search bar fantastic is that it is easy to find at the top of the screen in the center and the convenience of being able to do useful searches directly from your ADC dashboard. You do not have to go into the main portal to do a search. An additional aspect of the search that I love is that is saves my last few searches so I do not have to retype them.

Next, we will cover the toolbar at the top of the dashboard and the top of the portal screen.

Tool Bar

The previous section discussed some features on the Azure Data Catalog Dashboard. One of great features of the dashboard was its simple and clean GUI. In addition to keeping the GUIs easy to use and understand, Microsoft has made them consistent throughout ADC. ADC has the same tool bar in the dashboard and throughout the Portal.

Figure 16 – Azure Data Catalog tool bar

The tool bar contains all the administrative features of the data catalog.

The home button will take you back to the dashboard at any time.

The Publish button will take you to the **Publish your data now!** Screen that we discussed in the previous section. These buttons are more for navigation than for manipulation of any data.

The glossary is where the Business Glossary resides (available in the Standard Edition, not the free basic edition of Data Catalog). The Business Glossary allows the user to define business terms and create a common lexicon to be used throughout the Data Catalog. I will cover the Glossary in detail in a later section.

Settings are the tools that we use to set the general parameters when creating the catalog. These can also be changed in your Azure Portal but it is convenient to have access to them from within the Data Catalog Portal. With Settings, you can upgrade your subscription, or, change the location of the meta data for the catalog. Perhaps a new data center location comes on-line closer to your physical region and you would like to change you catalog location to that data center. You can do this in the Data Catalog Portal without having to go to your main Azure portal. You can also upgrade to the Standard Edition from this screen when you realize how badly you want that Glossary. All other settings that were created in the first section are here so you can make any modifications needed.

Chapter 1   **Azure Data** Catalog

The final button on the toolbar is the User button which displays details about the user and catalog you are using. The key features of this menu are the ability to clear Search History and Sign Out.

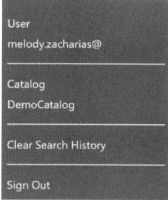

Figure 17 – Tool Bar

Just to have some fun I added a Portal Title to my Catalog and saved it in the settings. The change shows up immediately displaying my company name. This is done in the settings under Portal Title. Now I have a branded Catalog!

Figure 18 – Customized Company Name

Note: The text may not be displayed on displays with low resolutions settings.

The next step is to look at the attributes of an asset.

Asset Tiles

In the last section, we looked at the Tool bar. Although the tool bar dominates the real-estate at the top of the page, the majority of your window consists of the tiles that display your assets. These are located conveniently in the middle of the page

Figure 19 – Asset Tiles

Each tile in the main section of the page is an "asset". An asset is any object that stores or references data that is a part of the data source. For those familiar with Databases, a data source would be the database. The assets of that data source are the objects in the database. The tables, stored procedures, views and functions are all assets. When we first register a data source, Data Catalog reads the meta data and creates the tiles to represent the assets found within that data source. Let's take a closer look at what details are in each of these tiles.

When you click on a tile, you will see a small check box appear in the top right.

Chapter 1   **Azure Data** Catalog

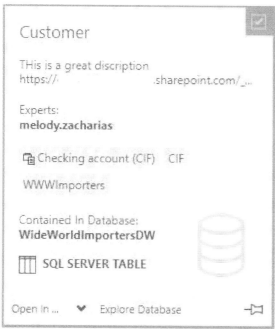

Figure 20 – Azure Data Catalog tile

Here highlighted in blue is the check box. Once the tile is clicked it will show the check mark, and open a details panel. There is a lot of information in the details panel, so we will cover that in a separate section.

The first line of the tile is the name of the asset that was registered; in this case "Customer". This name was automatically pulled from the meta data in the source.

The next line is a handy ***click tile to add a description*** message, if you have not already entered a description. Once you enter a description like I have, it shows the message. It invites you to click on it and if you do, you will be taken to that same details panel that we will discuss in a separate section.

By designating myself as the expert on this source, when data catalog registered this asset, it saved me typing the information by automatically listing me as the expert.

Below this is the name WWWImporters. This is the tag I entered during the registration process. I only entered one but I could have entered as many as were appropriate to all assets in the data source.

In this case, our source is the database WideWorldImportersDW, a data warehouse in SQL Server. The type of source is shown below the name.

On the bottom row are some action items. The first is **Open In…** this is the where you can choose to view the data in a separate application.

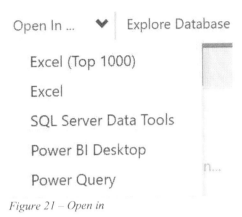

Figure 21 – Open in

The ability to view this data is only available to you if have been granted access to the original source.

The middle menu, **Explore Database**, opens a new window which gives you additional information about the source of the data. In this case, a database.

Figure 22 – Explore Database

The details panel gives you a high-level overview of all the assets in the source. In this case, it tells you there are 29 tables and 24 stored procedures in the database. The ← **Back to Catalog** link at the top of the box allows you to easily go back to your tile view.

In the bottom right corner of the assets tile, there is a pin. By choosing the pin, Data Catalog will pin the asset tile to your application page. This makes it very easy to find later and gives you quick access to the assets you use often.

Chapter 1 **Azure Data** Catalog

Details Panel Information pane

In the previous section, we looked at the asset tiles. Now let's look at the details within those tiles. When you are in the application, you can enter the details pane by clicking the tile. Regardless of the location of the tile when you choose it, the right-hand side of the application expands out to show you the details of that asset.

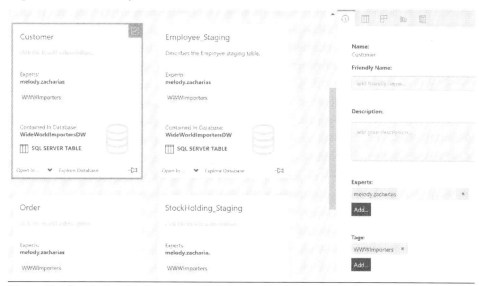

Figure 23 – Details Panel Information pane

The tile that is highlighted in blue is the tile that has its details pane exposed on the right of the screen. The universal icon for information (an "i" with a circle around it) identifies the information panel. We will look at the information panel in sections as each section has a specific purpose.

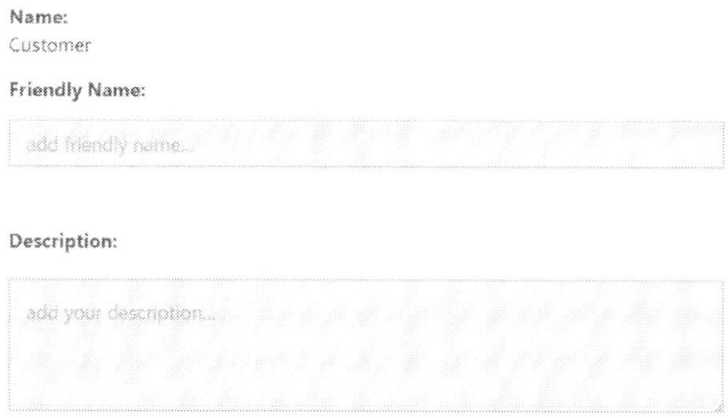

Figure 24 – Information Panel tile

This part is basic information. As I mentioned in the previous section, the Name is defaulted to the name of the asset as it is loaded. This is not always a very descriptive name so the Friendly Name is used to give a more user-friendly and descriptive name. The name comes from the source so in many legacy systems you may find abbreviations or other less obvious names that make it difficult for an end user understand.

For example, you may have a table named DIMAccount. This may be meaningful to a technology person but not necessarily to a business person. The Friendly Name "Account Dimension" should be more useful and descriptive so it is more universally understood. In addition to the names, there is space for a longer description. This description contains only text values. If you put a link in here it will only give you the text of the link. We will talk about how to put in hyper links in the next section.

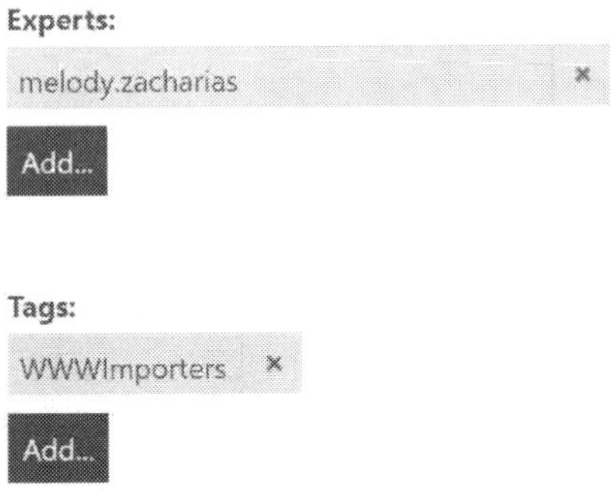

Figure 25 – Tags

The next part allows you to update modify and change the experts and tags that were entered in the registration phase. If you wanted to add additional experts to only some of the assets you registered or get more specific with tagging your assets, this is where you would do it.

The last section of the information panel is the Connection information;

Chapter 1 **Azure Data** Catalog

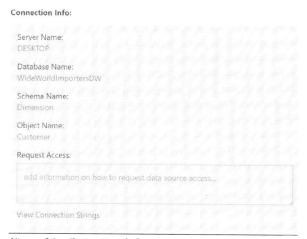

Figure 26 – Connection Information

This portion of the information panel is dedicated to connection information. This tells you where the data resides and even gives you multiple connection string data.

Finally, you can add in information on how to get access to the data.

This screen alone is worth every effort you put in to this product. It has numerous uses and is vital in keeping track of your data.

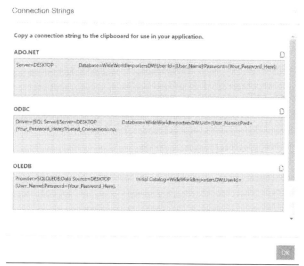

Figure 27 – Connection Strings

When you choose the Connection Strings link you are presented with all the different options of how to connect to this data. The small layered paper icon on the top right of each connection string detail allows you to quickly copy and paste the connection string into your code for use. Note the importance of {User_Name} and {Your_Password_Here} not only for its importance in reminding you where to place this information, but also due to the fact that it does not default to the current users' information or administrative names and passwords.

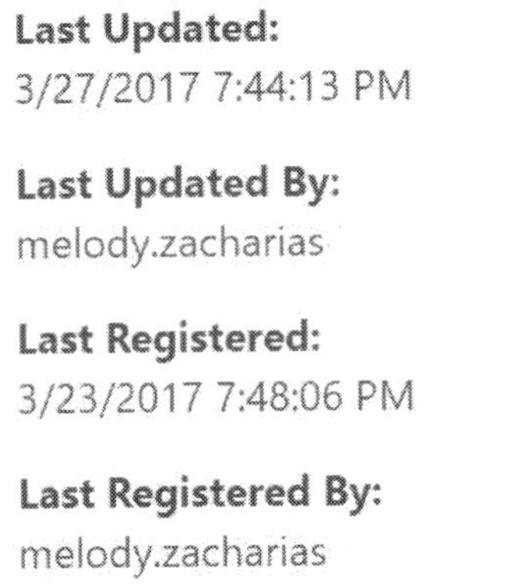

Last Updated:
3/27/2017 7:44:13 PM

Last Updated By:
melody.zacharias

Last Registered:
3/23/2017 7:48:06 PM

Last Registered By:
melody.zacharias

Figure 28 – Last Updated

This last section is automatically updated by ADC. This section tells you who did what, and when. In this example, it was me but as the catalog gets more use these will change and give you important information about who is using the catalog and when they used it.

Information panel Tabs

In the previous section we looked at the details pane. The focus was on the properties panel. There are 4 additional panels in that pane. In this section we will explore them.

Figure 29 – Information panel tabs.

Chapter 1   **Azure Data** Catalog

> **Note:** From left to right in the screen shot above the panels are:
>
> **Properties Documentation, Preview, Columns, and Data Profile.**

| Properties Documentation | Preview | Columns | Data Profile |

When viewing any of the panels you can hover your mouse over the edge of the panel on the left where it meets the main tile space until you see a double arrow "<->". You can use this to adjust the size if the panel.

The Preview pane is just as the name implies, a preview of the data that is in the asset you have selected.

Figure 30 – Preview Pane

This pane allows you to view the data that is in the asset. I mentioned before that if you do not have security access to the underlying data then you will not be able to see the data here. This is a view only screen and you cannot enter any data.

Chapter 1   Azure Data Catalog

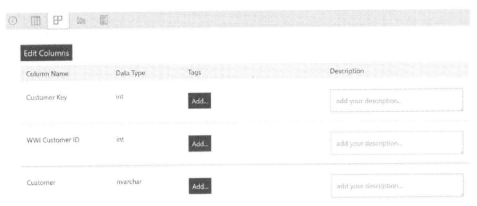

Figure 31 – Edit Columns

The Columns pane allows you to add a description of the various details that make up the asset. In this case we have Customer as the asset. The Customer asset contains details that are set out in rows, each row, representing a column in the customer table. The columns of the table, such as Customer key, WWI Customer ID, Customer, etc. are set out here as separate rows. Each of these rows can be annotated in this pane with tags and a description.

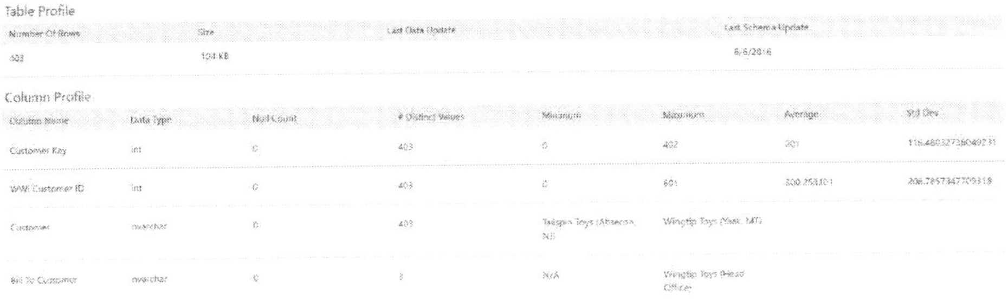

Figure 32 – Columns Pane

The Table Profile pane contains additional meta data. (Reminder: meta data is data about data, not the data itself.) In the case of our Customer Asset, this pane shows some details and even some statistics about the underlying data. It describes what is in the table. This can be very useful, particularly to those who do not have permission to view the actual data. The Top section describes the table with details such as;

Number of Rows – how much data is in the table

Size – how much space it takes up on disk

Last data update - the last time the data in the table was updated

Last Schema Update - this is when the last structural change was made to the table, so for example a column was added or the size of a column was changed.

The next section is all about the individual columns of data. This pane outlines the data type, which you would expect to learn from meta data but this panel goes much further, giving you some actual analysis about the data. We can see how many Null values are in each column as well as how many distinct values, the minimum and maximum values as well as averages and standard deviation for any numeric columns. (Reminder: A "null" value represents an absence of data, not a "zero" which is a value.)

Figure 33 – Individual Columns of Data

The final panel is the documentation panel. It is free form and has similar capabilities to other note applications from Microsoft. You will find the familiar basic formatting. In addition, there are buttons for;

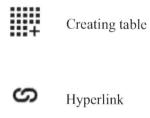

Creating table

Hyperlink

If your organization already has a start on the documentation for an asset, it is reassuring that it can still be referenced and used by linking to it here, making all documentation easier for everyone in the organization to find.

Now that we are familiar with what asset information we have we can move onto searching this information.

Search function Basics

In the last few sections, we looked at the different pieces of ADC. That overview was an important prerequisite to understanding this next piece: Searching. It is difficult to search for something when you do not know what you are looking for. This becomes more obvious the more data we need to search through. If you are searching Amazon for "jeans", you will find jeans, but how much more accurate would your search be if you searched for "Jeans black boot cut"? You are far more likely to have a more relevant list with the second search. Searching on ADC is no different. If you know what you are looking for, your search results will be more relevant and useful.

The main screen of ADC has two locations for easy searching. The first is the top of the screen on the left. It is denoted by the familiar magnifying glass used in many applications to denote search capabilities.

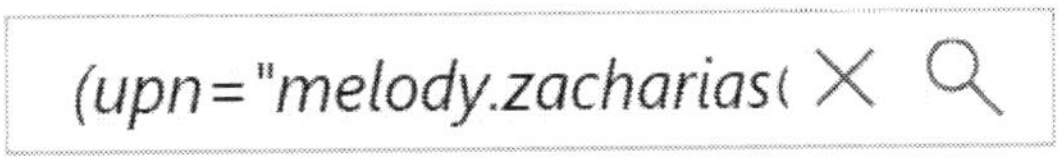

Figure 34 – Azure Data Catalog Easy Searching

The second is located on the left side of the screen. This search option is a menu of search capabilities.

Searches

▶ Current Search

▶ Filters

Figure 35 – Azure Data Catalog search capabilities

Chapter 1　**Azure Data** Catalog

Above is what it looks like when all the menu functions are minimized. I will talk about each individually. Below is an image of what the menu looks like when it is expanded out.

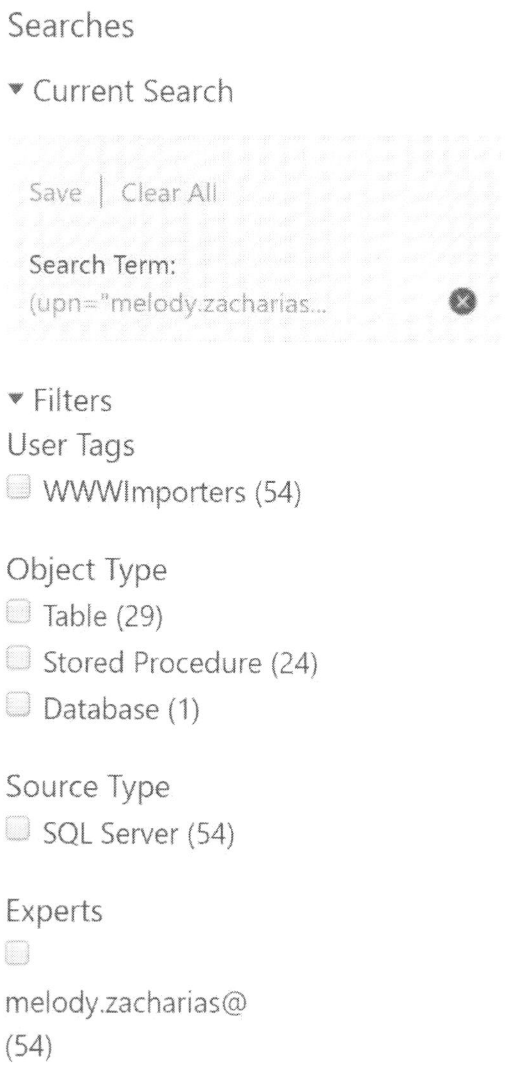

Searches

▼ Current Search

Save | Clear All

Search Term:
(upn="melody.zacharias...

▼ Filters
User Tags
☐ WWWImporters (54)

Object Type
☐ Table (29)
☐ Stored Procedure (24)
☐ Database (1)

Source Type
☐ SQL Server (54)

Experts
☐
melody.zacharias@
(54)

Figure 36 – Search Results

The first section is Current Search. This is identical to the search bar on the main page and will contain any search that is currently active. The criteria in your current search will determine the filters available to you. You can change or even save your current search from this menu. This is

45

a free form text search, making it more difficult to use because you must know the syntax, but it can be extremely useful once you get more comfortable with the syntax, and perhaps a coffee.

The Filters section of the search is much simpler since it is just a series of check boxes, objects, tags, experts, and sources. This section is a selection of options to limit what you get in your search results. The filters are presented as a way to limit your search results. As a Data Professional, I see it as more of a general grouping of the data. The filters are predetermined based on the type of meta data you have and can change based on the current search you are looking at.

Advanced Search functionality

In this section of our overview of ADC we are looking just at the advanced features in the search menu. This menu has some basic search options, however, when faced with looking for very specific data assets it is worth looking at the full complexity of the search functions. The search bar can be used for basic searches such as a word search like, *"finance"*. Or, you can make it more complex such as searching for a property with a specific term such as *"department:finance"*. Both of these are common in google, windows, and other programs with search capabilities. ADC expands on these with three additional options for searching;

Boolean – This is used to narrow a search *"finance **NOT** head office"*

Grouping – Grouping is done by using parentheses to group logic *"finance and "("head office" OR "main office")"*

Property – This is used to specify a type property type *"tag:cif"*

Comparison – This is used to make comparisons *"lastRegisteredTime > "03/15/2017 12:18:53 PM" **and** tag:cif"*

Has: and existence search has:description

Matching operators

Symbol	Explanation
:	Items where a specific property has the search term
=,<,>	Comparison operators these are used to compare values and can be combined. e.g. <=
" "	Quotations are used to group strings as a single unit value e.g. "finance department"
NOT, AND, OR	Boolean conditions.

Has:	Has is used as an existence search. If a given property has at least one element it will be returned by this operator.

The search operators are not case sensitive, however capitalizing the words for the Boolean conditions does make the search easier to read and understand. Should you limit your search too much or your search returns no data you will get this message:

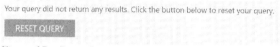

Figure 37 – Reset Query

Choosing the RESET QUERY box removes your entire query. If you feel you have simply made a typo, it is much easier to click in the search box and make your change so your entire query is not lost, forcing you to retype everything again.

Currently, exact match searching is not available. ADC uses Prefix Match Semantics. This means that when you search for Sale your search will return Sale, Sales, SaleData, and Salesman. The algorithms used by the search function could be the topic of an entire separate chapter. If you are curious and want to learn more information on the algorithm used for Prefix Match, it can be found here: https://pdfs.semanticscholar.org/c58a/b100d9a94b46bc6f2a868e53e7f32f008209.pdf

Saved search

Now that you know how to search and find what you need in your catalog, it is often worthwhile to save that search. There are times when you search just a word, or write simple comparison search and you may not need to save those. When you write a complex search or query, it can be helpful to save that search for use at another time. You save your search by choosing the save button in the Search panel as depicted below, it saves your entire search criteria.

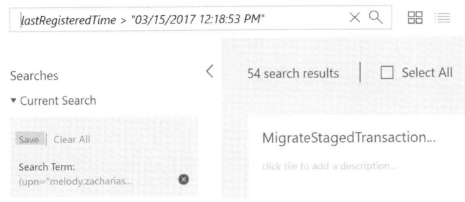

Figure 38 – Saved Search

The entire criteria includes any filters that were included as well as the specific operations that are listed in the search bar. Once you choose "save" you are given an opportunity to add a name to the search to make it easier to find in the future. By default, all searches are specific to the individual who created them. Should you wish to share them with others in your company, then be sure to check the share with company check box.

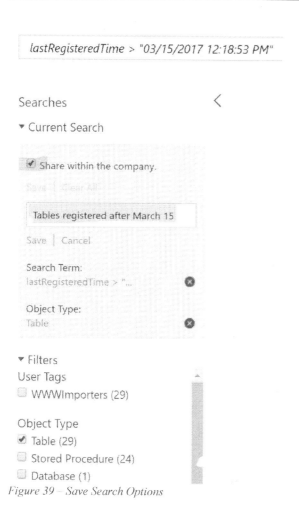
Figure 39 – Save Search Options

Once saved, the search shows up in my saved searches.

Figure 40 - Saved Search

The cog symbol allows you to access the saved search menu. This menu also allows you to manipulate the saved search. You can rename, delete or save this search as your default. The save as default is a particularly handy feature for when your catalog gets quite large and you want to focus on an area of particular interest.

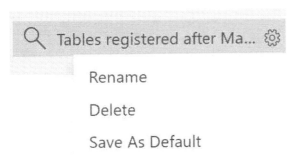

Figure 40 – Saved Search

Tagging

Tagging is the action of assigning a keyword or term to a piece of information. Tags are used to describe meta data items to allow them to be easily searched. They are determined by the creator of the tag. In ADC, the tags are located in the information pane. When you hover over a tag it gives information about the tag including who added it.

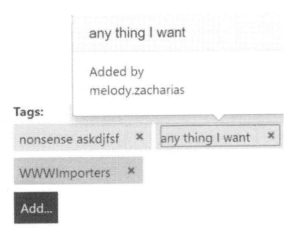

Figure 41 – Create a Tag

Note that anything can be added as a tag, even non-words. When adding a tag, if a tag already exists on that asset it will not add an additional identical one. This is true of a change in case as well; it will recognize "WWWImporters" and "wwwimporters" as the same tag and not include the second value.

Figure 42 -Tags

Even without adding in duplicates it can be easy to see with the above example how the sort order can cause issues with Tags. The value 11 comes before 2 whereas AAA comes before aa. I cannot add aaa as we already have AAA. None of these rules removes the risk of ending up with a mess in your tags. The best way to limit this issue and others is to have a Business Glossary. In the next section, we will look at setting up a Business Glossary in ADC.

Glossary Tags

I mentioned in the previous section how tagging in the free version is free form. There are no constraints or limitations on what you can use as a tag other than it limits duplicates. This free-for-all can of course lead to a shemozzle of tags that will quickly become more hindrance than helpful. The glossary will address this challenge. The glossary allows an organization to document key business terms and their definitions to create a custom business vocabulary. This enables consistency in the tag usage across the entire catalog. Once you have set up the terms they can be used in tagging. This enforces a governed approach to which tags are used, and provides specific meaning to those tags so everyone using the tags can be consistent.

Chapter 1   Azure Data Catalog

If you are still using the Free Edition, you get this message when you choose it from the menu.

Business Glossary is not available in the Free Edition

A business glossary allows users in your organization to document key business terms and their definitions to create a common business vocabulary across the Catalog. Learn More

Figure 43 – Glossary Tags

This is because the free edition of Data Catalog does not include the glossary. To update your subscription, go to Settings scroll down to pricing and choose "Standard Edition". At the time of the writing of this chapter it cost $1.22 per user per month for the standard edition of data catalog.

▼ Pricing: Standard Edition - Unlimited users, includes authorization. Up to 100,000 registered data assets.

The selected edition determines the number of users supported and the number of data assets that can be registered.

FREE EDITION	STANDARD EDITION	
Unlimited users Up to 5,000 registered data assets	Unlimited users, includes authorization Up to 100,000 registered data assets	1 users

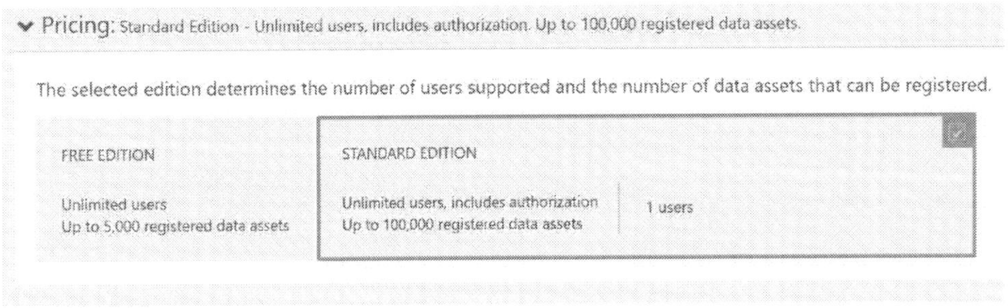

Figure 44 – Editions

Then choose to save. Now when I choose glossary I get this.

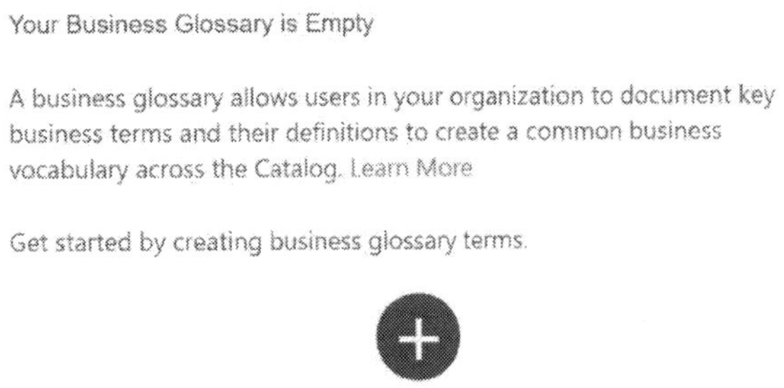

Your Business Glossary is Empty

A business glossary allows users in your organization to document key business terms and their definitions to create a common business vocabulary across the Catalog. Learn More

Get started by creating business glossary terms.

Figure 45 – Business Glossary

52

Chapter 1 Azure Data Catalog

Now you can start adding to your glossary.

> **Note:** Only glossary administrators and catalog administrators can create new glossary terms.

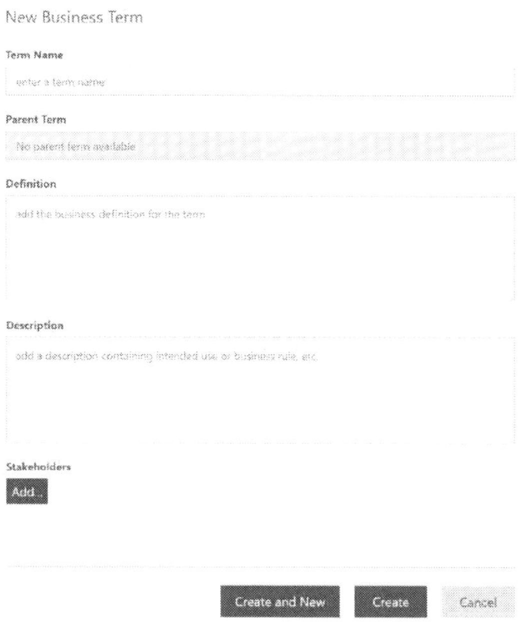

Figure 46 – New Business Term

The very first term you enter will not be able to have a Parent Term as a term needs to exist for it to be the parent, however all other fields can be entered. The Parent Term is a way to group data that is related like you would a family. A mother has a child. The Child is related to the mother but is a different entity. The child cannot exist without a mother. This is where the concept of Parent Term comes from. A Child term cannot exist without a Parent term. Another example would be a Magazine and a published date. You can have a Magazine that has not yet been published (Parent) but you cannot have a Published date (Child) without a Magazine.

Term Name – is the name of the Tag. This should be exactly what you want the tag to look like so if you want it to be an acronym, the acronym should be used here.

Parent Term – this is the name of the term you want the term to be a child of.

Definition – this is the definition of the business term

Description – This is different from the definition in that it is a description of the intended use of the term

Stakeholders – This is where you can tag your subject matter experts, people who know the most about a term.

Glossary Details

The glossary allows an organization to document key business terms and their definitions to create a custom business vocabulary. This enables consistency in the data usage across the entire catalog. Once you have set up the terms, they can be used in tagging.

The Glossary can then be set up in a hierarchy of items to show classifications. There is no limit to the number of levels in a hierarchy, however, Microsoft strongly suggests you limit the levels to "fewer than three" (in other words, "one or two") to keep it easy to understand. It is perfectly acceptable to have no hierarchies by simply leaving the parent term blank. Once you have added a few items you can review them in the main glossary page.

The left side of the glossary screen shows the terms you have added

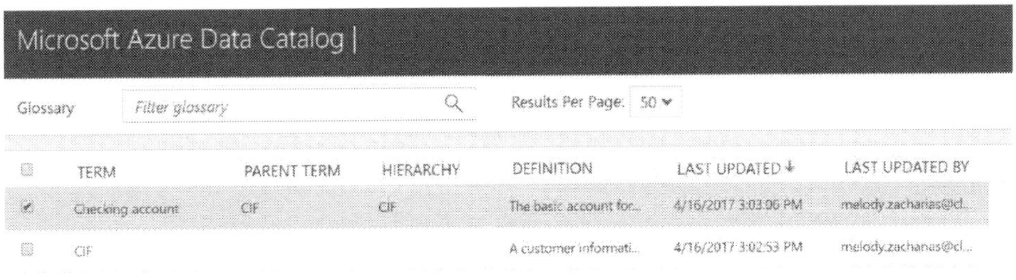

Figure 47 – Glossary Details

Here we see that a checking account is a child item of the CIF. I use this example to show a few things. The CIF is an acronym for Customer Information File. However, it is almost never referred to that in a bank. It is simply called a CIF. This is a good example of how an asset can then be tagged as a CIF without the entire name being needed. It also standardizes it as CIF, instead of having the numerous variations that people may come up with such as: cif, C.I.F etc. This is important when searching tags. Consistent tags make searches easier and more consistent.

There is additional information about the terms displayed in the table. The column sizes of each can be adjusted to allow you to view as much or as little of each column as you prefer. Above this table is the filter for the glossary and some results per page. As your glossary expands both of these will become very important in the management of your glossary.

The box to the left of each item can be checked to display the details of the item, if we check the CIF, the details look like this:

Chapter 1   **Azure Data** Catalog

Figure 48 – Glossary Details

This is displayed to the right of the glossary listing and displays the details of the checked item. Note at the top of the screen under the main Data Catalog menu is the glossary menu. These menu items are used as outlined here:

New term – allows you to create a new term

Add child – will add a child to an existing term automatically. This will bring up a new term window with the parent term filled in with the information of the term you were on when you choose add child.

Add admin – this allows you to add a glossary administrator. Note that security groups need to be set up for this to work.

Edit term – will allow you to edit the current term you are viewing.

Delete – this will delete the current term. Note that if the term is a parent then all children must be deleted <u>before</u> you can delete the parent. Microsoft was kind enough to ensure that we don't make what could be a huge mistake.

Toggle – this button expands and minimizes the detail view pane.

It is important to note that the glossary gives you not only information about the term but also how it is used and what it is related to by noting the relationships and assets associated to the term.

Glossary and tagging

As mentioned in the previous section, the glossary allows an organization to document key business terms and their definitions to create a custom business vocabulary. This enables consistency in the data usage across the entire catalog. Once you have set up the terms they can be used in tagging. This enforces a governed approach to how tags are used.

Once you have your glossary set up, you can use those terms to tag assets. The catalog is optimized to search the glossary as a term is typed into the tag bar.

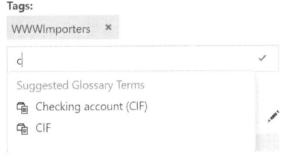

Figure 49 – Glossary Terms

You can see how when letters are typed you get suggestions directly from the glossary. This does not preclude a user from typing in their own term however. Terms that are simply typed in are called "user terms" and those that come from the glossary are "glossary terms".

Notice that Glossary Terms have an icon beside them in the list. This is still true in the catalog listing as seen here. The item, WWWImporters does not have an icon this is because it is not a glossary item. The Checking account has an icon because it is a glossary item.

Figure 50 – Glossary item example

When you hover over glossary items you also get additional details and a link to the glossary item.

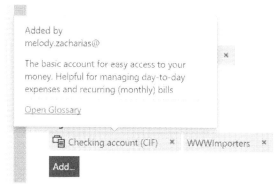

Figure 51 –Glossary item link

However, the non-glossary item has only the information about who added it.

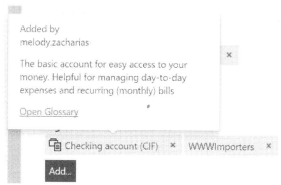

Figure 52– Description

Conclusion

In 2016 Microsoft acquired LinkedIn for 26.2 billion. LinkedIn had, at that time, approximately 100 million active users per month. Very few of those users pay anything for their use and access to LinkedIn. If we describe the purchase price as $260 per user, and those users pay nothing for the service, we are left scratching our heads as to why Microsoft paid so much. But the value of LinkedIn wasn't its user base, the value was in the data that user base generated. Microsoft obviously thought the data stream, not the revenue stream, was worth the purchase price.

We live in the Information Age. It is an age that recognizes that information is more important than physical things. Just compare Facebook with a valuation of around $200 billion and United Airlines with a valuation of around $34 billion. United owns billions of dollars' worth of assets in the form of airplanes, buildings, route licenses, and much more. Facebook by comparison, has very little in the way of hard assets. It's Facebook's information stream that makes its investors salivate. Today, information is leveraged more so than hard assets.

Data is the basic unit of information, but not the information itself. For data to become information, it must be organized, processed, and understood. Most companies are awash in data. In many cases that data is analogous to having stacks and stacks of papers sitting in boxes. In order for you to find the value in that information, it has to be organized so it can be processed and understood. Azure Data Catalog is the tool that will make the herculean job of organizing your data, possible.

What Microsoft did with the Azure Data Catalog, is produce a simplified way to collect Meta data. By crowd sourcing the addition of information to annotate your data, the enormous job of collecting and organizing company wide datasets becomes possible.

ADC is not currently well known, but the power it has to liberate information for companies, I believe, will soon make it a must-have tool for virtually every corporation. Familiarizing yourself with ADC is the sort of information that you will be able to leverage to advance your career.

What is the data in your company worth? How happy would your manager be if you were to unlock that value?

Chapter 2

Biml for Beginners: Script and Automate SQL Server Integration Services (SSIS) Development

By: Cathrine Wilhelmsen, Data Platform MVP and BimlHero Certified Expert

SQL Server Integration Services (SSIS) is a powerful tool for extracting, transforming and loading data, but creating and maintaining a large number of SSIS packages can be both tedious and time-consuming. Even if you use templates and follow best practices you often have to repeat the same steps over and over and over again during development. There are no easy ways to handle metadata and schema changes 3in your source databases, and for each new requirement you might have to go through every single package one more time to apply the changes.

Are you ready for a change? Say goodbye to repetitive work and hello to Biml, the markup language for Business Intelligence projects. By using Biml and BimlScript you can quickly generate SSIS packages from your source database metadata, and implement changes in multiple SSIS packages with just a few clicks.

Stop wasting your valuable time on doing the same things over and over and over again, and see how you can complete in a day what once took more than a week!

Traditional SSIS Development

Before we dive into the world of Biml, let us take a step back and look at traditional SSIS development and some of the more common pain points we may experience.

SSIS is a powerful tool that can be used for everything from a simple one-time copy of data between databases, to complex tasks like automating business transformations in Enterprise Data Warehouse loads. The graphical user interface allows you to create control flows and data flows with advanced tasks and transformations without writing a single line of code. For the new or occasional SSIS developer, this can make the tool easy to learn and use. But for experienced SSIS developers, working with a tool that relies heavily on a graphical user interface and mouse input, while having limited options for reuse and automation, is often a huge source of frustration.

You may even get to the point where you feel like repeatedly banging your head on the keyboard, but trust me, there is a better solution :)

Pain Point 1: Many SSIS Packages

One of the biggest pain points with traditional SSIS development is creating and maintaining a large number of SSIS packages. Many of these SSIS packages follow the same patterns, and you end up creating the same package over and over and over again with only minor changes to the source and destination.

There are ways you can reduce the time spent on creating and maintaining SSIS packages, but they each have their own drawbacks and limitations:

You can create package templates with standard connections, logging, error handling, flows and tasks, and create new packages from these templates instead of having to create all packages from scratch. This will save you time, but you will still have to manually create and customize each package from the template. And what happens if you need to change the template after you have created 100 packages? There is no way to change the template and apply the changes to the packages created from it. You will have to go through each package one more time, manually, to apply the changes.

You can create control flow package parts that contain commonly used tasks and data flows. Package parts can be inserted into multiple packages across multiple solutions, and changes to package parts will be applied to all the packages in which they are used. Package parts were introduced in SQL Server 2016, and were a huge step forward in making SSIS packages easier to maintain. However, you still have to manually create and customize each package.

You can create dynamic and reusable packages with parameters, configurations and variables, and use parent/child structures to control flow and executions. This can help reduce the number of packages needed in your project, but can quickly become a nightmare to debug, test and maintain.

All of the above can help reduce the time spent on creating and maintaining SSIS packages, but the development time is still fairly linear. If it takes one hour to create and test one package, it will take one hundred hours to create and test one hundred packages.

Pain Point 2: Frequent Source Changes

There is simply no easy way to handle source database changes in SSIS. A relatively small change, like your source system adding one new column in a table, can cause hours of extra work. In a typical Data Warehouse project, you have several layers from staging to data marts where the column needs to be added. You first have to add the column in all your SQL Server destination tables. Then you have to manually open up each package where the table is used, add the column, update all the tasks to ensure that the metadata changes are updated throughout the package, and test the changes. Finally, you have to deploy the SQL Server and SSIS changes simultaneously.

Having to spend so much time and effort on what should be simple changes makes it very tedious and time-consuming to work on projects with frequent source changes. It is difficult to be agile and work on SSIS projects in iterations, and it can be hard to justify the time and cost needed to your business users when all they want is a "simple change".

Pain Point 3: Slow Graphical User Interface

Even if you have few SSIS packages to maintain, you may experience frustrations with how SSIS relies on its graphical user interface. You have to spend a lot of time on what is often referred to as "plumbing": Dragging and dropping tasks and components on the design surface, connecting them, and aligning and resizing them to ensure that the package is visually easy to understand.

The control flow, data flow, parameters and event handlers are managed in separate panes. Variables and properties are managed in separate windows. Logging and task configurations are managed in various dialog boxes. This causes a lot of context switching back and forth, in addition to having to wait for design surfaces to load and dialog boxes to open. And if that was not enough, you often have to spend time on zooming in and out and adjusting dialog box sizes and grid widths to be able to do your work.

Take the Execute SQL task, for example. For something as simple as mapping parameters to a query, you have to open the Execute SQL Task editor, go through several dropdowns and dialog boxes to configure the connection and enter the SQL statement, switch to the Parameter Mapping tab, adjust the width of the parameter mapping grid, and go through several additional dropdowns. Doing this once might not a big deal. Doing this in 100 packages is, quite frankly, a huge waste of time.

Pain Point 4: SSIS .dtsx File Format

SSIS packages are meant to be created via the graphical user interface, and not by writing or editing the .dtsx code. While the .dtsx file format was improved to become more human readable in SQL Server 2012, it is still not entirely human writeable. The code is verbose, includes internal properties that you will not find in the design surface, and tracks objects using GUIDs and other IDs.

The .dtsx file format also tracks the layout information of the package. This makes it difficult, if not nearly impossible, to collaborate on SSIS projects using existing tools for code comparison, source control and change tracking. SSIS does not differentiate between an actual business logic change and a layout change. You can end up with multiple versions of the same SSIS package that is *logically* the same, but *visually* different.

Have you ever experienced this?

If you are an SSIS developer, you may have experienced the following scenario.

Chapter 2   Biml for Beginners:
Script and Automate SQL Server Integration Services (SSIS) Development

You have been working on a project for many weeks or maybe even months. You have created hundreds of SSIS packages. They have all been thoroughly tested, and you let out a little sigh of relief that you are finally done. It is almost happy hour time!

And then an architect or project manager walks in and says: "Great job, everyone! *But…*"

But *something* needs to be changed. Maybe you need to change your naming standards. Maybe you need to update the logging solution. Maybe you need to implement new requirements from your business users.

That *something* means that you have to spend the next couple of weeks going through *all* the SSIS packages one more time.

Your sigh of relief quickly turns into a sarcastic "Yay."

If you have experienced anything like this, you are probably ready for a change. And that change is Biml.

What is Biml?

Biml stands for Business Intelligence Markup Language. It is a human readable and writable XML language for automating and creating Business Intelligence and Data Warehouse solutions on the Microsoft Data Platform. It was created in 2008 by Scott Currie and his company Varigence.

Biml describes relational objects such as databases, schemas, tables, views and columns, as well as SSIS packages and SSAS cubes. By adding C# or VB code blocks, you can quickly generate entire Business Intelligence and Data Warehouse solutions from source database metadata instead of having to create each SQL script, SSIS package and SSAS cube manually. In this chapter, we will focus on Biml for SSIS.

Why use Biml?

Biml can help solve many of the pain points with traditional SSIS development. Instead of spending most of your time on "plumbing", such as dragging, dropping, connecting, aligning and resizing, you can focus on business logic. This will allow you to deliver more value to your business users in less time, while increasing your own value as an employee or consultant.

Chapter 2 **Biml for** Beginners:
Script and Automate SQL Server Integration Services (SSIS) Development

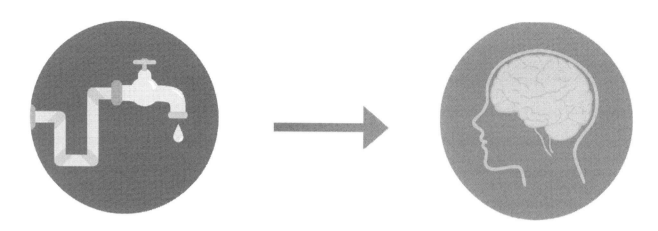

Will Biml solve *all* your pain points?

No, probably not. Biml is just one of many tools you can use in your Business Intelligence projects. Biml *is* a tool for generating SQL scripts and SSIS packages, and can help you speed up development time and increase productivity. Biml is *not* a pre-defined ETL framework or a tool for automating deployment. However, Biml can help solve *many* of your pain points. Let us take a look at how Biml can help solve the pain points with traditional SSIS development that were described earlier.

Solution 1: Many SSIS Packages

With Biml, you can create *one* Biml file that will generate hundreds and thousands of SSIS packages. When you need to change something, you simply update the Biml file and regenerate the SSIS packages. In just a few minutes, you can change your naming standards, update your logging solution, or implement a new requirement in *all* your SSIS packages across all your projects and solutions.

Solution 2: Frequent Source Changes

With Biml, you can generate SSIS packages based on your source database metadata. If your source database changes, you simply regenerate the SSIS packages to reflect the changes. You do not even need to tweak your Biml.

Solution 3: Slow Graphical User Interface

With Biml, you are no longer forced to work with the graphical user interface in SSIS. Instead of switching back and forth between windows, panes and dialog boxes, you can have everything in one Biml file. This also allows you to use code editor features like search and find/replace instead of having to manually go through a long list of properties to find what you need to change.

Solution 4: SSIS .dtsx File Format

With Biml, you can use existing tools for code comparison, source control and change tracking. Biml is a declarative language, so you do not need to specify default attributes and values. This keeps Biml files small and easy to read and write, and you know that each change to a Biml file is an actual change to business logic or package flow that you want to track. In addition, you can also separate code into multiple files and have multiple developers work on different parts of the same package. For example, one developer can be responsible for the entire logging framework, while others focus on the data flow and business transformations.

What do you need to start using Biml?

Biml is only used during development, so you do not need to install any software on your servers. All you need is a free add-in for Visual Studio / SQL Server Data Tools, you can use the free, online editor, or you can invest in a full-featured integrated development environment (IDE) for Biml projects that replaces Visual Studio / SQL Server Data Tools entirely.

BimlExpress

The free add-in for Visual Studio / SQL Server Data Tools is called BimlExpress. This add-in includes all the functionality needed for SSIS development, but not for SSAS development. It has a full code editor with syntax highlighting and Intellisense for Biml, and it is possible to enable Intellisense for C# / VB.

Download BimlExpress from Varigence: http://varigence.com/bimlexpress/

BimlOnline

The free, online editor for Biml projects is called BimlOnline. It has a full code editor with syntax highlighting and Intellisense for both Biml and C# / VB, SSAS support, a visual representation of your project and objects, a package and project importer for reverse-engineering, and an automated documentation feature.

Try BimlOnline: http://bimlonline.com/

BimlStudio

The full-featured integrated environment (IDE) for Biml projects is called BimlStudio. This is a licensed tool that replaces Visual Studio / SQL Server Data Tools entirely. It has a visual designer, full support for SSAS development and metadata modeling, a package and project importer for reverse-engineering, and full-stack automation tools.

Get a free trial of BimlStudio from Varigence: http://varigence.com/bimlstudio/

Chapter 2 **Biml for** Beginners:
Script and Automate SQL Server Integration Services (SSIS) Development

In this chapter, we will only use the free add-in BimlExpress.

How does Biml work?

You start by creating a Biml file, then you run the Biml file through the BimlCompiler. The BimlCompiler translates your Biml code into .dtsx code and generates the SSIS packages for you:

Figure 53 – BimlCompiler

The generated packages look and behave exactly like manually created packages, and are immediately readable, editable and usable with standard Microsoft tools. Biml is used for generating packages as an alternative to manually creating packages, and does not affect any of your existing processes. In fact, no one even has to know that you are using Biml!

After packages have been generated, you can execute and deploy them in the same way as your other SSIS packages and projects. This allows you to quickly start using Biml in one project or in parts of a project, and then gradually expand and improve your Biml solution as you learn more and get more experience working with Biml.

If you later find out that Biml is not the right tool for you, simply keep the SSIS packages you generated and go back to manual development.

Biml Syntax

Biml is an XML language. All XML documents must have a single root element that may have any number of child elements and attributes. Each child element may also have any number of child elements and attributes. To enforce which elements can be parents or children, which attributes are required or optional, and which values are acceptable for attributes, XML documents can have XML schemas that specifies the valid structure of the document. With XML schemas, code editors can provide Intellisense to make it easier to write valid code.

Biml Syntax Example

Below is an example of a very simple Biml file that creates two empty SSIS packages:

```
<Biml xmlns="http://schemas.varigence.com/biml.xsd">
    <Packages>
        <Package Name="EmptyPackage1"></Package>
        <Package Name="EmptyPackage2"/>
    </Packages>
</Biml>
```

Biml Syntax Example: Root Element

The root element is called Biml. It has an attribute that specifies the Biml XML schema:

```
<Biml xmlns="http://schemas.varigence.com/biml.xsd">
    <Packages>
        <Package Name="EmptyPackage1"></Package>
        <Package Name="EmptyPackage2"/>
    </Packages>
</Biml>
```

Biml Syntax Example: Collections of Elements

Inside the root element, we have collections of elements. These represent the main objects in our Biml projects, such as connections, databases, packages, tables and so on. In this example, we create a collection of packages:

```
<Biml xmlns="http://schemas.varigence.com/biml.xsd">
    <Packages>
        <Package Name="EmptyPackage1"></Package>
        <Package Name="EmptyPackage2"/>
    </Packages>
</Biml>
```

Biml Syntax Example: Elements

Inside the collections of elements, we have the actual elements, one element for each object in our Biml project. In this example, we create two different packages:

Chapter 2 Biml for Beginners:
Script and Automate SQL Server Integration Services (SSIS) Development

```
<Biml xmlns="http://schemas.varigence.com/biml.xsd">
    <Packages>
        <Package Name="EmptyPackage1"></Package>
        <Package Name="EmptyPackage2"/>
    </Packages>
</Biml>
```

Biml Syntax Example: Attributes

Elements can have attributes. Some of these attributes are required, while others are optional. Most elements have a required Name attribute. In SSIS, when we create a package or drag a task onto the design surface, they get assigned default names. In Biml, we need to specify these names:

```
<Biml xmlns="http://schemas.varigence.com/biml.xsd">
    <Packages>
        <Package Name="EmptyPackage1"></Package>
        <Package Name="EmptyPackage2"/>
    </Packages>
</Biml>
```

Biml Syntax Example: Full vs. Shorthand Syntax

All elements need to be opened and closed. The full syntax is to have one opening tag *<Package>* and one closing tag *</Package>*. If an element does not have any child elements, we can also use the shorthand syntax and place the closing slash inside the opening tag *<Package />*.

```
<Biml xmlns="http://schemas.varigence.com/biml.xsd">
    <Packages>
        <Package Name="EmptyPackage1"></Package>
        <Package Name="EmptyPackage2"/>
    </Packages>
</Biml>
```

Creating your first Biml Project

Now that you know how Biml can solve some of the pain points with traditional SSIS development, how it works and what the syntax looks like, it is time to create your first Biml project and get some hands-on experience.

For the examples in this chapter, we are using SQL Server 2016 with the WideWorldImporters database, and SQL Server Data Tools for Visual Studio 2015.

Chapter 2   Biml for Beginners:
Script and Automate SQL Server Integration Services (SSIS) Development

Install BimlExpress

Download and install BimlExpress from https://varigence.com/bimlexpress:

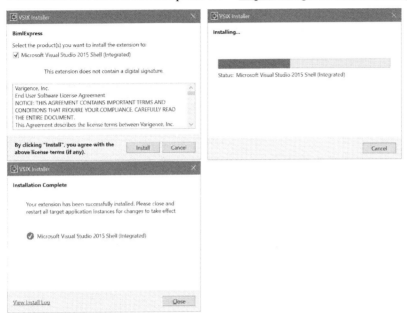

Figure 54 - Installation

When you open up Visual Studio / SQL Server Data Tools, you will see a new BimlExpress menu:

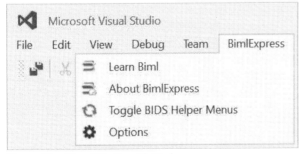

Figure 55 – Visual Studio with Biml

68

Chapter 2 **Biml for** Beginners:
Script and Automate SQL Server Integration Services (SSIS) Development

Click on About BimlExpress to activate your account. Enter your contact information and click Get Key:

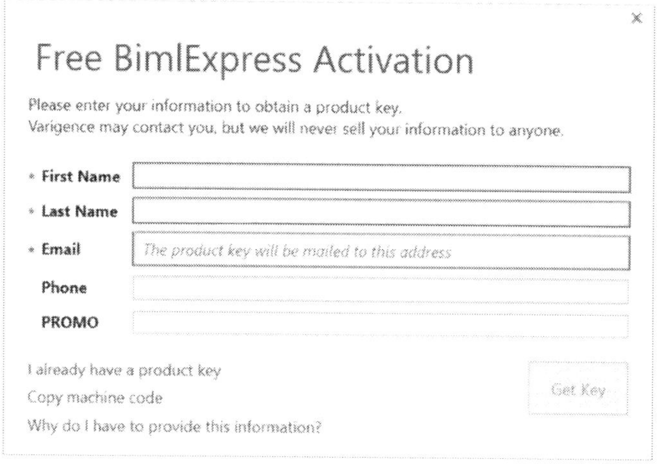

Figure 56 – BimlExpress

Insert the product key from the e-mail you received and click Continue:

Figure 57 - BimlExpress Licence

Your BimlExpress account is now activated.

Chapter 2   Biml for Beginners:
Script and Automate SQL Server Integration Services (SSIS) Development

Create New SSIS project

Create a new SSIS project and open it. When the project is open, you will see an expanded BimlExpress menu. You can now add Biml, C# and VB code files to your SSIS project:

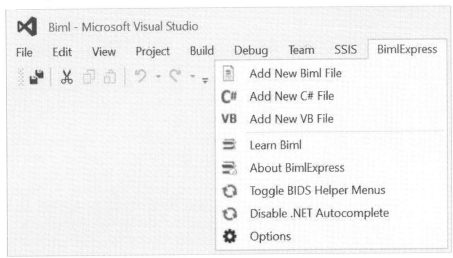

Figure 58 - BimlExpress Menu

Chapter 2 **Biml for** Beginners:
Script and Automate SQL Server Integration Services (SSIS) Development

Add New Biml File

There are two ways you can add Biml files to your SSIS project. You can click Add New Biml File from the BimlExpress menu, or you can right-click on the project in the Solution Explorer and click Add New Biml File:

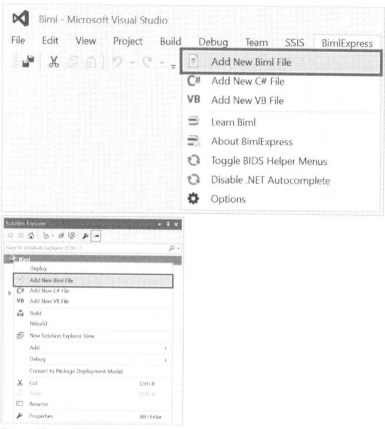

Figure 59 - Biml Solution

The new Biml file will be added under the Miscellaneous folder:

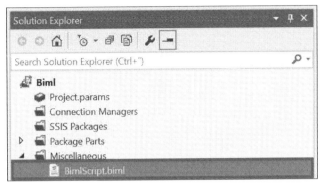

Figure 60 – Miscellaneous folder

Edit the Biml File

When you open a new Biml file, you will see that the root element <Biml> has already been added for you. When you start typing, the Biml Intellisense will show you all the valid elements for that specific location in the file. If the Intellisense disappears, click CTRL+Space to open it again:

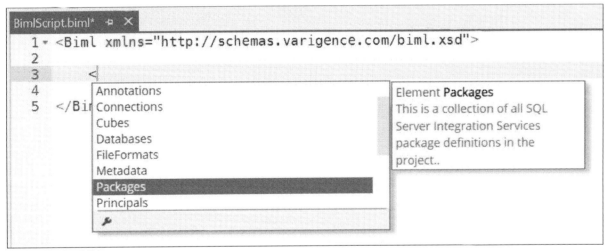

Figure 61 - Biml File

The Intellisense list is filtered based on what you type. A great way of learning Biml is to just start typing and see what comes up in the Intellisense and the tool tips for each element:

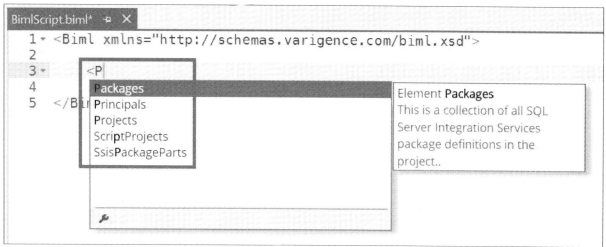

Figure 62 - Intellisense

Start with the very simple Biml file that creates two empty SSIS packages:

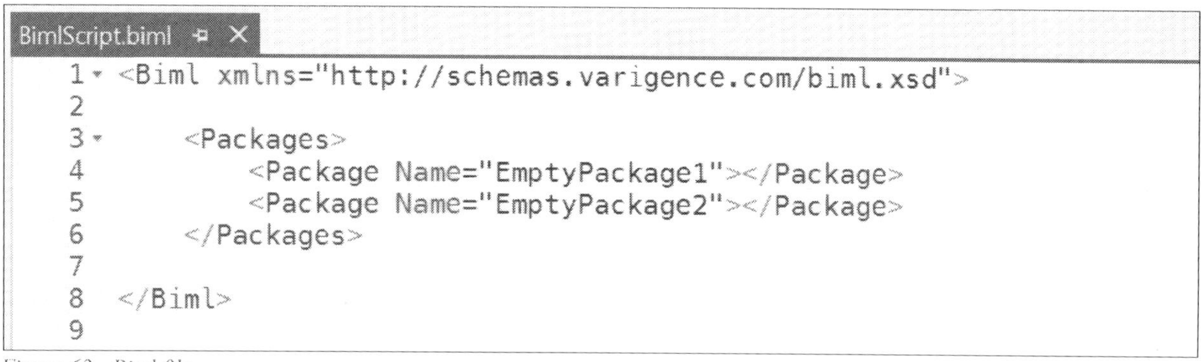

```
<Biml xmlns="http://schemas.varigence.com/biml.xsd">

    <Packages>
        <Package Name="EmptyPackage1"></Package>
        <Package Name="EmptyPackage2"></Package>
    </Packages>

</Biml>
```

Figure 63 - Biml file

Check Biml for Errors

While you are learning Biml, it is recommended that you check your Biml code for errors regularly to help with troubleshooting. While you have a Biml file open or selected in the Solution explorer you can click Check Biml For Errors from the BimlExpress menu, or you can right-click on the Biml file in the Solution Explorer and click Check Biml for Errors:

Chapter 2   Biml for Beginners:
Script and Automate SQL Server Integration Services (SSIS) Development

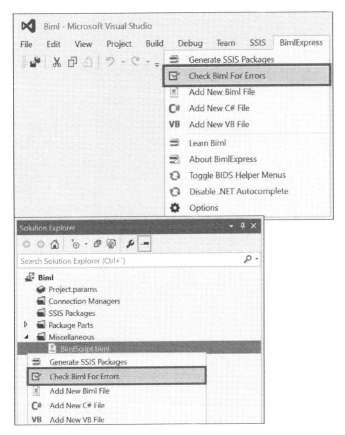

Figure 64 - Check for errors

Chapter 2 **Biml for** Beginners:
Script and Automate SQL Server Integration Services (SSIS) Development

If your code does not validate, you will get an error message with a description and the line number where the error is. For example, if you remove the name attribute from the Package element, you will get an error that says the required attribute Name is missing on line 5:

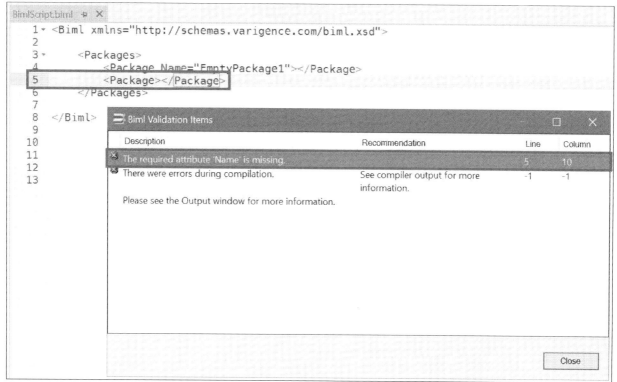

Figure 65 2ml Validation

If your code validates, you will get a No errors or warnings were found message:

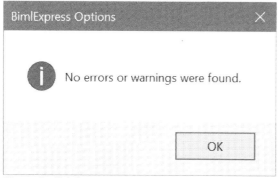

Figure 3 - Validation

Chapter 2 Biml for Beginners:
Script and Automate SQL Server Integration Services (SSIS) Development

Generate SSIS Packages

You are now ready to generate your first SSIS packages! While you have the Biml file open or selected in the Solution explorer you can click Generate SSIS Packages from the BimlExpress menu, or you can right-click on the Biml file in the Solution Explorer and click Generate SSIS Packages:

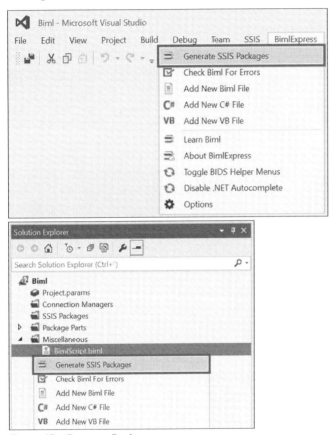

Figure 67 - Generate Package

While your packages are generating, you will see the progress in the bottom status bar:

Figure 68 -Status

When the packages have been generated, the bottom status bar changes to Ready, and the Output window says Biml expansion completed:

Chapter 2 **Biml for** Beginners:
Script and Automate SQL Server Integration Services (SSIS) Development

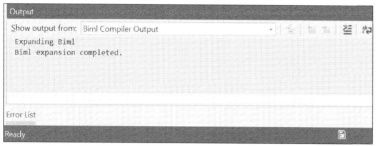

Figure 69 - Output

Congratulations! You have now generated your first two SSIS packages from Biml:

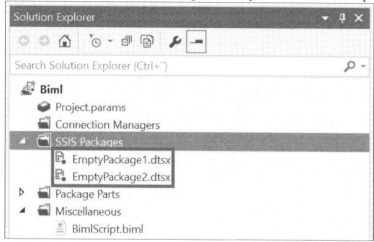

Figure 70 - Generated packages

77

Chapter 2 Biml for Beginners:
Script and Automate SQL Server Integration Services (SSIS) Development

Creating one Truncate and Load Package

You now have two empty packages in your Biml project, and yes, they are completely and utterly useless :) They only showed you how SSIS packages are generated from Biml. Delete the two packages, and we will create a new package that is actually useful.

Source and Destination Databases

For the next example, we will use the WideWorldImporters database (*left*) as our source database. It contains four schemas Application, Purchasing, Sales and Warehouse, and a number of tables in each schema. We will use the Staging database (*right*) as our destination database. It only contains one schema, but each table has the original schema name from the source database as a prefix:

Name	Schema
System Tables	
FileTables	
External Tables	
Cities (System-Versioned)	Application
Countries (System-Versioned)	Application
DeliveryMethods (System-Versioned)	Application
PaymentMethods (System-Versioned)	Application
People (System-Versioned)	Application
StateProvinces (System-Versioned)	Application
SystemParameters	Application
TransactionTypes (System-Versioned)	Application
PurchaseOrderLines	Purchasing
PurchaseOrders	Purchasing
SupplierCategories (System-Versioned)	Purchasing
Suppliers (System-Versioned)	Purchasing
SupplierTransactions	Purchasing
BuyingGroups (System-Versioned)	Sales
CustomerCategories (System-Versioned)	Sales
Customers (System-Versioned)	Sales
CustomerTransactions	Sales
InvoiceLines	Sales
Invoices	Sales
OrderLines	Sales
Orders	Sales
SpecialDeals	Sales
ColdRoomTemperatures (System-Versioned)	Warehouse
Colors (System-Versioned)	Warehouse
PackageTypes (System-Versioned)	Warehouse
StockGroups (System-Versioned)	Warehouse
StockItemHoldings	Warehouse
StockItems (System-Versioned)	Warehouse
StockItemStockGroups	Warehouse
StockItemTransactions	Warehouse
VehicleTemperatures	Warehouse

Figure 71 - Schema

Chapter 2 **Biml for** Beginners:
Script and Automate SQL Server Integration Services (SSIS) Development

Name	Schema
System Tables	
FileTables	
External Tables	
Application_Cities	wwi
Application_Countries	wwi
Application_DeliveryMethods	wwi
Application_PaymentMethods	wwi
Application_People	wwi
Application_StateProvinces	wwi
Application_SystemParameters	wwi
Application_TransactionTypes	wwi
Purchasing_PurchaseOrderLines	wwi
Purchasing_PurchaseOrders	wwi
Purchasing_SupplierCategories	wwi
Purchasing_Suppliers	wwi
Purchasing_SupplierTransactions	wwi
Sales_BuyingGroups	wwi
Sales_CustomerCategories	wwi
Sales_Customers	wwi
Sales_CustomerTransactions	wwi
Sales_InvoiceLines	wwi
Sales_Invoices	wwi
Sales_OrderLines	wwi
Sales_Orders	wwi
Sales_SpecialDeals	wwi
Warehouse_ColdRoomTemperatures	wwi
Warehouse_Colors	wwi
Warehouse_PackageTypes	wwi
Warehouse_StockGroups	wwi
Warehouse_StockItemHoldings	wwi
Warehouse_StockItems	wwi
Warehouse_StockItemStockGroups	wwi
Warehouse_StockItemTransactions	wwi
Warehouse_VehicleTemperatures	wwi

Figure 72 - Schema

We will create an SSIS package that first truncates the destination table Staging.wwi.Warehouse_Colors, then loads the data from WideWorldImporters.Warehouse.Colors, and finally logs the number of rows loaded to a custom logging table. This a is a common pattern for staging tables in Data Warehouse projects.

Biml Code

The following 60 lines of Biml code (43 lines of code, if you exclude the empty lines added for readability) is all that is needed to generate a truncate and load package.

Even if you are completely new to Biml, the code is readable and simple enough to give you an idea of what the SSIS package will look like in the end:

```xml
<Biml xmlns="http://schemas.varigence.com/biml.xsd">
    <Connections>
        <OleDbConnection Name="Admin" ConnectionString="Data Source=..." />
        <OleDbConnection Name="WWI" ConnectionString="Data Source=..." />
        <OleDbConnection Name="Staging" ConnectionString="Data Source=..." />
    </Connections>

    <Packages>

        <Package Name="Load_Warehouse_Colors" ConstraintMode="Linear">

            <Variables>
                <Variable Name="NewRows" DataType="Int32">0</Variable>
            </Variables>

            <Tasks>

                <ExecuteSQL Name="Truncate Warehouse Colors" ConnectionName="Staging">
                    <DirectInput>TRUNCATE TABLE wwi.Warehouse_Colors</DirectInput>
                </ExecuteSQL>

                <Dataflow Name="Load Warehouse Colors">
                    <Transformations>

                        <OleDbSource Name="Source Warehouse Colors" ConnectionName="WWI">
                            <ExternalTableInput Table="[Warehouse].[Colors]" />
                        </OleDbSource>

                        <DerivedColumns Name="Add LoadDate">
                            <Columns>
                                <Column Name="LoadDate" DataType="DateTime">@[System::StartTime]</Column>
                            </Columns>
                        </DerivedColumns>

                        <RowCount Name="Count NewRows" VariableName="User.NewRows" />

                        <OleDbDestination Name="Destination Warehouse Colors" ConnectionName="Staging">
                            <ExternalTableOutput Table="wwi.Warehouse_Colors" />
                        </OleDbDestination>

                    </Transformations>
                </Dataflow>

                <ExecuteSQL Name="Log Rows" ConnectionName="Admin">
                    <DirectInput>INSERT INTO dbo.SSISLog (StartTime, PackageName, NewRows) VALUES (?, ?,?)</DirectInput>
                    <Parameters>
                        <Parameter Name="0" VariableName="System.StartTime" DataType="DateTime2" Length="-1" />
                        <Parameter Name="1" VariableName="System.PackageName" DataType="AnsiString" Length="-1" />
                        <Parameter Name="2" VariableName="User.NewRows" DataType="Int32" Length="-1" />
                    </Parameters>
                </ExecuteSQL>

            </Tasks>

        </Package>

    </Packages>

</Biml>
```

Let us take a closer look at each part of the Biml code.

Chapter 2 **Biml for** Beginners:
Script and Automate SQL Server Integration Services (SSIS) Development

Biml Code: Connections

We first define three OLE DB Connections: Admin, WWI and Staging. (The ConnectionStrings have been truncated to ... in this example):

```
<Connections>
    <OleDbConnection Name="Admin" ConnectionString="Data Source=..." />
    <OleDbConnection Name="WWI" ConnectionString="Data Source=..." />
    <OleDbConnection Name="Staging" ConnectionString="Data Source=..." />
</Connections>
```

This generates the Connection Managers:

Figure 73 - Connection Manager

Biml Code: Packages with Variables

Then we define one package: Load_Warehouse_Colors. It has a ConstraintMode set to Linear, meaning that all control flow tasks will automatically be connected with Success precedence constraints in the order they are specified in the Biml code. You can also set ConstraintMode to Parallel and specify each precedence constraint manually.

Chapter 2 Biml for Beginners:
Script and Automate SQL Server Integration Services (SSIS) Development

The package has one variable named NewRows, of data type Int32 with a default value of 0:

```xml
<Packages>
    <Package Name="Load_Warehouse_Colors" ConstraintMode="Linear">

        <Variables>
            <Variable Name="NewRows" DataType="Int32">0</Variable>
        </Variables>

        <Tasks>
            ...
        </Tasks>

    </Package>
</Packages>
```

This generates the package and variable:

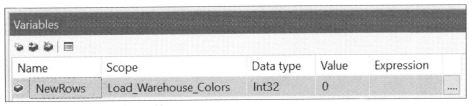

Figure 74 - Packages and Variables

Chapter 2 **Biml for** Beginners:
Script and Automate SQL Server Integration Services (SSIS) Development

Biml Code: Control Flow

The package has three control flow tasks. The first is an Execute SQL Task named Truncate Warehouse Colors that truncates the wwi.Warehouse_Colors table in the Staging database. The second is a Data Flow. The third is an Execute SQL Task named Log Rows that inserts a row into the custom logging table dbo.SSISLog in the Admin database:

```
<Tasks>

    <ExecuteSQL Name="Truncate Warehouse Colors" ConnectionName="Staging">
        <DirectInput>TRUNCATE TABLE wwi.Warehouse_Colors</DirectInput>
    </ExecuteSQL>

    <Dataflow Name="Load Warehouse Colors">
        <Transformations>
            ...
        </Transformations>
    </Dataflow>

    <ExecuteSQL Name="Log Rows" ConnectionName="Admin">
        <DirectInput>INSERT INTO dbo.SSISLog (StartTime, PackageName, NewRows) VALUES (?, ?,?)</DirectInput>
        <Parameters>
            <Parameter Name="0" VariableName="System.StartTime" DataType="DateTime2" Length="-1" />
            <Parameter Name="1" VariableName="System.PackageName" DataType="AnsiString" Length="-1" />
            <Parameter Name="2" VariableName="User.NewRows" DataType="Int32" Length="-1" />
        </Parameters>
    </ExecuteSQL>

</Tasks>
```

This generates the Control Flow:

Chapter 2   Biml for Beginners:
Script and Automate SQL Server Integration Services (SSIS) Development

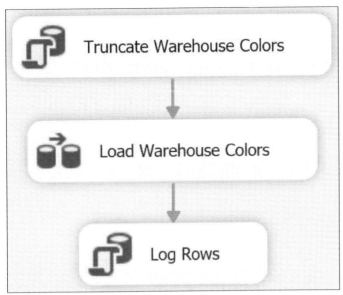

Figure 75 – Control Flow

Biml Code: Data Flow

The Data Flow has four transformations. The first is an OLE DB Source that gets all the data from the Warehouse.Colors table in the WideWorldImporters database. The second is a Derived Column that adds a column named LoadDate. The third is a Row Count. The fourth is an OLE DB Destination that loads all the data into the wwi.Warehouse_Colors table in the Staging database:

```
<Transformations>

    <OleDbSource Name="Source Warehouse Colors" ConnectionName="WWI">
        <ExternalTableInput Table="[Warehouse].[Colors]" />
    </OleDbSource>

    <DerivedColumns Name="Add LoadDate">
        <Columns>
            <Column Name="LoadDate" DataType="DateTime">@[System::StartTime]</Column>
        </Columns>
    </DerivedColumns>

    <RowCount Name="Count NewRows" VariableName="User.NewRows" />

    <OleDbDestination Name="Destination Warehouse Colors" ConnectionName="Staging">
        <ExternalTableOutput Table="wwi.Warehouse_Colors" />
    </OleDbDestination>

</Transformations>
```

This generates the Data Flow:

Chapter 2 **Biml for** Beginners:
Script and Automate SQL Server Integration Services (SSIS) Development

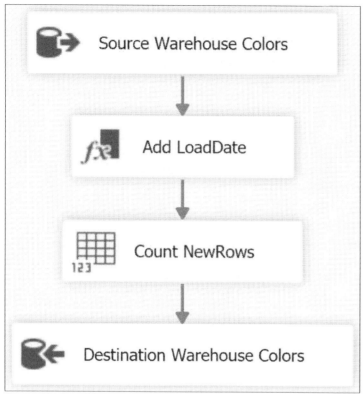

Figure 76 - Data Flow

Generated SSIS Package

The final, generated SSIS package looks like this:

Chapter 2 Biml for Beginners:
Script and Automate SQL Server Integration Services (SSIS) Development

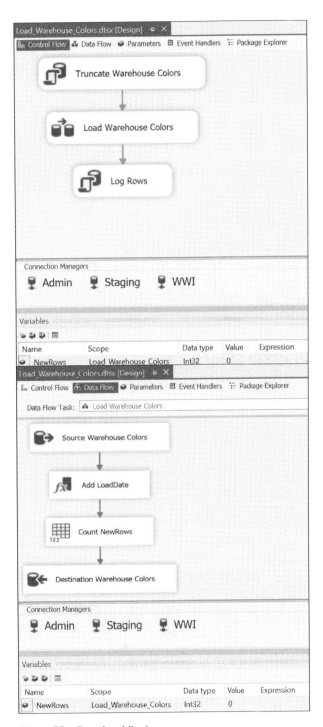

Figure 77 - Completed Package

Chapter 2 **Biml for** Beginners:
Script and Automate SQL Server Integration Services (SSIS) Development

Congratulations! You now have a package that is actually useful :) But you still only have *one* package for loading a single staging table. One of the advantages of using Biml is that you can create *many* packages from one Biml file. You do not want to create the same package over and over and over again, and you do not want to write the same Biml code over and over and over again. How do you solve that?

The Magic is in the BimlScript

So far, we have only created pure Biml files. The real power comes when you start extending your Biml files with BimlScript. BimlScript is C# or VB code blocks that you can add to generate, control and manipulate your Biml code, instead of writing all your Biml code manually.

With BimlScript, you can import your source database structure and metadata and use this metadata to create your entire Biml project. For example, you can loop over your metadata to generate an SSIS package or a Data Flow for each table in your source database, and replace all your static values with expressions.

BimlScript Syntax

BimlScript Code Blocks

There are five different kinds of code blocks you can use to add BimlScript to your Biml files:

`<# ... #>`	Control Blocks	Used for all C# / VB code to control logic, for example to import metadata, define variables, and create loops and if / else statements.
`<#= ... #>`	Text Blocks	Used to replace static values. Evaluates the C# / VB expression and replaces the expression with the string representation of the value.
`<#@ ... #>`	Directives	Used to provide instructions to the BimlCompiler, for example in which order to compile the Biml files or to include other Biml files in your project.
`<#+ ... #>`	Class Blocks	Used to create C# or VB classes and methods that can be called from multiple places in your Biml file, instead of copying and pasting the logic.

| `<#* ... *#>` | Comment Blocks | Used for commenting out your code, for example to add notes or for disabling code without deleting it. Supports multi-line comments. |

In this chapter, we will only use the Control and Text blocks.

BimlScript Syntax Example

Below is an example of a very simple Biml file with BimlScript that creates an empty SSIS package for each table in the source database. You will see that all the BimlScript code blocks have been highlighted with a yellow background:

```
<# var sourceConnection = SchemaManager.CreateConnectionNode(...); #>
<# var sourceMetadata = sourceConnection.GetDatabaseSchema(); #>
<Biml xmlns="http://schemas.varigence.com/biml.xsd">
    <Packages>
        <# foreach (var table in sourceMetadata.TableNodes) { #>
            <Package Name="Load_<#=table.Name#>"></Package>
        <# } #>
    </Packages>
</Biml>
```

BimlScript Syntax Example: Import Database Metadata

We first create a variable named sourceConnection, then we create a connection to our source database by calling SchemaManager.CreateConnectionNode. (The connection string has been

Chapter 2 Biml for Beginners:
Script and Automate SQL Server Integration Services (SSIS) Development

truncated to … in this example.) SchemaManager is a standard object that we can query without creating it first.

We also create a variable named sourceMetadata, and import all the database metadata by calling GetDatabaseSchema on our source connection. The sourceMetadata variable now contains all the information about our tables, views, columns, keys and indexes:

```
<# var sourceConnection = SchemaManager.CreateConnectionNode(...); #>
<# var sourceMetadata = sourceConnection.GetDatabaseSchema(); #>
<Biml xmlns="http://schemas.varigence.com/biml.xsd">
    <Packages>
        <# foreach (var table in sourceMetadata.TableNodes) { #>
            <Package Name="Load_<#=table.Name#>"></Package>
        <# } #>
    </Packages>
</Biml>
```

BimlScript Syntax Example: Looping over Tables

Then we create a loop around the Package element to generate one SSIS package for each table in our source database:

```
<# var sourceConnection = SchemaManager.CreateConnectionNode(...); #>
<# var sourceMetadata = sourceConnection.GetDatabaseSchema(); #>
<Biml xmlns="http://schemas.varigence.com/biml.xsd">
    <Packages>
        <# foreach (var table in sourceMetadata.TableNodes) { #>
            <Package Name="Load_<#=table.Name#>"></Package>
        <# } #>
    </Packages>
</Biml>
```

BimlScript Syntax Example: Replace Static Values with Expressions

Finally, we get the name of the table we are currently looping over, and use that as part of the package name:

Chapter 2 Biml for Beginners:
Script and Automate SQL Server Integration Services (SSIS) Development

```
<# var sourceConnection = SchemaManager.CreateConnectionNode(...); #>
<# var sourceMetadata = sourceConnection.GetDatabaseSchema(); #>
<Biml xmlns="http://schemas.varigence.com/biml.xsd">
    <Packages>
        <# foreach (var table in sourceMetadata.TableNodes) { #>
            <Package Name="Load_<#=table.Name#>"></Package>
        <# } #>
    </Packages>
</Biml>
```

Preview Expanded Biml

When you add BimlScript to your code, it can be very helpful to see the pure Biml to make sure that your loops and expressions are working as intended. To preview expanded Biml, click the Show Preview button:

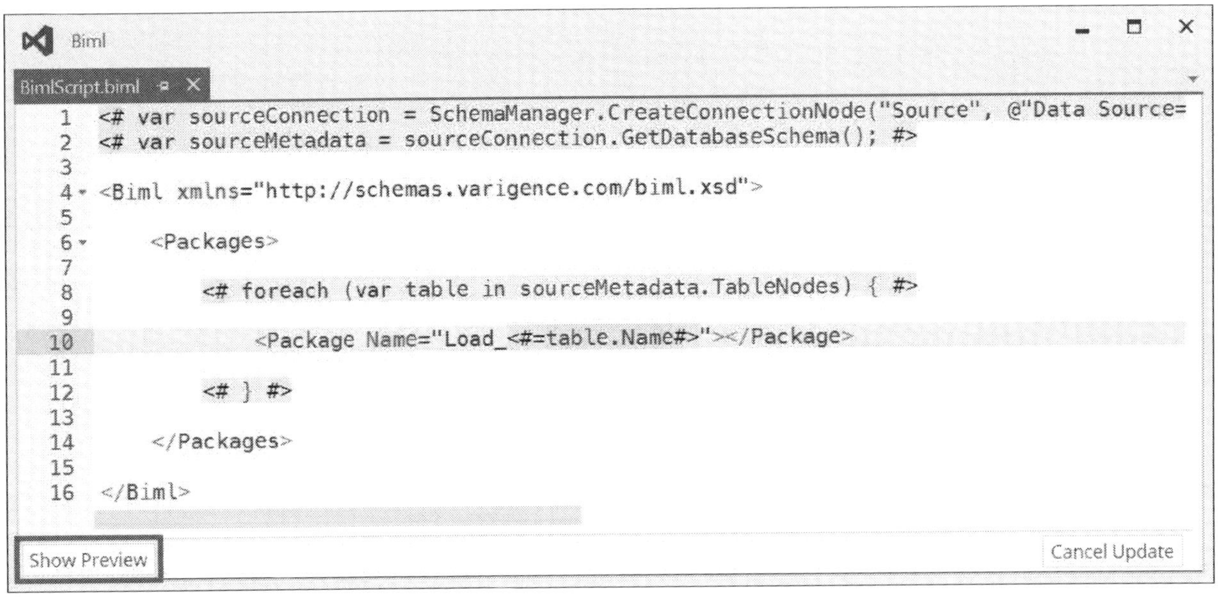

```
1  <# var sourceConnection = SchemaManager.CreateConnectionNode("Source", @"Data Source=
2  <# var sourceMetadata = sourceConnection.GetDatabaseSchema(); #>
3
4  <Biml xmlns="http://schemas.varigence.com/biml.xsd">
5
6      <Packages>
7
8          <# foreach (var table in sourceMetadata.TableNodes) { #>
9
10             <Package Name="Load_<#=table.Name#>"></Package>
11
12         <# } #>
13
14     </Packages>
15
16 </Biml>
```

Figure 78 - Show Preview

Chapter 2 **Biml for** Beginners:
Script and Automate SQL Server Integration Services (SSIS) Development

The preview pane will open, and the BimlCompiler will start compiling your BimlScript into pure Biml:

```
<# var sourceConnection = SchemaManager.CreateConnectionNode("Source", @"Data Sour
<# var sourceMetadata = sourceConnection.GetDatabaseSchema(); #>

<Biml xmlns="http://schemas.varigence.com/biml.xsd">

    <Packages>

        <# foreach (var table in sourceMetadata.TableNodes) { #>

            <Package Name="Load_<#=table.Name#>"></Package>

        <# } #>

    </Packages>

</Biml>
```

Compiling Biml...

Depending on your settings, you may have to click the Update button manually.

Chapter 2   Biml for Beginners:
Script and Automate SQL Server Integration Services (SSIS) Development

When the BimlScript has been compiled into pure Biml, you will see the results in the preview pane. In this example, we realize that we forgot to add the Schema name as part of our package name:

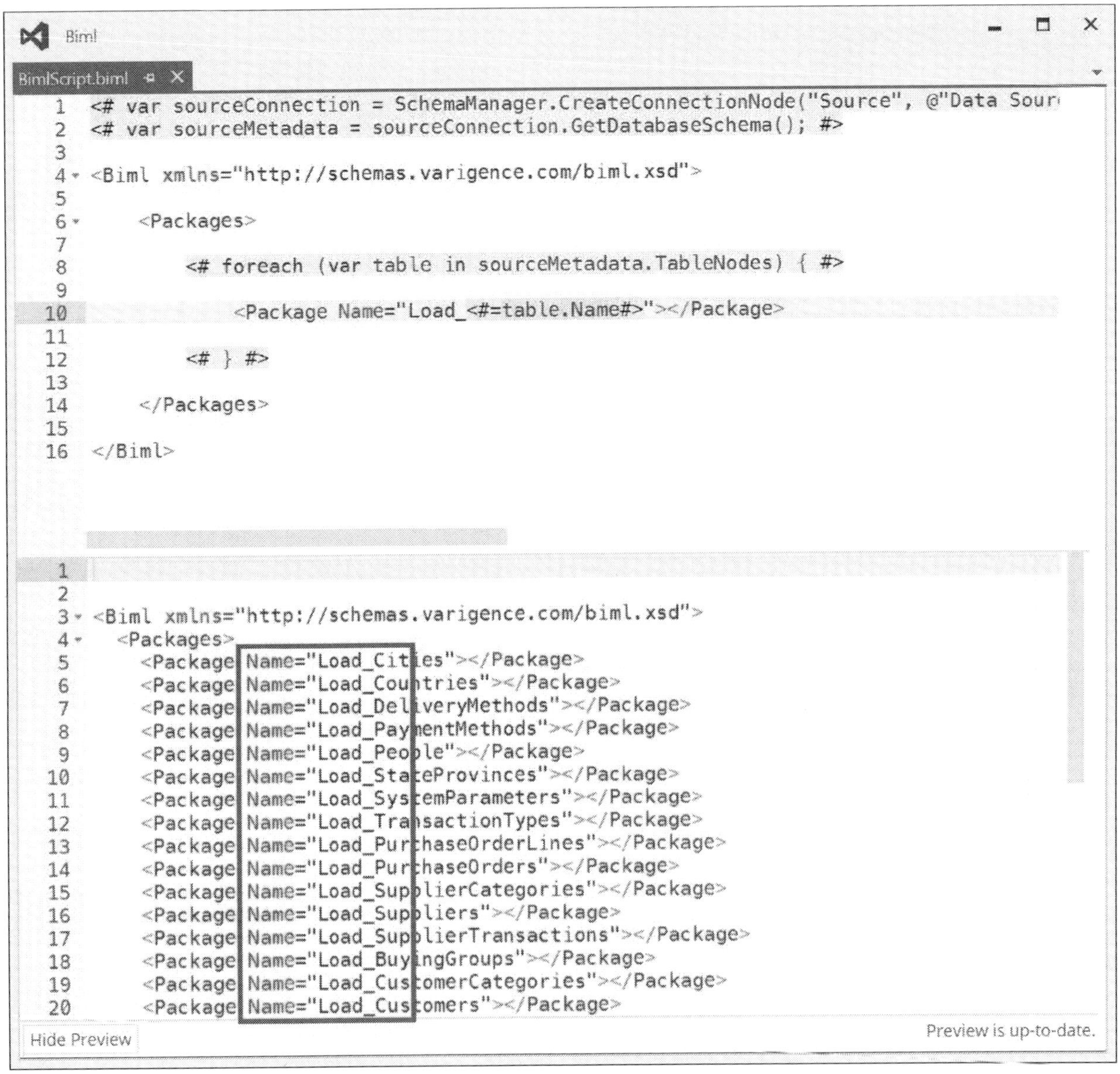

```
1  <# var sourceConnection = SchemaManager.CreateConnectionNode("Source", @"Data Sour
2  <# var sourceMetadata = sourceConnection.GetDatabaseSchema(); #>
3
4  <Biml xmlns="http://schemas.varigence.com/biml.xsd">
5
6      <Packages>
7
8          <# foreach (var table in sourceMetadata.TableNodes) { #>
9
10             <Package Name="Load_<#=table.Name#>"></Package>
11
12         <# } #>
13
14     </Packages>
15
16 </Biml>
```

```
1
2
3  <Biml xmlns="http://schemas.varigence.com/biml.xsd">
4      <Packages>
5          <Package Name="Load_Cities"></Package>
6          <Package Name="Load_Countries"></Package>
7          <Package Name="Load_DeliveryMethods"></Package>
8          <Package Name="Load_PaymentMethods"></Package>
9          <Package Name="Load_People"></Package>
10         <Package Name="Load_StateProvinces"></Package>
11         <Package Name="Load_SystemParameters"></Package>
12         <Package Name="Load_TransactionTypes"></Package>
13         <Package Name="Load_PurchaseOrderLines"></Package>
14         <Package Name="Load_PurchaseOrders"></Package>
15         <Package Name="Load_SupplierCategories"></Package>
16         <Package Name="Load_Suppliers"></Package>
17         <Package Name="Load_SupplierTransactions"></Package>
18         <Package Name="Load_BuyingGroups"></Package>
19         <Package Name="Load_CustomerCategories"></Package>
20         <Package Name="Load_Customers"></Package>
```

Figure 79 - Schema Name

Chapter 2 Biml for Beginners:
Script and Automate SQL Server Integration Services (SSIS) Development

We add the second BimlScript Text block to get the schema name, and update our preview to verify that the package names are now correct:

```biml
<# var sourceConnection = SchemaManager.CreateConnectionNode("Source", @"Data Sour
<# var sourceMetadata = sourceConnection.GetDatabaseSchema(); #>

<Biml xmlns="http://schemas.varigence.com/biml.xsd">

    <Packages>

        <# foreach (var table in sourceMetadata.TableNodes) { #>

            <Package Name="Load_<#=table.Schema#>_<#=table.Name#>"></Package>

        <# } #>

    </Packages>

</Biml>
```

```xml
<Biml xmlns="http://schemas.varigence.com/biml.xsd">
    <Packages>
        <Package Name="Load_Application_Cities"></Package>
        <Package Name="Load_Application_Countries"></Package>
        <Package Name="Load_Application_DeliveryMethods"></Package>
        <Package Name="Load_Application_PaymentMethods"></Package>
        <Package Name="Load_Application_People"></Package>
        <Package Name="Load_Application_StateProvinces"></Package>
        <Package Name="Load_Application_SystemParameters"></Package>
        <Package Name="Load_Application_TransactionTypes"></Package>
        <Package Name="Load_Purchasing_PurchaseOrderLines"></Package>
        <Package Name="Load_Purchasing_PurchaseOrders"></Package>
        <Package Name="Load_Purchasing_SupplierCategories"></Package>
        <Package Name="Load_Purchasing_Suppliers"></Package>
        <Package Name="Load_Purchasing_SupplierTransactions"></Package>
        <Package Name="Load_Sales_BuyingGroups"></Package>
        <Package Name="Load_Sales_CustomerCategories"></Package>
        <Package Name="Load_Sales_Customers"></Package>
```

Figure 80 - Preview

Creating all Truncate and Load SSIS Packages

By adding just a few lines of BimlScript to the original truncate and load package code, we can now create *all* SSIS packages from one Biml file:

```
<#
    var destinationSchema = "wwi";
    var sourceConnection = SchemaManager.CreateConnectionNode(...);
    var sourceMetadata = sourceConnection.GetDatabaseSchema();
#>
<Biml xmlns="http://schemas.varigence.com/biml.xsd">

    <Connections>
        <OleDbConnection Name="Admin" ConnectionString="Data Source=..." />
        <OleDbConnection Name="WWI" ConnectionString="Data Source=..." />
        <OleDbConnection Name="Staging" ConnectionString="Data Source=..." />
    </Connections>

    <Packages>

        <# foreach (var table in sourceMetadata.TableNodes) { #>

            <Package Name="Load_<#=table.Schema#>_<#=table.Name#>" ConstraintMode="Linear">

                <Variables>
                    <Variable Name="NewRows" DataType="Int32">0</Variable>
                </Variables>

                <Tasks>

                    <ExecuteSQL Name="Truncate <#=table.Schema#> <#=table.Name#>" ConnectionName="Staging">
                        <DirectInput>TRUNCATE TABLE <#=destinationSchema#>.<#=table.Schema#>_<#=table.Name#></DirectInput>
                    </ExecuteSQL>

                    <Dataflow Name="Load <#=table.Schema#> <#=table.Name#>">
                        <Transformations>

                            <OleDbSource Name="Source <#=table.Schema#> <#=table.Name#>" ConnectionName="WWI">
                                <ExternalTableInput Table="<#=table.SchemaQualifiedName#>" />
                            </OleDbSource>

                            <DerivedColumns Name="Add LoadDate">
                                <Columns>
                                    <Column Name="LoadDate" DataType="DateTime">@[System::StartTime]</Column>
                                </Columns>
                            </DerivedColumns>

                            <RowCount Name="Count NewRows" VariableName="User.NewRows" />

                            <OleDbDestination Name="Destination <#=table.Schema#> <#=table.Name#>" ConnectionName="Staging">
                                <ExternalTableOutput Table="<#=destinationSchema#>.<#=table.Schema#>_<#=table.Name#>" />
                            </OleDbDestination>

                        </Transformations>
                    </Dataflow>

                    <ExecuteSQL Name="Log Rows" ConnectionName="Admin">
                        <DirectInput>INSERT INTO dbo.SSISLog (StartTime, PackageName, NewRows) VALUES (?, ?, ?)</DirectInput>
                        <Parameters>
                            <Parameter Name="0" VariableName="System.StartTime" DataType="DateTime2" Length="-1" />
                            <Parameter Name="1" VariableName="System.PackageName" DataType="AnsiString" Length="-1" />
                            <Parameter Name="2" VariableName="User.NewRows" DataType="Int32" Length="-1" />
                        </Parameters>
                    </ExecuteSQL>

                </Tasks>

            </Package>

        <# } #>

    </Packages>

</Biml>
```

Chapter 2 **Biml** for Beginners:
Script and Automate SQL Server Integration Services (SSIS) Development

These 70 lines of Biml and BimlScript code expands into 1063 lines of pure Biml code:

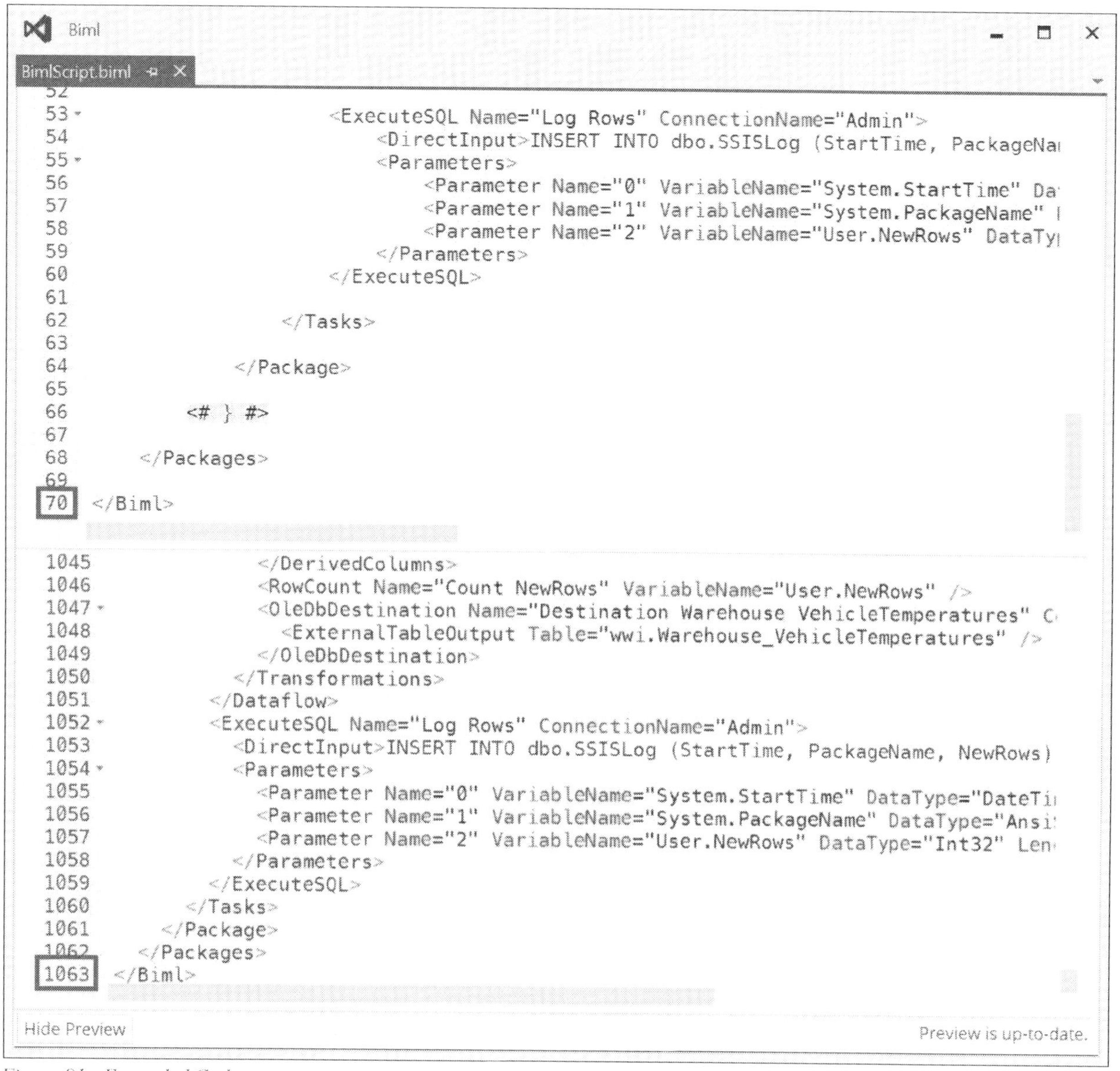

Figure 81 - Expanded Code

The 1063 lines of pure Biml code generates 31 truncate and load SSIS packages:

95

Chapter 2   Biml for Beginners:
Script and Automate SQL Server Integration Services (SSIS) Development

Figure 82 - Resulting Packages

That is a lot of Biml code you do not have to write manually, and even less dragging and dropping and connecting and aligning and resizing you do not have to do in SSIS!

Summary

In this chapter, you have learned how Biml can help solve many of the pain points with traditional SSIS development, what the Biml and BimlScript syntax looks like, and how to create a Biml project to generate SSIS packages to truncate and load all the tables in a Data Warehouse staging environment.

By writing just 70 lines of Biml and BimlScript code, we generated 31 SSIS packages in a few minutes. We could just as easily have created hundreds and thousands of packages in the same time with the same amount of code. Imagine the time saved compared to creating each of these packages manually by dragging, dropping, connecting, aligning and resizing over and over and over again!

What are the next steps?

The goal of this chapter has been to give you a very basic introduction to Biml and to show you how using Biml can help you save time and become a more efficient SSIS developer.

If your interest has been piqued and you want to learn more Biml, go to http://www.bimlscript.com. The website is created by Varigence, the creators of Biml, and has more in-depth lessons that you can work through in your own pace.

You can also find my Biml resources, recorded sessions, slide decks and demo code on my blog: https://www.cathrinewilhelmsen.net/biml/. If you have any questions whatsoever, please feel free to contact me, I will be happy to help! :)

It is your turn to experience this

If you start using Biml, you may experience the following scenario.

You have been working on a project the whole day. You have created a handful of Biml patterns that generate hundreds of SSIS packages. Everything has been thoroughly tested, and you let out a little sigh of relief that you are finally done. It is almost happy hour time!

And then an architect or project manager walks in and says: "Great job, everyone! *But...*"

But *something* needs to be changed. Maybe you need to change your naming standards. Maybe you need to update the logging solution. Maybe you need to implement new requirements from your business users.

Chapter 2   Biml for Beginners:
Script and Automate SQL Server Integration Services (SSIS) Development

That *something* means that you have to spend a couple of minutes tweaking your Biml patterns.

You smile as you tweak the code, click Generate SSIS Packages and tell yourself "It is Monday, and I'm done for the week!"

Chapter 3
Care and Feeding of a SQL Server

By: Jennifer McCown, Microsoft Certified Master in SQL Server, CEO of MinionWare

Data lives in a database. Someone has to design the database, and someone must create a way for the data to get in and out.

All that is good solid work, but here's the tricky bit: someone also must take care of the database, *and* the server it sits on. Since "maintaining the server" isn't nearly as sexy as "creating systems and programs", the care and feeding of a server tends to get short-changed or neglected entirely, even by database administrators (who happen to be the people responsible for such things).

You, on the other hand, had the foresight to have picked up this book, and turned to this chapter in particular. Well done! You will be well prepared to handle the big five administration tasks:

- **Backups** – Keep copies of all the data and objects in case of loss or screw-up.
- **Integrity checks** – Servers occasionally scramble bits and ruin databases, so you must regularly check for this.
- **Index maintenance** – Databases, like cars, need regular maintenance to keep them going. Think of index maintenance like regular oil changes.
- **Disk management** – Databases grow, and backup files stack up. Find out about full disks before they happen.
- **Alerting** – You don't know *anything* if you have to go searching for the information. Get alerted.

> **Note**: Many would argue, and they're right, that "**Performance**" belongs on this list. A database administrator is one of the people in charge of performance monitoring, tracking, and improvement. This is such a large topic, however, that we simply don't have space for it in this chapter.

For performance, I recommend everyone begin with Grant Fritchey's book, "SQL Server Query Performance Tuning", and just about anything (blog, book, or podcast) by Kendra Little. And of course, read the chapter *Indexing for Beginners* in this very book!

Backups

A backup "**copies the data or log records** from a SQL Server database or its transaction log to a backup device, such as a disk, to create a data backup or log backup."[1]

A backup is a copy. It's a sophisticated copy, and they've added some interesting features to the process, but remember that in essence, a backup is a copy of your database.

Backing up your database is the most important thing you will do as a DBA, because disasters happen. Servers self-destruct. Data gets accidentally deleted or overwritten by overenthusiastic technologists (or end users with too much access). Backups are insurance for your database, and yes, they are *mandatory*.

Before we really get started, let's talk about the database and the transaction log.

Databases and their transaction logs

Any SQL Server database will have at least one **data** file – where all the tables, objects, and data are stored – and a transaction **log** file – which records every single change that is done to, and in, the database.

---

[1] "Backup Overview (SQL Server)", *Microsoft*. https://docs.microsoft.com/en-us/sql/relational-databases/backup-restore/backup-overview-sql-server

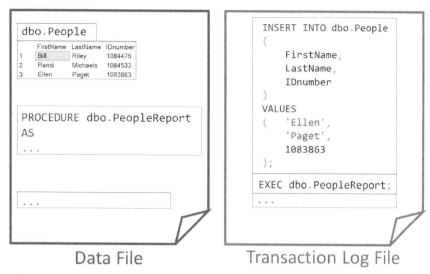

Figure 83– SQL Server Database Structure

In figure 83 above, the data file contains the table dbo.People, and the data in it; the procedure dbo.PeopleReport; and more. The transaction log file has a record of an INSERT statement and an execution of the dbo.PeopleReport procedure, and more. Data files contain things, and transaction log files contain a record of actions.

By the way, neither of these files is directly readable by humans. They're internally formatted specifically for SQL Server's use, not ours!

It's important to know the difference between data and log files, because there are different backup types.

Backup Types

There are three basic backup types:

- A **full backup**, backs up the data file (and the active part of the log file).

- A **differential backup**, a.k.a. "diff backup", backs up the differences in the data file that have occurred since the last full backup. For a diff backup to be any use, you must also have the most recent full backup on hand. We'll talk about why this is useful in the Restoring Backups section, below.

- A **transaction log backup**, backs up everything that happened in the transaction log *since the last transaction log backup*. These happen more frequently than full or diff backups, and tend to produce smaller backup files. (After all, what "weighs" more: the entire database, or all the changes performed on the database in the last hour?) Transaction log backups are of use in conjunction with a full backup, because you must have a starting place!

Study this bullet list. It takes some time to really absorb the information, when you're new to SQL Server. Most people get very confused about transaction log backups – which most people call log backups, so listen: **a log backup *itself* does not care, ever-ever-ever, about full backups.** It doesn't care, it doesn't pay attention. A log backup only cares about the last log backup, so it can pick up the sequence of changes where it left off. *You* care about both full and log backups, but **a full backup does not affect how a log backup behaves.** Clear? Awesome.

How to back up a database

How do we perform a backup? The full syntax of a backup command is a little heavy[2], but the basics are simple.

Here's how we would take a full backup of the database "MyDatabaseName", and save the file to the D:\ drive:

```
BACKUP DATABASE [MyDatabaseName]
TO DISK = 'D:\SQLBackups\MyDatabaseName20170421.bak';
```

At its simplest, the command is just:

- "BACKUP DATABASE", then
- the database name (I highly recommend brackets), then
- TO DISK, and
- a path and file name (I recommend using the date and time as part of the file name).

Similarly, to take a log backup for the same database, we might use:

```
BACKUP LOG [MyDatabaseName]
TO DISK = 'D:\SQLBackups\MyDatabaseName201704211130.trn';
```

Notice the statements above use *.bak* for the full backup's file extension, and *.trn* for the log. These extensions are not required, but it's good industry practice that allows you to tell your files apart at a glance.

To take a differential backup for the same database:

> BACKUP DATABASE MyDatabaseName
>
> TO DISK = 'D:\SQLBackups\MyDatabaseNameDIFF20170421.bak' WITH DIFFERENTIAL;

---

[2] See "Backups (Transact-SQL)". https://docs.microsoft.com/en-us/sql/t-sql/statements/backup-transact-sql

Chapter 3   **Care and** Feeding of a SQL Server

> **Important**: You *can* take multiple backups to a single backup file; if you back up to 'D:\SQLBackups\MyDatabaseName.bak' twice in a row, each backup will be contained in that one file. But most DBAs prefer to use separate backup files for each successive backup. If you choose to use separate backup files for each backup, I recommend making each file name unique with the backup date and time; and, I recommend using the keywords WITH INIT, FORMAT in your backup statement, to ensure the file contains only one backup.

It's no big deal to back up a database. The big deal is handling schedules, logging, options, manageability, and more. For a complete solution that manages all these issues, I recommend you use a T-SQL based solution. My company's free backup tool is Minion Backup[3], and I believe it's the best option available. But no matter what you use, it should include these principles:

- Schedule backups. Never count on regular manual backups!
- Use native SQL Server backups.
- Keep logs of all backup activity.
- Clean up old backup files as they age out. (We don't want to keep backup files forever!)
- Generate alerts on missing backups.
- Handle errors gracefully, and log them.

> **Important: Never** use the built-in SQL Server maintenance plans. They lack configuration, logging, and manageability. What's worse, maintenance plans often stop working without warning!

So, we've covered how to back up a database. But when should you use a full backup, a log backup, or a differential backup? Different backup types matter more, less, or not at all depending on the *database recovery model*.

Full vs Simple Recovery Model

Every SQL Server database writes transactions –*things done* to the database, like insert and create statements – to the transaction log. But different **recovery models** handle certain things in different ways.

A database can be in one of three recovery models:

- **Full model** – Saves all transactions to the transaction log, and *keeps* every one until they're backed up with a transaction log backup.

---

[3] See "Minion Backup". http://MinionWare.net/Backup/

- **Bulk-logged**[4] – Nearly the same as Full model, but in bulk logged, certain large operations *may* not be recorded fully; for those, instead of logging each transaction, it logs the data pages[5] that were changed. This is the least often used of the three, and we will mostly ignore it in this chapter.
- **Simple model** – Saves all transactions to the transaction log, until there's no chance that the given transaction will be *rolled back* (undone). Then, the system is free to clear out old recorded transactions on its own schedule (through a process called "checkpoint"). So, we cannot take log backups on a database in simple model!

> **Important:** Because databases in full model (or bulk-logged model) keep everything that's written to the transaction log, these databases must have both full backups and log backups. If you only took full backups of these databases, the transaction log would continue to grow and grow, eventually filling up the log file – or, if the file has auto grow enabled, filling up the disk that the log sits on! Regular transaction log backups keep the log file at a reasonable size.

Find out what recovery model a database is in by querying sys.databases:

```sql
SELECT name
     , database_id
     , state_desc
     , recovery_model
     , recovery_model_desc
FROM sys.databases;
```

	name	database_id	state_desc	recovery_model	recovery_model_desc
1	master	1	ONLINE	3	SIMPLE
2	tempdb	2	ONLINE	3	SIMPLE
3	model	3	ONLINE	1	FULL
4	msdb	4	ONLINE	3	SIMPLE
5	ReportServer	5	ONLINE	1	FULL
6	ReportServerTempDB	6	ONLINE	3	SIMPLE
7	Minion	7	ONLINE	1	FULL
8	AdventureWorks2008	8	ONLINE	3	SIMPLE

Figure 84 – SQL Server Recovery Models

---

[4] For more information on bulk logged model, see "Backup Under the Bulk-Logged Recovery Model", https://technet.microsoft.com/en-us/library/ms190692(v=sql.105).aspx

[5] SQL Server stores data on disk in the form of "pages". A **page** is an 8 KB block of data that gets written or read as a unit. Data in tables are stored in "data pages", and the data in an index is stored in "index pages". See "Understanding Pages and Extents". https://technet.microsoft.com/en-us/library/ms190969(v=sql.105).aspx

Chapter 3 **Care and** Feeding of a SQL Server

For databases in full or bulk logged recovery, you must take full backups *and* log backups. The full backups let you restore your database to the state it was in when the backup happened. We know from the last section that log backups keep the transaction log at a reasonable size. But, log backups also let you replay every action that happened after that full backup, all the way to the most recent log backup. That means less loss of data in the case of a database problem!

If that doesn't make any sense, then it's time to talk about restoring backups.

Restoring backups

In the last section, I said a database in full or bulk logged recovery mode needs full backups *and* log backups. Why?

Scenario 1: Let's say we perform a full backup of the database each night at 10:00 p.m. Now it's Monday at 2:00 p.m., and the server goes down and won't come back up! *Restore* that full backup to another server, and we have a restored database that looks just like it did on Sunday night. The good news is that we haven't lost all our data; the bad news is that we've lost all the changes to the database that happened since 10:00 p.m. the day before.

This is where log backups come in. Full backups are too big and expensive to take every five minutes, or even every hour. But log backups are more lightweight.

Scenario 2: We are still taking full backups every night, but we're also taking log backups every 15 minutes. The server breaks at 2:00 p.m. and won't come up, so we restore the full backup using the keyword WITH NORECOVERY, so the database is still in a restoring state. Then, we start restoring log backups, starting with the first log backup taken after 10:00 p.m. Sunday, and then restoring each successive log backup one after that. Now we have lost *at most* 15 minutes of data!

Even better, if the server were accessible at all, we could try to back up the "*tail of the log*"[6] and get all the data back!

Let's write the code to restore, as in scenario 2.

First, restore the full backup with NORECOVERY:
```
RESTORE DATABASE [MyDatabaseName]
FROM DISK = 'D:\SQLBackups\MyDatabaseName20170421.bak' WITH NORECOVERY;
```

Then restore each transaction log backup after that, with NORECOVERY:
```
RESTORE LOG [MyDatabaseName]
FROM DISK = 'D:\SQLBackups\MyDatabaseName20170421_1015.trn' WITH
NORECOVERY;
RESTORE LOG [MyDatabaseName]
```

---

[6] See "Tail-Log Backups (SQL Server)". https://docs.microsoft.com/en-us/sql/relational-databases/backup-restore/tail-log-backups-sql-server

```
FROM DISK = 'D:\SQLBackups\MyDatabaseName20170421_1030.trn' WITH
NORECOVERY;
RESTORE LOG [MyDatabaseName]
FROM DISK = 'D:\SQLBackups\MyDatabaseName20170421_1045.trn' WITH
NORECOVERY;
... [a whole lot more log restore statements] ...
RESTORE LOG [MyDatabaseName]
FROM DISK = 'D:\SQLBackups\MyDatabaseName20170422_1345.trn' WITH
RECOVERY;
```

Notice that the final RESTORE statement has WITH RECOVERY, because at this point we're done restoring and want to make the database usable.

But, we said we'd talk about differential backups too, right?

Scenario 3: Now we've decided to take daily full backups, log backups every 15 minutes, and differential backups every 4 hours. And the server breaks at 2:00 p.m. Let's walk through the restore scenario, and then talk about it.

First, restore the full backup with NORECOVERY:

```
RESTORE DATABASE [MyDatabaseName]
FROM DISK = 'D:\SQLBackups\MyDatabaseName20170421.bak' WITH NORECOVERY;
```

Then restore the *most recent* differential backup; in our case, the most recent differential backup happened at noon on April 22:

```
RESTORE DATABASE [MyDatabaseName]
FROM DISK = 'D:\SQLBackups\MyDatabaseNameDIFF20170422_1200.bak' WITH
NORECOVERY;
```

Then restore each transaction log backup that happened *after* that last differential, with NORECOVERY:

```
RESTORE LOG [MyDatabaseName]
FROM DISK = 'D:\SQLBackups\MyDatabaseName20170422_1315.trn' WITH
NORECOVERY;
RESTORE LOG [MyDatabaseName]
FROM DISK = 'D:\SQLBackups\MyDatabaseName20170422_1330.trn' WITH
NORECOVERY;
RESTORE LOG [MyDatabaseName]
FROM DISK = 'D:\SQLBackups\MyDatabaseName20170422_1345.trn' WITH
NORECOVERY;
```

So, what's the difference between scenarios 2 and 3? The difference is the number of RESTORE LOG statements we had to write and run. The differential backup saved us a fair amount of time, both in coding and in the restore process.

Differential backups aren't strictly *necessary*, but if you have the room for them on disk, they can be a very big nice to have.

Review

Database files:

- Databases have one or more data file, and typically one transaction log file.
- The data file holds objects and data.
- The log file holds *changes done* to the database, like inserts and creates.

Backup types:

- There are three types of backups, but we're ignoring "bulk logged".
- Full backups back up the database data file(s).
- Log backups back up everything that happened in the log *since the last log backup.*

Recovery models:

- A database can be set to one of three recovery models. For now, we're mostly interested in FULL and SIMPLE recovery.
- **Full recovery mode** – If your database is in FULL mode, you must implement *both* full and log backups. (Differential backups are optional.)
- **Simple mode** – A database in SIMPLE mode gets only FULL backups. (Differential backups are optional.)

Important notes:

- Log backups are not at all affected by full backups. But, to restore log backups, you need a full backup restored with NORECOVERY as a starting place.
- I recommend one backup per backup file. I also recommend naming your backup file with the backup date and time.
- Every database with full model recovery requires both full and log backups!

Integrity Checks

Data can be written to disk incorrectly – or fouled up once it's on disk – which is called *data corruption*. The internal mechanisms don't really matter for this discussion, but be aware that it can happen.

When data corruption happens in a database, it can be absolutely devastating; it *can* make the database entirely unusable. There are three basic scenarios for how the aftermath of corruption goes:

1. **You're diligent and very lucky** – You have regular integrity checks with alerts, so you detect corruption right away, and can take steps to fix it.

2. **You're diligent but unlucky** – You have integrity checks, and you detect the corruption, but it's one of the bad kinds of corruption. Here, the best solution is to restore the database from backup…which you can do, because you have good backups.

3. **You weren't diligent** – You don't have integrity checks, so the corruption goes on getting worse and worse, undetected. Someone finally notices when the database starts throwing weird errors or becomes entirely unusable. You don't have backups. Your only recourse is to dig through what's left of the database at the page[5] level, painstakingly retrieving a ridiculously small amount of data, if any.

Which one sounds good to you? Scenario 1? I think so too, but we'll cover both 1 and 2 here: regular integrity checks and good backups.

Taking Integrity Checks

The way to check the "physical and logical integrity" of your databases is to run a DBCC CHECKDB[7] on each one of them, on a regular basis. (I recommend daily or weekly integrity checks, as time and maintenance windows allow.)

As with anything, and especially any maintenance system, this seems relatively simple at first: "Just run the CHECKDB on each database! We can put the statements in a job!" But we quickly run into issues:

- What if the CHECKDB operation takes too long, and starts to impact resource usage during "prime time"?
- What if a new database is added, or an existing one removed?
- How will we be alerted if corruption happens? Or if an error happens during the process?
- What if we want to see a history of CHECKDB operations, how long they took, etc.?

Of course, I recommend the free tool Minion CheckDB[8], along with an alert, to handle most of this for you. There are other solutions out there, too. Whatever you choose, be sure you are performing regular, automated integrity checks!

For now, though, we'll take the simplest possible case: you want to run integrity checks on your own laptop, on which you have a single user database: MyDatabaseName. At a minimum, we need to set up a recurring job, and configure an alert.

---

[7] See "DBCC CHECKDB". https://docs.microsoft.com/en-us/sql/t-sql/database-console-commands/dbcc-checkdb-transact-sql

[8] See "Minion CheckDB". http://MinionWare.net/CheckDB

First, then, create a job to run daily DBCC CHECKDBs on all databases. The code would look like this:

```
DBCC CHECKDB ('master');
DBCC CHECKDB ('msdb');
DBCC CHECKDB ('model');
DBCC CHECKDB ('tempdb');
DBCC CHECKDB ('MyDatabaseName');
```

Note: Yes, we ran DBCC CHECKDB against the SQL work database, TempDB. You can, and you should, check TempDB for corruption. Corruption in TempDB might point to issues with the underlying storage (that is, the disk system) …and that means danger for anything else sitting on that storage!

When this job runs, it will output the results of the check to the SQL Server log. While that's nice – it's good to have a log of found errors! – this is not at all a complete solution. You need an alert to tell you that corruption has been found. See the "Alerting" section below – and especially the "Integrity Check Alert" subsection – for more.

Recovering from Corruption

If DBCC CHECKDB finds corruption errors in a database, you have several levels of recovery action available to you. Choose the least impactful option that will fix the corruption:

1. **Repair indexes** – if the corruption is within an index (or more specifically, within index pages[5]), you can either **drop and recreate** the index, or **disable and rebuild** the index[9]. Then, run the DBCC CHECKDB again to make sure all is well.

2. **Restore from backup** – "Microsoft always recommends a user restore from the last known good backup as the primary method to recover from errors reported by DBCC CHECKDB."[10]

3. **REPAIR_REBUILD** – This DBCC CHECKDB option allows you to correct corruption "without the possibility of data loss"[10]. Unfortunately, it won't always be possible to fix corruption with this option.

4. **REPAIR_ALLOW_DATA_LOSS** – There is another DBCC CHECKDB option that will fix corruption: REPAIR_ALLOW_DATA_LOSS. This option, as you might guess,

---

[9] "…you may be able to repair the index inconsistencies by rebuilding the nonclustered index offline." See "ALTER INDEX (Transact-SQL)". https://docs.microsoft.com/en-us/sql/t-sql/statements/alter-index-transact-sql

[10] See "DBCC CHECKDB (Transact-SQL)". https://docs.microsoft.com/en-us/sql/t-sql/database-console-commands/dbcc-checkdb-transact-sql

poses the risk of losing actual data[11].

Some of this may sound like gibberish to you, and that's fine. Fixing corruption is a very complex topic, and it's going to take you some further reading. People have devoted white papers, conference sessions, and entire training courses to handling database corruption. See the additional reading list in this section's review, below.

For now, understand that there are a handful of tools available to you for recovering from corruption, and they increase in both effectiveness and consequences.

Review

Important points:

- Your best defense against corruption is regular backups, and regular integrity checks with alerting.
- Fixing corruption is an incredibly complex topic. Read more, and practice corruption recovery, to be well prepared.
- Get a great third-party tool for integrity checks, so you don't have to completely reinvent the wheel.

Additional reading:

- Anything tagged "CheckDB" http://littlekendra.com/tag/checkdb/
- Fixing a Corrupt TempDB, http://www.sqlsoldier.com/wp/sqlserver/day14of31daysofdisasterrecoveryfixingacorruptTempDB
- Error 823, https://support.microsoft.com/en-us/help/2015755/how-to-troubleshoot-a-msg-823-error-in-sql-server
- Error 824, https://support.microsoft.com/en-us/help/2015756/how-to-troubleshoot-msg-824-in-sql-server
- Error 825, https://support.microsoft.com/en-us/help/2015757/how-to-troubleshoot-msg-825-read-retry-in-sql-server

---

[11] See "Does Repair_Allow_Data_Loss cause data loss?", *SQL in the Wild.* http://www.sqlinthewild.co.za/index.php/2009/06/03/does-repair_allow_data_loss-cause-data-loss/

Index Maintenance

Your databases have tables and views. Most likely, some of those have indexes on them. And indexes need maintenance. Why? Let's ask Microsoft[12]:

> *"Over time these modifications can cause the information in the index to become scattered in the database (fragmented). Fragmentation exists when indexes have pages in which the logical ordering, based on the key value, does not match the physical ordering inside the data file. Heavily fragmented indexes can degrade query performance and cause your application to respond slowly."*

This excerpt basically says that data that *should be* in order on disk, but it gets out of order, and that this impedes performance. (By the way, you can't see fragmentation by looking at the data in the table; we'll look at detecting fragmentation later in this section.)

Let's go a step further and think about *how* data pages become fragmented. To visualize this, think about a library shelf full of DVDs. The shelf (*page*) that holds movies (*data*) that start with the letter "M" is completely full:

Figure 85 – Fragmentation

So then, what happens when a new "M" movie comes in? Well, there are empty shelves on either side. So, the librarian decides to shelve the new movie where it belongs, and move about half of the movies to the next shelf, to make room.

Figure 86 - Fragmentation causing a page split

---

[12] "Reorganize and Rebuild Indexes", *Mircosoft*. https://docs.microsoft.com/en-us/sql/relational-databases/indexes/reorganize-and-rebuild-indexes

In database parlance, we have experienced a **page split**. Splitting one page – or a library shelf – takes up a little time, but if it doesn't happen all the time, it won't make a big impact.

Now, what if the same thing happens when the neighboring shelves are full?

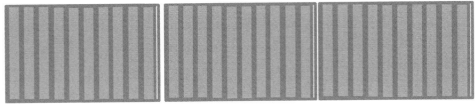

Figure 87– Full pages

The librarian is *absolutely dedicated* to shelving the movie where it belongs, so they do the same thing as before…except that about half the movies go to a shelf *somewhere else in the library*. The movies are now out of order; we have **fragmentation**.

After the library closes for the day, of course, the library staff can spend the necessary time to shift all the movies down by one shelf, and reshelve the displaced "M" movies back where they're supposed to be – in other words, they can *defragment* the shelves.

Even better, we have a particularly *smart* library staff. They decide that, as long as they're moving everything around, they should make sure that each shelf is no more than 80% full. That extra

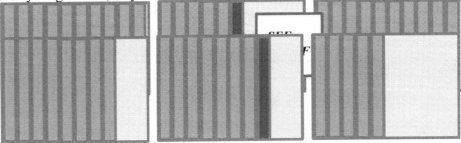

Figure 88– Fragmentation % full

space will let them go quite a long time without having to perform the defragmenting chore again:

This idea of leaving extra space on each shelf – or page – to prevent fragmentation is **fill factor.**

Prevent Index Fragmentation

I recommend some level of fill factor for most indexes in your databases. A good starting place is 90%, meaning that when an index is rebuilt, SQL Server will only fill each page up to 90%.

You can set the fill factor for indexes in several ways:

- **When you create the index.** This is a good bet for new indexes that are likely to fragment often.

    ```
    CREATE NONCLUSTERED INDEX ix2 ON dbo.DiskSpace (ExecutionDateTime)
    WITH (FILLFACTOR = 90, PAD_INDEX=ON);
    ```

- **When you rebuild the index**. This is the best option for indexes that have *proved* to fragment often.
    ```
    ALTER INDEX ix2 ON dbo.DiskSpace REBUILD
    WITH (FILLFACTOR=90, PAD_INDEX=ON);
    ```

- **System-wide, when any index is created.** Once this takes effect, any new database created will have the specified fill factor. This works well for systems that are likely to experience fragmentation in every database, and in almost all tables.

    ```
    EXEC sp_configure 'fill factor (%)', 90; -- requires restart to take effect
    RECONFIGURE;
    ```

I said "most" indexes should have fill factor; some don't need it. Specifically, indexes that don't experience page splits don't need a fill factor:

- **Any index where data will only ever be added at the end (of the index).** For example, the index on a date column in a log table: each successive insert will be a higher date, so it will go at the end of the index.

- **"Read only" indexes.** These include any index on a table that is functionally read only, or on a table in a read only database.

Defragment Indexes

Even if we configure good fill factor levels, fragmentation will still (eventually) occur. How do we go about maintaining our indexes, then? The plan starts out simple: every week or so, find out which indexes are fragmented, and run index maintenance (REORGANIZE or REBUILD statements) as appropriate.

And of course, just like with backups and integrity checks, index maintenance in the real world runs into a familiar set of issues:

- What if the index maintenance operation takes too long, and starts to impact resource usage during "prime time"?
- What if a new database is added, or an existing one removed? Will the routine automatically maintain that new database (or, avoid erroring out over a missing database)?
- How will we be alerted if index maintenance fails, or doesn't start? How are errors handled and logged?
- What if we want to see a history of index maintenance operations, how long they took, etc.?

And again, I recommend one of our free tools - Minion Reindex[13] – along with an alert, to handle most of these issues for you. There are also other free and paid tools available.

For now, though, we'll develop our own solution against the simplest possible case, to learn the principals involved. The simplest case here is: index maintenance on a single SQL Server instance, on a single user database (MyDatabaseName).

This process must include a recurring job which:

1. Detects fragmentation.
2. Generates and runs the defragment statements.

Before we build that process, we really should learn more about those defragment statements: REORGANIZE and REBUILD.

REORGANIZE vs REBUILD

The short version of REORGANIZE vs REBUILD is:

- **REORGANIZE** is a lightweight, online operation that's good for defragmenting lightly fragmented indexes.
- **REBUILD** is a heavier, *often* offline operation that's better for heavily fragmented indexes.

Remembering which one is which is easy: is it a bigger job to *reorganize* your kitchen – which might leave the room in a functional state –or to *rebuild* your kitchen? Conceptually at least, reorganizing is a lighter job.

Of course, there's more to know:

---

[13] See "Minion Reindex". http://MinionWare.net/Reindex

- **You can't REORGANIZE a heap** (a table with no clustered index). You can REBUILD it, or create a clustered index on it and reorg or rebuild *that*. (Be aware that adding a clustered index to a heap rewrites the whole table[14], and so it may take a while.)

- **"Rebuilding an index drops and re-creates the index.** This removes fragmentation, reclaims disk space by compacting the pages[5] based on the specified or existing fill factor setting, and reorders the index rows in contiguous pages. When ALL is specified, all indexes on the table are dropped and rebuilt in a single transaction." [12]

- **You can REBUILD or REORGANIZE all indexes – clustered and nonclustered – on a table** if you use ALTER INDEX ALL. For example, ALTER INDEX ALL ON dbo.TableName REBUILD;

- **If you're running SQL Server Enterprise Edition, you can perform online REBUILD operations**, with the option WITH (ONLINE = ON). For example, ALTER INDEX IndexName ON dbo.TableName REBUILD WITH (ONLINE = ON);

- **Extremely small indexes don't see much – if any – benefit from index maintenance.** The Microsoft article *Reorganize and Rebuild Indexes*[15] says, "fragmentation in a small index might not be reduced after reorganizing or rebuilding the index". I recommend excluding small indexes (anything under 1000 pages / 7 MB).

- **Index maintenance on FULL model databases can use up a lot of transaction log space**. To guard against this, take regular log backups during the maintenance, or switch the database to BULK_LOGGED model before the maintenance. Just remember to switch it back to FULL model after.

Detect Fragmentation

SQL Server provides a number of "dynamic management views", or DMVs, to offer insight into the system itself. Use the **sys.dm_db_index_physical_stats**[16] DMV to identify highly fragmented indexes.

> **NOTE**: What constitutes "highly fragmented" is a matter of some debate in the SQL community. On one hand, the "Reorganize and Rebuild Indexes" article noted above recommends that you reorganize indexes that are lightly fragmented (between 5% and 30%), and that you rebuild indexes that are heavily fragmented (more than 30%). But how did Microsoft arrive at that number? One expert from the development team said he gave

---

[14] See "Heaps (Tables without Clustered Indexes)". https://docs.microsoft.com/en-us/sql/relational-databases/indexes/heaps-tables-without-clustered-indexes

[15] "Reorganize and Rebuild Indexes", *Microsoft*. https://docs.microsoft.com/en-us/sql/relational-databases/indexes/reorganize-and-rebuild-indexes

[16] See "sys.dm_db_index_physical_stats (Transact-SQL)". https://docs.microsoft.com/en-us/sql/relational-databases/system-dynamic-management-views/sys-dm-db-index-physical-stats-transact-sql

the number simply because *they had to put a number down*. In other words: those numbers are arbitrary.

I tend to reorganize indexes up to 20% fragmentation, and rebuild indexes over that number.

To find highly fragmented indexes in a single database, query sys.dm_db_index_physical_stats, passing in the database ID as the first parameter:

```
SELECT object_id, index_id, avg_fragmentation_in_percent, fragment_count,
page_count
FROM sys.dm_db_index_physical_stats(DB_ID('MyDatabaseName'), NULL, NULL,
NULL, NULL)
WHERE avg_fragmentation_in_percent > 20;
```

This will return a set of data that includes the index fragmentation level, as noted in the avg_fragmentation_in_percent column:

object_id	index_id	avg_fragmentation_in_percent	fragment_count	page_count
389576426	2	57.1428571428571	5	7
437576597	2	60	4	5
437576597	3	83.3333333333333	6	6
485576768	1	30.7692307692308	5	13

Note that querying sys.dm_db_index_physical_stats can take quite a while for large databases, or if you decide to query it for all databases (by passing in NULL as the first parameter). This may well be a query you only want to run after peak times are over! Also note that the query uses the system function DB_ID() to get the ID of database "MyDatabaseName".

Using the result set returned by the query above, we can generate and run REORDER statements just for those highly fragmented indexes! This is exactly how free and third-party tools determine which indexes need maintenance.

Remember that extremely small indexes don't see much – if any – benefit from index maintenance. So, we can exclude small indexes – say, anything under 1000 pages (7 MB):

```
SELECT object_id, index_id, avg_fragmentation_in_percent, fragment_count,
page_count
FROM sys.dm_db_index_physical_stats(DB_ID('MyDatabaseName'), NULL, NULL,
NULL, NULL)
WHERE avg_fragmentation_in_percent > 20
    AND page_count > 1000;
```

We can alter this query easily to find indexes to reorganize – those with 5 to 30% fragmentation. And while we're at it, let's add joins to sys.tables and sys.indexes so we can get the table and index names:

```
SELECT dm.object_id, dm.index_id, avg_fragmentation_in_percent,
fragment_count, page_count
```

Chapter 3 Care and Feeding of a SQL Server

```
FROM sys.dm_db_index_physical_stats(DB_ID('MyDatabaseName'), NULL, NULL,
NULL, NULL) AS dm
INNER JOIN sys.indexes AS i ON i.object_id = dm.object_id AND i.index_id
= dm.index_id
INNER JOIN sys.tables AS t ON dm.object_id = t.object_id
WHERE dm.avg_fragmentation_in_percent BETWEEN 5 AND 30
    AND dm.page_count > 1000;
```

Generate and Run Statements

To rebuild a single index, we run a statement like this:

```
ALTER INDEX [IndexName] ON [dbo].[TableName] REBUILD ;
```

Note that if you're running SQL Server enterprise, you can perform online index rebuilds using the ONLINE option:

```
ALTER INDEX [IndexName] ON [dbo].[TableName] REBUILD WITH (ONLINE = ON);
```

And to reorganize an index, use the REORGANIZE keyword:

```
ALTER INDEX [IndexName] ON [dbo].[TableName] REORGANIZE;
```

So, we can alter the queries from the last section to generate these statements for indexes that need maintenance. First, REBUILD statements:

```
SELECT 'ALTER INDEX [' + i.name + '] ON ['
    + SCHEMA_NAME(t.schema_id) + '].[' + t.name
    + '] REBUILD;'
FROM sys.dm_db_index_physical_stats(DB_ID('MyDatabaseName'), NULL, NULL,
NULL, NULL) AS dm
INNER JOIN sys.indexes AS i ON i.object_id = dm.object_id AND i.index_id
= dm.index_id
INNER JOIN sys.tables AS t ON dm.object_id = t.object_id
WHERE dm.avg_fragmentation_in_percent > 20
    AND dm.page_count > 1000
    AND i.type_desc <> 'HEAP';
```

Note: This query excludes heaps (tables without clustered indexes). We certainly *can* rebuild fragmented heaps, but remember that this will also rebuild all of the nonclustered indexes on those tables. Also, a heap rebuild takes a different syntax (ALTER TABLE [TableName] REBUILD). For the purposes of this example, I'd rather not incur that cost by default. You can certainly write a query to generate heap rebuilds, if that's what works best in your environment (and by that, I mean if the extra rebuild cost doesn't take up too much time or resources).

And next, REORGANIZE statements:

```
SELECT 'ALTER INDEX [' + i.name + '] ON ['
    + SCHEMA_NAME(t.schema_id) + '].[' + t.name
    + '] REORGANIZE;'
```

```
FROM sys.dm_db_index_physical_stats(DB_ID('MyDatabaseName'), NULL, NULL,
NULL, NULL) AS dm
INNER JOIN sys.indexes AS i ON i.object_id = dm.object_id AND i.index_id
= dm.index_id
INNER JOIN sys.tables AS t ON dm.object_id = t.object_id
WHERE dm.avg_fragmentation_in_percent BETWEEN 5 AND 30
    AND dm.page_count > 1000
    AND i.type_desc <> 'HEAP';   -- Can't reorganize a heap.
```

Procedure dbo.SimpleIndexMaintenance

The final, simple solution is a parameterized stored procedure (SP) that uses a query like those above to generate statements for a given database:

```
CREATE PROCEDURE dbo.SimpleIndexMaintenance
    @DBName sysname
AS
BEGIN
    DECLARE @i INT = 1,
            @max INT,
            @sql NVARCHAR(MAX);

    CREATE TABLE #Statements (
        ID INT IDENTITY(1, 1),
        stmt NVARCHAR(MAX)
    );

    ---- GENERATE STATEMENTS ----
    SET @SQL = 'SELECT CASE
                    WHEN dm.avg_fragmentation_in_percent > 20
THEN
                        ''ALTER INDEX ['' + i.name + '']
ON ['' + SCHEMA_NAME(t.schema_id) + ''].['' + t.name + ''] REBUILD WITH
(ONLINE = ON);''
                    WHEN dm.avg_fragmentation_in_percent BETWEEN
5 AND 30 THEN
                        ''ALTER INDEX ['' + i.name + '']
ON ['' + SCHEMA_NAME(t.schema_id) + ''].['' + t.name + ''] REORGANIZE ;''
                END AS stmt
        FROM [' + @DBName + '].sys.dm_db_index_physical_stats(DB_ID(''' +
@DBName + '''), NULL, NULL, NULL, NULL) AS dm
            INNER JOIN [' + @DBName + '].sys.indexes AS i
                ON i.object_id = dm.object_id
                AND i.index_id = dm.index_id
            INNER JOIN [' + @DBName + '].sys.tables AS t
                ON dm.object_id = t.object_id
        WHERE dm.avg_fragmentation_in_percent >= 5
            AND dm.page_count > 1000
            AND i.type_desc <> ''HEAP'';'
```

```
        INSERT INTO #Statements ( stmt )
        EXEC (@sql);

        -- Add the "USE databasename" statement:
        UPDATE #Statements SET stmt = 'USE [' + @DBname + ']; ' + stmt;

        ---- RUN STATEMENTS ----
        SELECT @max = MAX(id) FROM #Statements;
        WHILE @i <= @max
        BEGIN
                SELECT @sql = stmt FROM #Statements WHERE ID = @i;
                PRINT @sql;
                IF @sql IS NOT NULL
                        EXEC (@sql);
                SET @i = @i + 1;
        END;

        DROP TABLE #Statements;
END;
```

Earlier, I listed several issues with simple systems like this: overrunning the maintenance window, failing to deal with new and dropped databases, alerting, and lack of logging. The solution you use should also provide better configuration options, including:

- Thresholds for REORGANIZE and REBUILD.

- Fill factor and pad index.

- Exclusions. For example, maybe you *never* want to maintain indexes in database "Temp1".

- Options per database, table, or even index – as opposed to our solution, which allows one setting across the board.

All these limitations are a very big deal, which is why I recommend downloading a good third-party solution. You absolutely need to understand index maintenance, but you don't have to rewrite the whole process yourself.

Review

Important points:

- Indexes become fragmented, which degrades performance. So, it is important to prevent fragmentation, and to perform regular index maintenance.

- Prevent index fragmentation by configuring fill factor. 90% is a good starting point.

- Maintain indexes using REORGANIZE and REBUILD statements, preferably via a complete third-party tool that includes scheduling, logging, and configuration options.

- Determining what is "highly fragmented" is a matter of debate. Reorganizing indexes fragmented above 5%, and rebuilding indexes fragmented above 20%, is a good starting point.
- Querying sys.dm_db_index_physical_stats can take a long time. You may want to do this outside of peak database usage times.

Further reading:

- SQL Server Heaps, and Their Fragmentation, https://www.simple-talk.com/sql/database-administration/sql-server-heaps-and-their-fragmentation/
- A SQL Server DBA myth a day: (29/30) fixing heap fragmentation, https://www.sqlskills.com/blogs/paul/a-sql-server-dba-myth-a-day-2930-fixing-heap-fragmentation/

Disk Management

In a small, informal Twitter poll in 2016 I asked the SQL Server community what their biggest database administrative headache was, fully expecting to hear "backups" or something similar. But the biggest problem reported was *disk management*, a.k.a. "disk free space monitoring".

In retrospect, this makes sense. We as DBAs aren't usually in control of ordering or parceling out disk space, but the systems we're in charge of typically take up more space than anything else in the company.

So, we have a great storm brewing:

- Database and backup files take up a ton of space.
- DBAs usually don't manage disk space allocation, and must request space.
- There is no automatic space monitor/alert/management that comes installed with the OS, or with SQL Server.

We're absolutely primed for disks to run out of space, bringing down databases or ruining backup solutions. What's to be done?

The only two possible answers are: create your own solution, or get the company to buy a third-party solution. Here, we'll present another simple, "first step" solution that you can build on.

There is no super easy way to get disk space information from T-SQL, and so we turn to PowerShell. Once you know some PowerShell, it's relatively simple to get all the information you need. Here we'll go step by step to retrieve the information, make it usable, and store it in a table (which will make it easier to alert on!).

Disk Space Information via PowerShell

This PowerShell command gets a list of drives from the computer, and capacity and free space information for each:

```
Get-WmiObject Win32_Volume
```

If you open a PowerShell window and run that command, you'll get the right information back, but it will also include "system drives" that we don't use or control. Let's filter those out:

```
Get-WmiObject Win32_Volume | WHERE{ $_.DriveType -eq 3 -and $_.name -notmatch "\?" }
```

This code gets those same drives, and then passes ("pipes") the information to a WHERE filter. DriveType 3 means "fixed drives" – no USB or floppy disks – and the name -notmatch "\?" filters out those system drives.

The output is still a bit messy, though:

```
__GENUS                 : 2
__CLASS                 : Win32_Volume
__SUPERCLASS            : CIM_StorageVolume
...
Capacity                : 511048306688
Caption                 : C:\
Compressed              : False
ConfigManagerErrorCode  :
ConfigManagerUserConfig :
CreationClassName       :
Description             :
DeviceID                : \\?\Volume{3eff9ded-0000-0000-0000-501f00000000}\
DirtyBitSet             :
DriveLetter             : C:
DriveType               : 3
ErrorCleared            :
ErrorDescription        :
ErrorMethodology        :
FileSystem              : NTFS
FreeSpace               : 142568759296
IndexingEnabled         : True
...
```

That's not a pretty output at all. Let's just pull back the data that we need: drive letter, capacity, and free space. And, we'll calculate the percent space free, while we're at it:

```
Get-WmiObject Win32_Volume | `
WHERE{ $_.DriveType -eq 3 -and $_.name -notmatch "\?" } | `
select DriveLetter, Capacity, FreeSpace,
@{LABEL='FreeSpacePct';EXPRESSION={$_.FreeSpace*100/$_.Capacity} }
```

See how we're using the same command as before, and piping that output to a PowerShell "select" statement. The output from this command looks better:

```
DriveLetter     Capacity        FreeSpace       FreeSpacePct
-----------     --------        ---------       ------------
C:              511048306688    142671421440    27.917404200911
```

One last thing: let's convert Capacity and FreeSpace to GB, to make those numbers easier to read:

```
Get-WmiObject Win32_Volume | `
WHERE{ $_.DriveType -eq 3 -and $_.name -notmatch "\?" } | `
select DriveLetter, @{LABEL='CapacityGB';EXPRESSION={"{0:N2}" -f ($_.Capacity/1GB)} }, `
@{LABEL='FreeSpaceGB';EXPRESSION={"{0:N2}" -f ($_.FreeSpace/1GB)} }, `
@{LABEL='FreeSpacePct';EXPRESSION={$_.FreeSpace*100/$_.Capacity} }
```

Saving the Data to SQL Server

That PowerShell command does look like a mess, but we got there step by step. Now, we need to get that data into a SQL table. Create the table:

```
CREATE TABLE dbo.DiskSpace
(
    ExecutionDateTime DATETIME2,
    DriveLetter NVARCHAR(10),
    Capacity FLOAT,
    FreeSpace FLOAT,
    FreeSpacePct FLOAT
);
Create the final script that retrieves the data, formats it, and inserts
it to the table:
$DriveList = Get-WmiObject Win32_Volume | WHERE{ $_.DriveType -eq 3 -and
$_.name -notmatch "\?" } | select DriveLetter,
@{LABEL='CapacityGB';EXPRESSION={"{0:N2}" -f ($_.Capacity/1GB)} },
@{LABEL='FreeSpaceGB';EXPRESSION={"{0:N2}" -f ($_.FreeSpace/1GB)} },
@{LABEL='FreeSpacePct';EXPRESSION={"{0:N2}" -f
($_.FreeSpace*100/$_.Capacity)} }

$ExecutionDateTime = Get-Date -Format "%M/%d/%y %H:m:ss";

$DriveList | %{ # Loop through each drive

            $DriveLetter = $_.DriveLetter;
            $CapacityGB = $_.CapacityGB;
            $FreeSpaceGB = $_.FreeSpaceGB;
    $FreeSpacePct = $_.FreeSpacePct;

            # Create the insert query
```

```
        $InsertQuery = "INSERT INTO dbo.DiskSpace ( ExecutionDateTime ,
DriveLetter , Capacity , FreeSpace , FreeSpacePct ) VALUES
('$ExecutionDateTime', '$DriveLetter', $CapacityGB, $FreeSpaceGB,
$FreeSpacePct);"

        # Run the insert query
        Invoke-Sqlcmd -ServerInstance . -Database MyDBName -Query
$InsertQuery -SuppressProviderContextWarning
    }
```

That Powershell script can go straight into a job step (make sure the step is of type Powershell). From then on, you can use the data in the DiskSpace table to alert you on low disk space! We'll talk about the alerting piece in "Alerting", below.

We can do more with this solution, so let's talk about future upgrades.

Upgrade Your Solution

If you create your own solution, it should have a few key features:

- Collect disk space usage data into SQL Server tables.
- Use that data to project when the disk is likely to become full (or better still, 80% or 90% full).
- Delete old data as it ages out. (After all, nobody wants 10 years of disk space data on hand.)
- Automatically alert the DBA team.

Note that I stress "alert", because there are solutions that require you to have a dashboard up and running, and for you to notice a pop up alert, or a dashboard light changing. This isn't effective *at all*, and it's not scalable. "Alert" means an active alert, like an email.

There are other features that would be beneficial – such as the ability to exclude disks from alerting, configurable alert thresholds, centralized data storage, and so on. But you're a DBA with limited time, and so we're talking about creating a first step, bare-bones disk management system.

How to create a comprehensive system is an entire book unto itself, and so I leave you with the other solution: get the company to pay for something good.

Review

Important Points:

- Disk management, or disk free space monitoring, is one of the biggest challenges faced by DBAs.

- T-SQL has no easy insight into disk free space, so use PowerShell and SQL tables. Or, convince the company to buy a disk free space monitoring solution.
- Configure an alert for low disk space.

Further reading:

- Video: Beginning PowerShell for DBAs 1, http://midnightdba.itbookworm.com/Video/Watch?VideoId=25
- Video: PowerShell Cmdlets for DBAs, http://midnightdba.itbookworm.com/EventVids/OKC2014/SQLSatOKC2014_Powershell CmdletsDBAscamrec.wmv
- Stairway to SQL PowerShell Level 1, http://www.sqlservercentral.com/articles/Stairway+Series/90381/

Alerting

In live, production SQL shops, I have seen alerts directed automatically to the "deleted" folder; alerts ignored for months; and alerts for *positive* events, like "The DB1 transaction log backup completed at 4:45pm". These are not effective alerts.

An alert is a signal that something is wrong, and that you should do something to handle the issue. Alerts should be *actionable*.

Many alerts have a far too narrow scope. For example, every shop I've ever worked in has an alert for failed backups, but very few have had an alert for missing backups. After all, a backup might be considered missing if the job failed, or never started, or never existed in the first place!

Alerts should be actionable, and they should have a broad scope. With these principles in mind, let's look at alerts for backups, integrity checks, index maintenance, and disk management.

Note: So far, the solutions we've developed have been relatively simple – even primitive. So, we'll develop simple alerting solutions to go along with our simple backups, integrity checks, index maintenance, and disk management.

Important: All these alerting solutions depend on the SQL Agent to be up and running. If Agent is stopped for any reason, you won't receive any alerts! The way to prevent this is to have a central server dedicated to monitoring your instances and providing alerts. But again, that's a whole other book!

First: Set up Mail

To send mail from SQL Server, you must configure Database Mail, along with a mail profile[17] (an account used as the "from" address for Database Mail). Use the instructions in the "Configure Database Mail" article on Docs.Microsoft.com[18], or use the script SQL Magazine provides on Database Mail[19].

To use standard SQL Agent alerts, we would need to configure an Operator[20] to be on the receiving end of the alerts. Instead, we're going to use the system stored procedure **sp_send_dbmail**.

Backup Alerts

Ideally, an alert system would use backup and maintenance logs to determine if the process had kicked off, if any errors occurred, if a database were missing from the process, or if a database hadn't been backed up within a reasonable time. With those logs, it's a fairly simple matter to develop the right queries, and then send out an email with the results when necessary.

For now, we'll proceed as if we're making everything from scratch, and we don't have this kind of logging yet. Once logging *is* in place, it won't be difficult to refactor the queries to use that log data.

Looking at the list of possible backup failures above, we can reduce our backup alert needs down to this concept: **alert me if any database hasn't been backed up in X hours.** If full backups run daily, and log backups run every fifteen minutes, it would be reasonable to get alerts for:

- Any database without a full backup in the last 24 hours
- Any database without a log backup in the last hour.

Let's break this up into steps.

First, what databases are online? Let's save the list of database names, and their recovery model descriptions, to a temporary table:

```
SELECT name, recovery_model_desc
INTO #DBs
```

---

[17] See "Create a Database Mail Profile" https://docs.microsoft.com/en-us/sql/relational-databases/database-mail/create-a-database-mail-profile

[18] See "Configure Database Mail". https://docs.microsoft.com/en-us/sql/relational-databases/database-mail/configure-database-mail

[19] See "How to Set Up SQL Server Database Mail in One Easy Script". http://sqlmag.com/database-administration/how-set-sql-server-database-mail-one-easy-script

[20] See "Operators". https://docs.microsoft.com/en-us/sql/ssms/agent/operators

Chapter 3   Care and Feeding of a SQL Server

```
FROM sys.databases
WHERE [state] = 0 -- ONLINE
      AND name <> 'tempdb';
```

Second, when was the latest full backup for each database? Add two columns to the temporary table – one each for full and log backups – and update them.

```
ALTER TABLE #DBs ADD LastFullBackupDate datetime;
ALTER TABLE #DBs ADD LastLogBackupDate datetime;

-- Find the last full backup date for all DBs:
UPDATE DB
SET LastFullBackupDate = D.BackupDate
FROM #DBs AS DB
INNER JOIN (
    SELECT B.database_name,
           MAX(B.backup_finish_date) AS BackupDate
    FROM msdb.dbo.backupset AS B
    WHERE B.type = 'D'   -- Full backups
    GROUP BY B.database_name ) AS D ON D.database_name = DB.name;

-- Find the last log backup date for all non-SIMPLE model DBs:
UPDATE DB
SET LastLogBackupDate = D.BackupDate
FROM #DBs AS DB
INNER JOIN (
    SELECT B.database_name,
           MAX(B.backup_finish_date) AS BackupDate
    FROM msdb.dbo.backupset AS B
    WHERE B.type = 'L'   -- Log backups
    GROUP BY B.database_name ) AS D ON D.database_name = DB.name
WHERE DB.recovery_model_desc <> 'SIMPLE'; -- SIMPLE databases can't do
log backups.
```

Now we have a set of data that looks like this:

name	recovery_model_desc	LastFullBackupDate	LastLogBackupDate
master	SIMPLE	2017-06-29 22:00:04.000	*NULL*
model	FULL	2017-06-29 22:00:06.000	2017-06-29 22:15:22.000
msdb	SIMPLE	2017-06-29 22:00:10.000	*NULL*
DB1	FULL	2017-06-29 19:27:03.000	2017-06-29 22:30:19.000
DB2	SIMPLE	*NULL*	*NULL*

Third, are any of the backups out of date or missing? Use one query per backup type:

Chapter 3   Care and Feeding of a SQL Server

```sql
-- Missing or old full backups:
SELECT name, LastFullBackupDate,
    DATEDIFF(HOUR, LastFullBackupDate,  GETDATE()) AS
HoursSinceFullBackup
FROM #DBs
WHERE ISNULL(LastFullBackupDate, '1/1/1950') < DATEADD(HOUR, -24,
GETDATE());

-- Missing or old log backups:
SELECT name, LastLogBackupDate,
    DATEDIFF(HOUR, LastLogBackupDate,  GETDATE()) AS HoursSinceLogBackup
    , recovery_model_desc
FROM #DBs
WHERE ISNULL(LastLogBackupDate, '1/1/1950') < DATEADD(HOUR, -1,
GETDATE());
```

Finally, send an alert about any missing or old backups. Create one job to run full backup alerts daily:

```sql
DECLARE @Subject NVARCHAR(200), @Query NVARCHAR(MAX);
SELECT @Subject = 'ALERT: [' + @@SERVERNAME + '] missing backups-FULL';
-- [ Here, set @Query = the "Missing or old full backups" query from
above ]

IF EXISTS (SELECT * FROM #DBs
WHERE ISNULL(LastFullBackupDate, '1/1/1950') < DATEADD(HOUR, -24,
GETDATE()))
EXEC msdb.dbo.sp_send_dbmail
    @profile_name = 'YourProfileName',
    @recipients = 'Email@Address.com',
    @query = @Query,
    @Subject = @Subject,
    @attach_query_result_as_file = 1;
DROP TABLE #DBs;
```

Create a second job to run log backup alerts hourly:

```sql
DECLARE @Subject NVARCHAR(200), @Query NVARCHAR(MAX);
SELECT @Subject = 'ALERT: [' + @@SERVERNAME + '] missing backups-LOG;'
-- [ Here, set @Query = the "Missing or old log backups" query from above
]

IF EXISTS (SELECT * FROM #DBs
WHERE ISNULL(LastLogBackupDate, '1/1/1950') < DATEADD(HOUR, -1,
GETDATE()))
EXEC msdb.dbo.sp_send_dbmail
    @profile_name = 'YourProfileName',
    @recipients = 'Email@Address.com',
    @query = @Query,
    @Subject = @Subject,
    @attach_query_result_as_file = 1;
```

```
DROP TABLE #DBs;
```

From now on, as long as the SQL Agent service is running, you will receive an email with a list of missing backups any time backups fail for any reason!

Integrity Check Alerts

Just like with backup alerts, integrity check alerts are much easier to accomplish in conjunction with a system that includes logging (like Minion CheckDB). And just like the last section, we'll work here as if we don't have access to a system like that.

What we need from integrity check alerts is slightly different. What we need to know is twofold:

- Have integrity checks been missed?
- Has an integrity check revealed any corruption?

First, find out if an integrity check has been missed. Some of this script will be brand new, because we're using xp_ReadErrorLog to search the SQL log for CHECKDB events. The rest of the script will look a lot like the backup alerts, above, because we will populate and update a #DBs temporary table with the latest operation date:

```sql
-- Get CheckDB actions from the current log:
CREATE TABLE #ErrorLog
(
    LogDate DATETIME,
    ProcessInfo NVARCHAR(200),
    Text NVARCHAR(MAX)
);

INSERT INTO #ErrorLog
    ( LogDate, ProcessInfo, Text )
EXEC sys.xp_readerrorlog 0, 1, N'CHECKDB';

DELETE FROM #ErrorLog WHERE [Text] NOT LIKE 'DBCC CHECKDB (%';

-- Isolate the database name:
ALTER TABLE #ErrorLog ADD DBName NVARCHAR(MAX);
UPDATE #ErrorLog SET DBName = REPLACE([Text] , 'DBCC CHECKDB (', '');
UPDATE #ErrorLog SET DBName = LEFT(DBName, CHARINDEX(') ', DBName)-1);
```

The #ErrorLog table now contains data that looks like this:

LogDate	ProcessInfo	Text	DBName
2017-06-29 14:02:46.890	spid51	DBCC CHECKDB (MinionDev) executed by MIDNIGHT\Jen found 0 errors and repaired 0 errors. …	MinionDev

Chapter 3   **Care and** Feeding of a SQL Server

We can use the DBName and the LogDate, along with a list of online databases (from sys.databases), to generate a query of old or missed CHECKDBs:

```sql
-- Find the last CHECKDB date for all DBs:
SELECT name, CAST(NULL AS DATETIME) AS LastCheckDBDate
INTO #DBs
FROM sys.databases
WHERE [state] = 0; -- ONLINE

UPDATE DB
SET LastCheckDBDate = D.LogDate
FROM #DBs AS DB
INNER JOIN (
    SELECT MAX(LogDate) AS LogDate, DBName
    FROM #ErrorLog
    GROUP BY DBName ) AS D ON D.DBName = DB.name;

-- Missing or old CheckDBs:
SELECT name, LastCheckDBDate,
    DATEDIFF(HOUR, LastCheckDBDate, GETDATE()) AS DaysSinceCheckDB
FROM #DBs
WHERE ISNULL(LastCheckDBDate, '1/1/1950') < DATEADD(DAY, -7, GETDATE());
```

Just like with backups, we will create a job to run missed CheckDB alerts weekly:

```sql
DECLARE @Subject NVARCHAR(200), @Query NVARCHAR(MAX);
SELECT @Subject = 'ALERT: [' + @@SERVERNAME + '] missing CHECKDB';
-- [ Here, set @Query = the "Missing or old CheckDBs" query from above ]

IF EXISTS (SELECT * FROM #DBs
WHERE ISNULL(LastCheckDBDate, '1/1/1950') < DATEADD(DAY, -7, GETDATE()))
EXEC msdb.dbo.sp_send_dbmail
    @profile_name = 'YourProfileName',
    @recipients = 'Email@Address.com',
    @query = @Query,
    @Subject = @Subject,
    @attach_query_result_as_file = 1;
DROP TABLE #ErrorLog;
DROP TABLE #DBs;
```

Second, alert for corruption: xp_ReadErrorLog will let us see if any corruption has been discovered. Corruption will show up as an Error 823, Error 824, or Error 825, so we search for all three.

```sql
-- Get corruption errors from the current log:
CREATE TABLE #ErrorLog
(
    LogDate DATETIME,
    ProcessInfo NVARCHAR(200),
    Text NVARCHAR(MAX)
```

129

```
);

INSERT INTO #ErrorLog
        ( LogDate, ProcessInfo, Text )
EXEC sys.xp_readerrorlog 0, 1, N'Error', N'823';
INSERT INTO #ErrorLog
        ( LogDate, ProcessInfo, Text )
EXEC sys.xp_readerrorlog 0, 1, N'Error', N'824';
INSERT INTO #ErrorLog
        ( LogDate, ProcessInfo, Text )
EXEC sys.xp_readerrorlog 0, 1, N'Error', N'825';

-- If there are errors, send an alert
DECLARE @Subject NVARCHAR(200), @Query NVARCHAR(MAX);
SELECT @Subject = 'ALERT: [' + @@SERVERNAME + '] CORRUPTION ERRORS';
SET @Query = 'SELECT * FROM #ErrorLog;'

IF EXISTS (SELECT * FROM #ErrorLog)
EXEC msdb.dbo.sp_send_dbmail
    @profile_name = 'YourProfileName',
    @recipients = 'Email@Address.com',
    @query = @Query,
    @Subject = @Subject,
    @attach_query_result_as_file = 1;
DROP TABLE #ErrorLog;
```

Index Maintenance Alerts

Index maintenance is important, but not nearly as critical as backups, integrity checks, and disk management. If index maintenance doesn't happen for a few rounds, often the only consequence is some extra performance degradation. Whereas, with the other three, data is destroyed, left vulnerable, or made inaccessible!

The point is that for index maintenance, the only alert we truly need is for the circumstance when the job has not run in some time.

Find the most recent, successful index maintenance job run time: We can find the last successful run date for the job in the MSDB table *sysjobhistory*, and save that data to a temporary table:

```
SELECT TOP 1
    job.name,
    CONVERT(DATETIME, CONVERT(VARCHAR(10), history.run_date)) AS
SuccessRunDate
INTO #MaintenanceHistory
FROM msdb..sysjobhistory AS history
INNER JOIN msdb..sysjobs AS job ON job.job_id = history.job_id
WHERE job.name = 'IndexMaintenance'
    AND history.run_status = 1 -- Succeeded
ORDER BY SuccessRunDate DESC;
```

Note that we're not bothering with the most recent run *time*. The majority of index maintenance processes run at most once per day, though we could easily modify this to get the most recent run time.

Second, alert for no recent index maintenance: If the index maintenance job hasn't run recently – for example, within the last three days – send an alert:

```
DECLARE @Subject NVARCHAR(200), @Query NVARCHAR(MAX);
SELECT @Subject = 'ALERT: [' + @@SERVERNAME + '] Index Maintenance
Overdue';
SET @Query = 'SELECT * FROM #MaintenanceHistory WHERE SuccessRunDate >
DateAdd(Day, -3, GetDate());'

IF EXISTS (SELECT * FROM #MaintenanceHistory WHERE SuccessRunDate >
DateAdd(Day, -3, GetDate()))
EXEC msdb.dbo.sp_send_dbmail
    @profile_name = 'YourProfileName',
    @recipients = 'Email@Address.com',
    @query = @Query,
    @Subject = @Subject,
    @attach_query_result_as_file = 1;
DROP TABLE #MaintenanceHistory;
```

Disk Management Alerts

In the "Disk Management" section, we developed a solution that retrieves disk capacity and use information, and saves it to the SQL Server table dbo.DiskSpace.

For this alert, we simply check the most recent data collection (as defined by the most recent ExecutionDateTime), and see if the free space percentage is low (say, below 15%).

First, get the most recent disk space collection: If any disks are low on space (as of the last collection), save the data to a temporary table:

```
SELECT ExecutionDateTime
     , DriveLetter
     , Capacity
     , FreeSpace
     , FreeSpacePct
INTO #DiskSpace
WHERE ExecutionDateTime =
      ( SELECT MAX(ExecutionDateTime) FROM dbo.DiskSpace )
    AND FreeSpacePct < 15;
```

Second, alert for low disk space: If a disk is under the free space threshold, send an alert:

```
DECLARE @Subject NVARCHAR(200), @Query NVARCHAR(MAX);
SELECT @Subject = 'ALERT: [' + @@SERVERNAME + '] Low Disk Space';
SET @Query = 'SELECT * FROM #DiskSpace;'

IF EXISTS (SELECT * FROM #DiskSpace)
    EXEC msdb.dbo.sp_send_dbmail
                @profile_name = 'YourProfileName',
                @recipients = 'Email@Address.com',
                @query = @Query,
                @Subject = @Subject,
                @attach_query_result_as_file = 1;
DROP TABLE #DiskSpace;
```

Review

Important notes:

- Alerts should be *actionable*. Any alert that isn't actionable is just spam.
- Alerts should have a broad scope, to catch as many types of failure as possible.
- All the presented alert solutions depend on SQL Agent. If Agent is stopped, you won't receive alerts!
- Alerting is far easier if you're working with backup and maintenance systems that provide logging.
- Implement alerting consistently across all your SQL Server instances.

Further reading:

- Configure Database Mail, https://docs.microsoft.com/en-us/sql/relational-databases/database-mail/configure-database-mail
- Create a Database Mail Profile, https://docs.microsoft.com/en-us/sql/relational-databases/database-mail/create-a-database-mail-profile
- How to Set Up SQL Server Database Mail in One Easy Scrip", http://sqlmag.com/database-administration/how-set-sql-server-database-mail-one-easy-script
- Operators, https://docs.microsoft.com/en-us/sql/ssms/agent/operators

Chapter Review

So, to review:

- It's vitally important to back up, maintain, and alert on your SQL Server instances.
- Let someone else do most of the work: download good, free, third-party software for backups, index maintenance, and integrity checks.
- But, have a good working understanding of the principals involved!
- Configure actionable alerts that have a good, broad scope (so that they catch as many *types* of process failures as possible).
- Make sure you set up backup, maintenance, and alerting on all your SQL Server instances!

Chapter 4
Indexing for Beginners

By: Kathi Kellenberger, Data Platform MVP

To the novice, indexes can seem like magic. The right indexes can dramatically improve the performance of queries, but determining what those indexes are is not an easy task. Or is it? This chapter explains how indexes work and how to figure out which indexes to create.

Introduction

Fifteen years ago, I found myself as the database administrator at a large law firm. I did have some experience with SQL Server, even earning the MCDBA certification at the time. As a developer, there was much I had to learn.

One of the most important applications in the firm was annoyingly slow. Shortly after I took the job, my manager asked me if there were indexes in the application's database. I confirmed there were, but I didn't know if those indexes were right for the queries or even how to figure that out. Eventually, I determined that there were some issues with the storage configuration and there was no index maintenance job set up. After correcting those two problems, the application performance improved, but I still had a lot to learn about indexes.

Data rows and indexes are stored on disk in an object called a page. This page holds 8 K bytes. In order for SQL Server to read the data, the page must be copied into memory. The fewer pages needed, the faster the query will run. Indexes help because of this fact. Without an index, the database engine may need to load all the pages of a table into memory. This could be thousands or even millions of pages. An index could potentially decrease this to just a handful of pages, dramatically improving the performance. CPU, I/O, and memory pressure are all reduced when effective indexes are in place. That's why it's so important that DBAs and developers understand why indexes are needed and how to take advantage of them.

This chapter covers traditional tables and indexes. Other types of indexes include XML, spatial, full-text, column store, and the indexes of in-memory tables. None of these will be covered. When the words **table** and **index** are used in this chapter, they will refer to the traditional objects.

Dictionaries, Novels, and Textbooks

I have presented my "Indexing for Beginners" session at PASS Summit and at a few SQL Saturdays. I've also taught the topic many times during T-SQL classes. My favorite part of teaching indexing is the many parallels to real life. Indexes on database tables make more sense to beginners once they imagine using these common objects. Sadly, some of these objects, such as phone books, aren't used much anymore.

Chapter 4 Indexing for Beginners

When talking about indexes, we must take a step back and talk about tables. A table may be one of two structures: a heap or a clustered index. You may hear someone say they are adding a clustered index to a table. That is actually incorrect. They are turning the table into a clustered index. That's right. A clustered index is a particular table structure. A common interview question is "How many clustered indexes can you have on a table?" The answer is one because the clustered index is the table, not something added to it.

I've used a phone book to represent clustered indexes for years, but recently I decided that a dictionary is better. When I was a kid, we always had a dictionary in our desk. I remember using it multiple times a day. At home, my dad had a larger dictionary that I loved using. I found out from my grandson Thomas that he had a personal dictionary in his desk in school in 3rd grade. Outside of that, the classrooms have a dictionary or two to share among the students.

Dictionaries are organized alphabetically by the words defined inside. You will find all the words that begin with **A** at the beginning and all the words beginning with **Z** at the end. You will also find pronunciations, origins, and definitions for each entry. If the defined words were stored randomly instead of in alphabetic order, it would be very difficult to find the word you were interested in. You would have to read or scan the entire dictionary to find the word. Instead, you can quickly locate the desired word. Imagine that you need the definition of **database**. You would open the dictionary about a fourth of the way in. You would go back and forth until you found the correct page. Then you would quickly locate the word on that page. It would take seconds. Reading every entry in the dictionary would take…well, you would probably lose interest long before finding the word.

The phone book is also similar to a clustered index. The names are in order, and additional information such as the address and phone number are included.

Tables that do not have clustered indexes are called **heaps**. Heaps are like novels. Imagine that you tried to read a novel with alphabetized words. It wouldn't make sense at all. The order of the words in a novel do make sense because they form sentences that combine into a story. You read the novel in order starting at page one and continue until you reach the end. Well, most of us read novels that way.

The third type of structure you'll learn about in this chapter is a **nonclustered index**. A nonclustered index is a separate object that points to a table. They can point to both heaps and clustered indexes. Think of a text book. The main section of the book is a heap. There is an index in the back, a smaller alphabetized structure that tells you which page contains information about a topic. Each key in a nonclustered index points to one or more pages of a table. I really like how the data in a book and in a table are both stored in pages!

At this point, we have barely begun talking about indexes in a SQL Server database, but I hope you can see how indexes save time in the physical world. In a SQL Server database, the right indexes make all the difference.

Heaps

In the last section, I compared a heap to a novel or the main section of a textbook. The words are found inside the book in the order that the author adds them. The rows of a heap are found in pages in the order that they have been inserted into the table. To find any particular word, you must look at every word. You can't even stop when you locate the word you need because it may be found in the heap more than once. Figure 89 is an example. The letters have been added in order, and you must look all seven letters to find the As.

Figure 89 – The rows in a heap

> **Note**: This figure, like all the others in this chapter, is a simplistic illustration meant to describe a concept not to be completely correct.

I am often asked about the best table structure: heaps or clustered indexes. Of course, the answer is "It depends." For the most part, clustered indexes are recommended for SQL Server database tables, but there are situations where heaps make more sense. For example, a staging database where data from other systems is copied each night before the data is loaded into a data warehouse may be more efficient as a heap. Another example is temp tables. You can create clustered index temp tables, but often temp tables are heaps.

Listing 1 is an example of creating a heap table.

Listing 1: Create a heap
```
CREATE TABLE [dbo].[HeapExample] (
[ID] INT NOT NULL,
[TheValue] VARCHAR(30) NULL
);
```

Clustered Indexes

The clustered index is the table. The table is the clustered index. I have occasionally run into folks during my presentations who have argued this point with me, but it is the truth. A clustered index is organized by a key. The key will be composed of one or more columns from the table. Most of the time, that key will also be the primary key of the table. When you search that table by the key, only a small number of pages will be read. If you search by another column, the database engine will read every row trying to find the value.

Picture that dictionary again. If you search for a particular word to learn what it means, the word is easy to find. You can estimate which part of the book it's in and then, by trial and error, you can locate the page. Within a few seconds, you find the word and read the definition.

Imagine that you have the definition but not the word. You could still find the entry in the dictionary, but it would require reading every entry. I'm sure you would give up long before you found it. Fortunately, SQL Server doesn't give up so easily.

Figure 90 is the simplified structure of a clustered index. It's called a balanced tree or B-tree. The clustered index is divided into two parts: the non-leaf levels and the leaf level. The index structure is an upside down tree. The root is at the top, and the leaves are at the bottom. The non-leaf levels contain the key columns and pointers to other pages in the index. This figure shows just a fraction of the pointers, represented by arrows, which are found in the index, but it should be enough to help you understand how the index works. Another difference between this figure and reality, is that the non-leaf levels are much flatter than this. A small table may have only one non-leaf level. You'll see this when we query the index metadata later in the chapter.

The leaf levels contain another copy of the keys and the non-key column values. In our dictionary analogy, the entries are the keys and they are stored in the non-leaf levels. The leaf level repeats the keys and contains the definitions, origins, and pronunciations.

In a clustered index, if the cluster key is not unique, SQL Server will add a uniqueifier to the rows. This ensures that each key is unique within the clustered index, but the uniqueifier is not a value that you will actually see or need to care about.

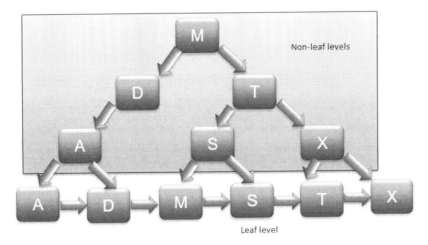

Figure 90 – Simplified index structure

In the heap example, we had to look at seven values to find the As. To find the As in this simplistic clustered index, you start at the root and then go left or right until finding the value. In this case, you would start at M, go left since A is less than M. At D, you would go left again. Now you have found A, and you just need to continue to the leaf level page. You have read four pages instead of seven. In a real table, the difference will usually be tens of thousands of pages.

When I do a live presentation on this topic, I always run a simulation of finding a value in a heap compared to an index. For the heap, my simulation searches each value in a table filled with random values. To simulate the index, I do a binary search. A binary search begins searching a sorted list in the middle. It continues to break the list in half, either higher or lower than the last value, until the desired value is found. I usually search a heap of 10,000 rows, and the number of searches could be any number between 1 and 10,000. For the index, I'll continue to increase the number of sorted values to 1 million. Every time I search for a number within a list of one million, my number is found in about 20 guesses. That is the log base 2 of one million. SQL Server is even more efficient than a binary search as we will find out in the examples to follow.

Listing 2 is an example of using the clustered index key to find a row. The Sales.SalesOrderDetail table in the AdventureWorks2014 database has a primary key and clustered index key on SalesOrderID + SalesOrderDetailID. In this case, the combination of the two columns makes the rows unique.

When searching for a row by SalesOrderID, the clustered index key is used. Before running this query, press CTRL + M to turn on the Actual Execution Plan. If you open another query window before completing the chapter, be sure to do this each time.

Listing 2: Using a clustered index

```
SET STATISTICS IO ON;
USE AdventureWorks2014;
GO
SELECT SalesOrderID, SalesOrderDetailID,
        CarrierTrackingNumber
FROM Sales.SalesOrderDetail
WHERE SalesOrderID = 43659;
```

The first line enables you to see the number of pages that SQL Server had to read to find and return the requested rows. This query returns one row. Figure 91 show the statistics IO output found on the Messages tab.

```
(12 row(s) affected)
Table 'SalesOrderDetail'. Scan count 1, logical reads 3, physical reads 2, read-ahead reads 0,
```

Figure 91 – The Logical reads

Chapter 4 Indexing for Beginners

The logical reads value is the number of pages that the database engine had to read to return the results. In this case, that is 3 pages. Remember that the lower number of pages SQL Server must access, the faster the query will run. Two of the pages were in the non-leaf level and one page was the row in the leaf level. If the search were a binary search, the logical reads would most likely have been higher.

Figure 92 displays the execution plan. The query used the cluster key to efficiently find the row by using a clustered index seek.

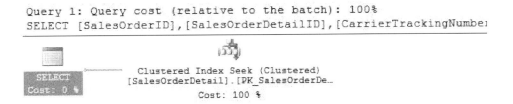

Figure 92 - The execution plan of a clustered index seek

Listing 3 is a query that uses the CarrierTrackingNumber column to find the same row.

Listing 3: Query by CarrierTrackingNumber
```
SELECT SalesOrderID, SalesOrderDetailID,
         CarrierTrackingNumber
FROM Sales.SalesOrderDetail
WHERE CarrierTrackingNumber = '4911-403C-98';
```

Figure 93 displays the logical reads for the query.

```
(12 row(s) affected)
Table 'SalesOrderDetail'. Scan count 1, logical reads 1246, physical reads 0, read-ahead reads 565,
```

Figure 93 – The logical reads when filtering on CarrierTrackingNumber

The logical reads have increased from 2 to 1246. More than one row is stored on a page, but the database engine had to search every page to find the values. Even when the all the rows were located, the database engine had to continue searching to the end of the table just in case there were more values.

Figure 94 shows the execution plan.

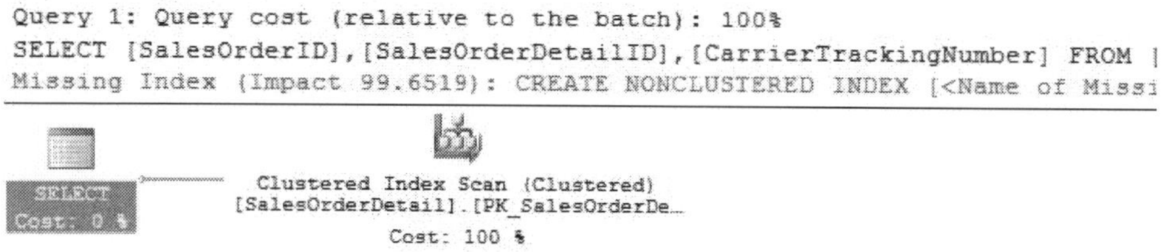

```
Query 1: Query cost (relative to the batch): 100%
SELECT [SalesOrderID],[SalesOrderDetailID],[CarrierTrackingNumber] FROM [
Missing Index (Impact 99.6519): CREATE NONCLUSTERED INDEX [<Name of Missi
```

               Clustered Index Scan (Clustered)
    SELECT   [SalesOrderDetail].[PK_SalesOrderDe...
    Cost: 0 %   Cost: 100 %

Figure 94 – The execution plan when filtering on CarrierTrackingNumber

The execution plan confirms that a clustered index scan was used. This means that the entire table was scanned to find the rows since there is no index on CarrierTrackingNumber. There is also a missing index suggestion. We'll take a look at missing index suggestions later in the chapter.

If you create a table with a primary key, the database engine will automatically make that table a clustered index. It's possible to override that behavior, but most of the time the behavior is accepted. If you add a primary key to an existing table, the database engine will also create a clustered index by default if one is not already in place. You can also turn a heap into a clustered index with the CREATE INDEX command. Listing 4 shows two ways to create clustered indexes.

Listing 4: Creating clustered indexes

```sql
--Automatically creates a clustered index because of primary key
CREATE TABLE [dbo].[PKExample] (
        [ID] INT NOT NULL PRIMARY KEY,
        [TheValue] VARCHAR(30) NULL
);

--Doesn't create clustered index
CREATE TABLE [dbo].[StartsAsAHeap] (
        [ID] INT NOT NULL PRIMARY KEY NONCLUSTERED,
        [TheValue] VARCHAR(30) NULL
);
--Create the clustered index later
CREATE CLUSTERED INDEX [CI_StartsAsAHeap] ON [dbo].[StartsAsAHeap]
([TheValue]);
```

The figure below shows how these tables look in SQL Server Management Studio (SSMS). Notice that SQL Server will provide an ugly name for your index if you do not name the index or the primary key constraint. Even though SQL Server created an index for the primary key in the StartsAsAHeap table, it is not clustered since that is what was specified in the CREATE TABLE command.

Chapter 4 Indexing for Beginners

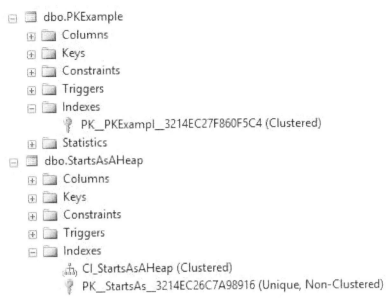

Figure 95 – The SSMS view of two tables

As I mentioned, the primary key is usually the cluster key, but it doesn't have to be. Should it be? Again, that depends. What is the most common column used to access the data? That could be a column that is used in the WHERE clause in every query for the table. That column may make a better choice for the clustered index than the primary key. Is the data mostly queried by a range of dates? Maybe that date column would make a good cluster key since the rows would be close together. Even if there is just one row in a page that is needed, the entire page must be read into memory. If the required rows are in the same small set of pages, the query will be faster.

There are a few rules of thumb you can follow when determining the cluster key. Again, there is no absolute right or wrong here.

- The cluster key should be narrow
- The cluster key should be ever increasing
- The cluster key should be static
- The cluster key should be unique

These are no hard and fast rules, and, in fact, there are often online arguments among developers about the best clustered index key. The GUID, or globally unique identifier data type (UNIQUEIDENTIFIER in SQL Server), is a favorite among developers, but it makes a terrible cluster key. It's a wide data type. You will learn in the next section that wide cluster keys affect the sizes of nonclustered indexes. For example, say that the combination of ten columns makes a row unique and is the natural primary key. Instead of using ten columns as the cluster key, it would be more efficient to create an integer ID column for the cluster key and possibly the primary key as well. You can always create a unique nonclustered index to enforce the uniqueness on the actual unique key columns.

An increasing cluster key would be an IDENTITY column, for example, that increases automatically as new rows are added. This cuts down on fragmentation since the rows are organized in the order that they are inserted. Some people argue that it creates a hotspot in the one page at the end as new rows are added. Which one to choose? I have seen good results using the ever increasing column, but it may cause problems for some workloads where many rows are added at once.

Most experts agree that having a static cluster key is a good idea. If the value is changed, then the row will potentially belong in a different page. Again, this is a cause of fragmentation.

A unique cluster key is not absolutely required, but let's consider the other end of the spectrum. Imagine using a bit column for the cluster key. Assuming an even distribution of 1 and 0, searching for 1 will eliminate only half the rows. It would be more efficient to eliminate the majority of the rows if possible. The more granular the values of the cluster key, the better.

As I mentioned, the structure is much more compact than shown in Figure 90. Listing 5 uses the sys.dm_db_index_physical_stats function to see the clustered index of the Production.Product table.

Listing 5: The clustered index of the Production.Product table

```
SELECT object_name(i.[object_id]) AS TableName,
i.name AS IndexName, Page_count,index_type_desc,  index_depth,index_level
FROM sys.indexes AS I
CROSS APPLY sys.dm_db_index_physical_stats(DB_ID(), i.object_id,
          i.index_id , NULL,'detailed')
WHERE I.object_id = object_id('Production.Product') AND I.index_id = 1;
```

Each index has an Index_id, and clustered indexes are always 1. Heaps can also be seen with this query, but they have an Index_id of 0.

TableName	IndexName	Page_count	index_type_desc	index_depth	index_level
Product	PK_Product_ProductID	13	CLUSTERED INDEX	2	0
Product	PK_Product_ProductID	1	CLUSTERED INDEX	2	1

Figure 96 – The index levels of a the clustered index of ProductionPilot

By using the detailed option, you can see all the index levels. The sys.dm_db_index_physical_stats function is mostly used to find the fragmentation state of the index. When it is used this way, the last parameter is usually set to "limited". When set to limited, only one row will be returned. By using "detailed" you can see each level and the number of pages in each level.

Index level 0 is the leaf level. All the rows in the table are stored in 13 pages in this level. The non-leaf level is only 1 page.

Listing 6 is another example looking at the largest table in the AdventureWorks2014 database, the Sales.SalesOrderDetail table.

Listing 6: The clustered index of the Sales.SalesOrderDetail table

```sql
SELECT object_name(i.[object_id]) AS TableName,
i.name AS IndexName, Page_count,index_type_desc,  index_depth,index_level
FROM sys.indexes AS I
CROSS APPLY sys.dm_db_index_physical_stats(DB_ID(), i.object_id,
          i.index_id , NULL,'detailed')
WHERE I.object_id = object_id('Sales.SalesOrderDetail') AND I.index_id = 1;
```

TableName	IndexName	Page_count	index_type_desc	index_depth	index_level
SalesOrderDetail	PK_SalesOrderDetail_SalesOrder...	1237	CLUSTERED INDEX	3	0
SalesOrderDetail	PK_SalesOrderDetail_SalesOrder...	7	CLUSTERED INDEX	3	1
SalesOrderDetail	PK_SalesOrderDetail_SalesOrder...	1	CLUSTERED INDEX	3	2

Figure 97 – The levels of the Sales.SalesOrderDetail clustered index

This table has just two non-leaf levels totaling 8 pages. The leaf level storing all the rows is just 1237 pages.

Nonclustered Indexes

A nonclustered index is a separate object that is associated with a table. The table can be a heap or a clustered index. You may hear about **index tuning** which usually means figuring out which nonclustered indexes are beneficial for the workload. When a query can fully take advantage of a nonclustered index, SQL Server will not need to access the table at all. Even if SQL Server must inspect every entry in the nonclustered index, it will still be easier than scanning the entire table. Imagine reading through the entire index of a text book. Maybe it doesn't sound that appealing, but it shouldn't take too long.

Another analogy I love is the library card catalog. I spent hours looking up books in those cabinets as a child. If I remember correctly, there were at least three indexes: author, title, and subject. The cards in the author index are organized by author, of course. If you had a favorite author, say Stephen King, you could find the cards for all of his books together in the drawer. Well, if you were a true Stephen King fan, you would also know he wrote under the pen name Richard Bachmann. You can answer quite a few queries just from those cards. For example, you can count the cards and create a list of the books along with their publish dates. If you need to know something that is not on the card, you will need to walk to the shelf to get the answer.

The structure of nonclustered indexes is like that of clustered indexes. Again, it is an upside down tree with the root on top and the leaf level on the bottom. The non-leaf levels contain one or more

Chapter 4 Indexing for Beginners

columns that make up the key. The leaf level repeats the key and contains additional columns *included* with the index. The leaf level pages also have pointers to the rows of the tables. In the case of a clustered index, the pointer is the cluster key. In the case of a heap, the pointer is called a *row identifier* or RID.

When the nonclustered index points to a clustered index table, the cluster key is stored in the leaf level pages. During the discussion of clustered indexes, I mentioned that narrow cluster keys are better. Wide cluster keys increase the size of nonclustered indexes. Smaller objects provide better performance, so narrower cluster keys are better.

When a query is submitted to SQL Server, a component called the query optimizer decides the best way to run the query. It can choose between the clustered and nonclustered indexes that exist on the table. It must not take too long to figure this out, though, or it may take more time than running the query.

Listing 7 is a query that uses a nonclustered index to find rows of the Person.Person table with the last name of "Duffy."

Listing 7: Query using the nonclustered index

```
SELECT BusinessEntityID, FirstName, MiddleName, LastName
FROM Person.Person
WHERE LastName = 'Duffy';
```

This query takes 2 logical reads. Figure 98 is the execution plan.

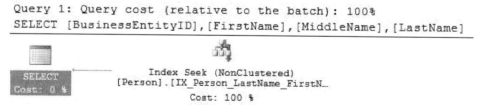

Figure 98 – The execution plan of using nonclustered index

The query optimizer decided to use a seek operation on the IX_Person_LastName_FirstName_MiddleName index to return the results. The seek operation uses the non-leaf level of the index to quickly locate the correct leaf level pages.

Listing 8 is the index definition.

Listing 8: The IX_Person_LastName_FirstName_MiddleName index

```
CREATE NONCLUSTERED INDEX [IX_Person_LastName_FirstName_MiddleName] ON
[Person].[Person]
(
        [LastName] ASC,
        [FirstName] ASC,
        [MiddleName] ASC
);
```

All the columns needed for the query are contained within the index. The BusinessEntityId column is the cluster key so it's automatically part of the leaf level pages. The other columns needed in the query are keys in the index.

Listing 9 is another query against the Person.Person table. This time, the filter is on the FirstName column.

Listing 9: Filtering on FirstName

SELECT BusinessEntityID, FirstName, MiddleName, LastName

FROM Person.Person

WHERE FirstName = 'Terri';

This query took 109 logical reads. The execution plan can be seen in Figure 99.

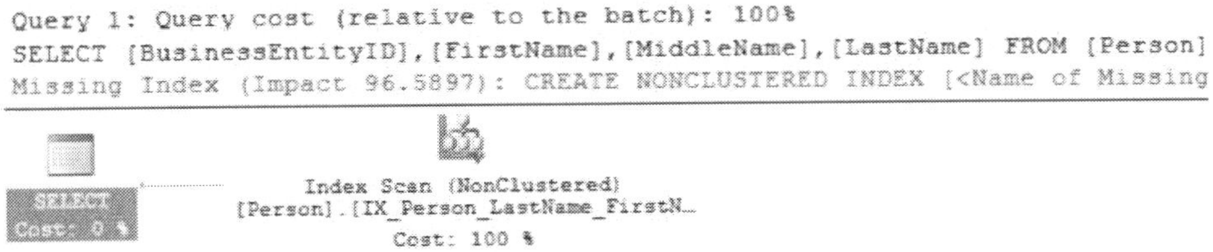

```
Query 1: Query cost (relative to the batch): 100%
SELECT [BusinessEntityID],[FirstName],[MiddleName],[LastName] FROM [Person]
Missing Index (Impact 96.5897): CREATE NONCLUSTERED INDEX [<Name of Missing
```

```
   SELECT           Index Scan (NonClustered)
   Cost: 0 %       [Person].[IX_Person_LastName_FirstN...
                           Cost: 100 %
```

Figure 99 – The execution plan when filtering on FirstName

The same index is used but the query optimizer decided to scan the index leaf level pages instead of performing a seek against the non-leaf levels to find the rows. A possible index to improve the performance of the query is also suggested. Even though the index was scanned, it was still more efficient than scanning the table.

In addition to the index keys, you can also include additional columns that will be helpful in the query. These included columns are found only in the leaf level. This is like the publication date found on the book's card in the card catalog. Listing 10 is an example.

Listing 10: An index with an included column

```
CREATE NONCLUSTERED INDEX [IX_ProductReview_ProductID_Name] ON
[Production].[ProductReview]
(
         [ProductID] ASC,
         [ReviewerName] ASC
)
INCLUDE ([Comments]);
```

I often think of a nonclustered index with included columns as a small copy of the table. You can't query the index directly, but query optimizer can select the index for the query. If all columns needed for the query are found in the index, the table doesn't need to be touched and the query performance will most likely be good.

Usually, the included columns are used in SELECT or ORDER BY clauses of the query, but they can be used anywhere, even the WHERE clause. If, for example, you searched the Production.ProductReview table and filtered on the Comments column, the index would be scanned. This is still usually a better option than scanning the table.

I mentioned fragmentation briefly in the Clustered Indexes section. Fragmentation affects nonclustered indexes as well. When rows in the table are inserted, updated, or deleted, the nonclustered indexes must be kept up to date. That is one reason why it's not a great idea to randomly add lots of indexes in hopes that they will improve the queries. It takes resources to keep the indexes up to date. Whenever the index keys themselves are modified, the index becomes fragmented. While designing the clustered index key to cut down on fragmentation is possible, it's not possible to design nonclustered indexes this way. If you need an index on a column that changes frequently, well, you need that index. You will have to just plan maintenance on the indexes to run on a periodic basis.

NOTE: Index maintenance is beyond the scope of this chapter.

You can have one clustered index per table, but the limit for nonclustered indexes is 999. Should you have that many? Well, it depends... There are situations where that many indexes could be helpful, but most of the time, ten or twelve indexes per table is usually good enough. How do you know which indexes to add? Here are a few guidelines:

- Index foreign key columns
- Index columns used in WHERE clauses
- Index JOIN columns
- Include columns that will appear in the SELECT list

Covering Indexes

When the database engine can get all the columns from the table needed from the nonclustered index for a query, the index is called a *covering* index. While I love having covering indexes for my queries, I do not like the actual term. It sounds to me like there is a covering property that can be turned on or off. The term refers to a specific situation not a type of index. The index covers this particular query. If you add another column to the query, the index may no longer be covering, and the database engine will need to get that column from the actual table. Unfortunately, this can be an expensive operation. In some situations, this is more expensive than scanning the entire table.

This operation is called a *bookmark lookup*. You may also hear the term *key lookup*. A key lookup refers to retrieving one or more columns from a clustered index. A *rid lookup* refers to retrieving columns from a heap.

The library card catalog is a good example. There is quite a bit of information located on the card. But, say you need to know the first paragraph of page 42 of "The Shining." You must make a trip to the bookshelf and look at the book, which is much more effort than standing at the card catalog. You might think that is not such a big deal. What if you need to find the first paragraph of page 42 of all the Stephen King books? As a human, you will be able to realize that the books are in the same couple of shelves in the fiction section and make one trip. There is no guarantee that the rows will be located together in a query. SQL Server will need to make a trip to the table for each key.

Listing 11 is a query that has a bookmark lookup because the Color column is not part of the index.

Listing 11: A query with a bookmark lookup

```
SELECT ProductID, Name, Color
FROM Production.Product
WHERE name LIKE 'Long-Sleeve%';
```

Figure 100 – The execution plan for A query with a bookmark lookup

The query optimizer decided to use the AK_Product_Name index which has a key on the Name column. Notice that the key lookup is more than 50% of the query effort. This query returns just four rows so the effort to retrieve the color is not too bad. The query in Listing 12 retrieves 46 rows.

Listing 12: A query that returns 46 rows

```
SELECT ProductID, Name, Color
FROM Production.Product
WHERE Name LIKE 'Road%';
```

```
Query 1: Query cost (relative to the batch): 100%
SELECT ProductID, Name, Color FROM Production.Product WHERE Name LIKE 'Road%'

    SELECT         Clustered Index Scan (Clustered)
    Cost: 0 %      [Product].[PK_Product_ProductID]
                              Cost: 100 %
```

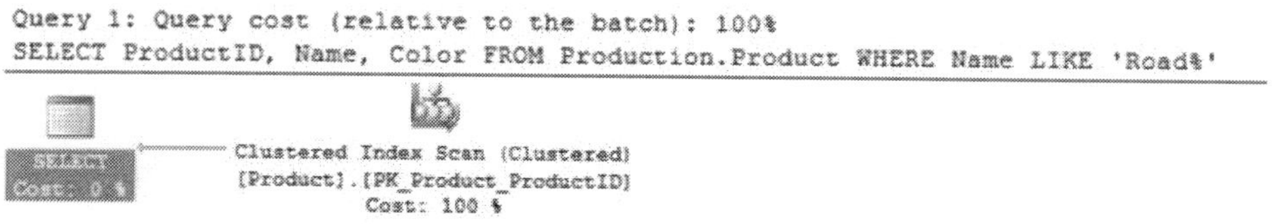

Figure 101 – The execution plan when 46 rows are returned

Notice that the query optimizer decided to scan the clustered index when 46 rows were returned. It was more effort to do a bookmark lookup on 46 rows than to scan the clustered index.

If you decided to add Color to the AK_Product_Name index, the query would use an index seek with no key lookup.

Sargability

Even if an index covers a query, it's still possible to cause the index to be scanned. The term **sargable** stands for Search ARGument ABLE. This means that the predicate in the WHERE clause has been written so that a seek of the index is possible. Understanding the phone book is helpful when learning the difference between sargable and non-sargable expressions.

Imagine that you meet Terri Duffy at a party. If you remember her last name is "Duffy", it's easy to find her name in the phone book. If you remember only her last name starts with "D" you may decide to use the LEFT function to find the name. You will have to apply the function to every row. If, instead, you looked for rows where the name is LIKE "D%", then finding the name will be much quicker. Listing 13 shows the two queries.

Listing 13: Finding names that start with D

Chapter 4 Indexing for Beginners

```
SELECT FirstName, LastName
FROM Person.Person
WHERE LEFT(LastName,1) = 'D';

SELECT FirstName, LastName
FROM Person.Person
WHERE LastName LIKE 'D%';
```

Each query returns 556 rows. The first query using LEFT took 109 logical reads. The second query using LIKE took only 6 logical reads. The predicate using LIKE is sargible while the predicate using LEFT is non-sargible. Figure 102 shows the execution plans.

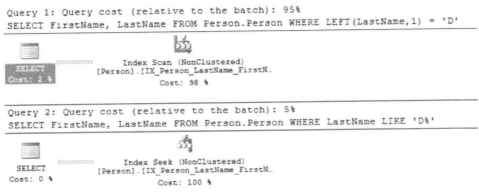

Figure 102 – The execution plans for finding names that start with D.

Notice that the first query took 95% of the effort because it had to scan the index, applying the function to each value, instead of performing a more efficient seek. The benefit of using LIKE only applies when the first character is known. Listing 14 is a query that uses a wildcard at the front of the value.

Listing 14: Using LIKE with the wildcard in front

```
SELECT FirstName, LastName
FROM Person.Person
WHERE LastName LIKE '%uffy';
```

In this case, the logical reads are 109 and the execution plan is identical to the plan when the LEFT function is used, an index scan. If you tried to find the name in the phone book but didn't know the first letter, you would also need to read every entry.

If you are not searching on the leading column, the query optimizer will not have a choice but to do a scan. If you search for "Terri" in the FirstName column, the index will be scanned just as if you looked for a first name in the phone book.

As a rule of thumb, when functions are applied to columns in the leading position of the index the predicate is non-sargable. A frequent issue is with dates. I didn't find an index with a leading date or time column, so Listing 15 adds a new index to the Sales.SalesOrderHeader table. The two queries show how to find all the rows from 2012.

Listing 15: Create an index and find all the rows from 2012

```
CREATE INDEX INDEX_CHAPTER_SARGABILITY_TEST ON Sales.SalesOrderHeader
(OrderDate);

SELECT SalesOrderID, OrderDate
FROM Sales.SalesOrderHeader
WHERE YEAR(OrderDate) = 2012;

SELECT SalesOrderID, OrderDate
FROM Sales.SalesOrderHeader
WHERE OrderDate >= '1/1/2012' AND OrderDate < '1/1/2013';

DROP INDEX_CHAPTER_SARGABILITY_TEST ON Sales.SalesOrderHeader;
```

The first query is much easier to write, but the second query is much more efficient if there is an index on OrderDate. Figure 103 shows the execution plans for the two queries.

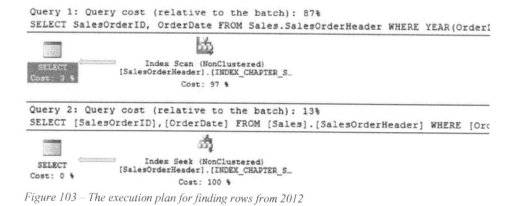

Figure 103 – The execution plan for finding rows from 2012

Another cause of non-sargability is implicit conversions. For example, if you have a varchar column that contains numbers, when you search using an integer variable, the varchar values will

Chapter 4 Indexing for Beginners

be implicitly converted to integers. Run the script in Listing 16 to create a table and run a script with this issue.

Listing 16: Implicit conversions

```sql
CREATE TABLE ImplicitConversion(
         ID NVARCHAR(10) NOT NULL PRIMARY KEY,
         Name NVARCHAR(50));

INSERT INTO ImplicitConversion(ID, Name)
SELECT ProductID, Name
FROM Production.Product;

DECLARE @ID INT = 517;

SELECT  ID, Name
FROM ImplicitConversion
WHERE ID = @ID;

GO

DECLARE @ID NVARCHAR(10) = '517';

SELECT  ID, Name
FROM ImplicitConversion
WHERE ID = @ID;
```

Figure 104 – The execution plans demonstrating an implicit conversion

Because each value of ID had to be converted to an integer before comparing to the variable, the index was scanned in the first example. In the second example, the data type of the column matched the variable so a seek was performed. Whenever declaring variables or defining parameters, make sure they match the data type of the column. Also note that there is a caution symbol in the first query. If you hover your mouse over the SELECT operator, you will see the warning about the explicit conversion.

If the situation were reversed, an integer column and an nvarchar variable, the conversion would not be a problem. In this case, the variable would be converted to an integer. If two tables are joined on columns with different data types, you can imagine how that would slow the query down.

Data types are converted based on a precedence list that can be found at https://docs.microsoft.com/en-us/sql/t-sql/data-types/data-type-precedence-transact-sql. Data types are always implicitly converted up the list.

Filtered Indexes

The filtered index feature is not frequently used, but they are often very useful. A filtered index has a WHERE clause, and only rows that meet the criteria are included in the index. If there is a small fraction of rows in the index, the filtered index is much smaller and more efficient. This is especially useful when a column has a small number of non-NULL values.

Listing 17 creates a filtered index on the Production.Product table and uses it in a query.

Listing 17: Create and use a filtered index

```
CREATE INDEX FILTERED_INDEX ON Production.Product
(Color)
INCLUDE (Size,Name)
WHERE Color = 'Blue';

SELECT ProductID, Name, Color, Size
FROM Production.Product
WHERE Color = 'Blue';

DROP INDEX FILTERED_INDEX ON Production.Product;
```

Unique Indexes

I mentioned that the primary key is not always the best clustered index key. When you do not use the primary key as the cluster key, you can still define the key as primary key. SQL Server will automatically create an index for the primary key. Listing 4 in the Clustered Indexes section contains an example of this. You can also create additional unique indexes by specifying that the index should be unique. The Sales.SalesOrderHeader table has a unique SalesOrderHeader column. Listing 18 is the definition for the unique index on this column.

Listing 18: The unique index on SalesOrderNumber

```sql
CREATE UNIQUE NONCLUSTERED INDEX [AK_SalesOrderHeader_SalesOrderNumber] ON
[Sales].[SalesOrderHeader]
(
        [SalesOrderNumber] ASC
);
```

Joining Tables

So far, all the sample queries have been just one table. In the real world, most queries involve multiple tables. The query optimizer must select the best index for each table. If an index is available for the joining column, the data will be pre-sorted to make joining easier. If there are filters on another column, then an index that starts with the column in the predicate may be more useful allowing the data to be filtered before joining instead of after. Listing 19 contains a query that join tables.

Listing 19: A query that joins two tables

```sql
SELECT SalesOrderId, SalesOrderDetailID, Prod.ProductID, Prod.Name
FROM Sales.SalesOrderDetail AS SOD
JOIN Production.Product AS Prod ON SOD.ProductID = Prod.ProductID
WHERE Name = 'Road-450 Red, 48';
```

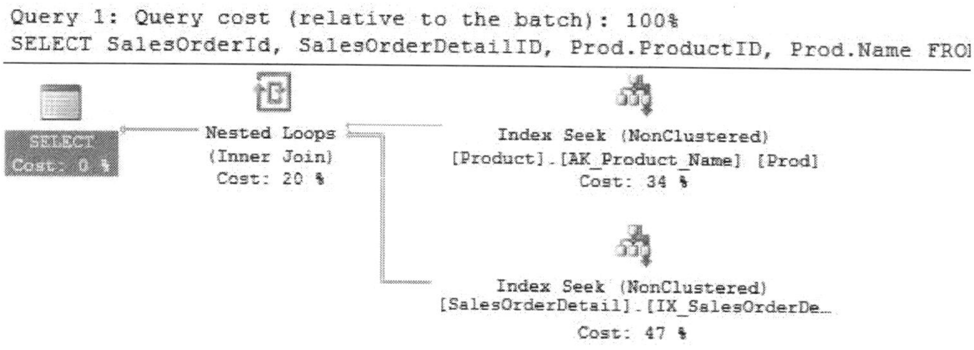

Chapter 4 Indexing for Beginners

```
Query 1: Query cost (relative to the batch): 100%
SELECT SalesOrderId, SalesOrderDetailID, Prod.ProductID, Prod.Name FRO|
```

```
    SELECT  ──  Nested Loops  ──  Index Seek (NonClustered)
   Cost: 0 %     (Inner Join)      [Product].[AK_Product_Name] [Prod]
                 Cost: 20 %                Cost: 34 %

                              ──  Index Seek (NonClustered)
                                  [SalesOrderDetail].[IX_SalesOrderDe...
                                           Cost: 47 %
```

Figure 105 – The execution plan of a query that joins two tables

The query optimizer decided to use the AK_Product_Name index because there was a filter on the Name column. The rows were filtered before joining to the Sales.SalesOrderDetail table.

Missing Index Hints

In the Clustered Indexes section, I showed you an execution plan with a missing index suggestion (Figure 106). The optimizer will sometimes provide the create statement for an index that would improve the performance of the query. That information is also saved in the sys.dm_db_missing_index_details DMV. Listing 20 shows the query used to see the missing index details. Note that this information is lost each time that SQL Server is restarted.

Listing 20: The missing index details

```
SELECT DB_NAME(database_id) AS DatabaseName,
       statement, equality_columns, inequality_columns, included_columns
FROM sys.dm_db_missing_index_details;
```

DatabaseName	statement	equality_columns	inequality_columns	included_columns
AdventureWorks2014	[AdventureWorks2014].[Sales].[SalesOrderDetail]	[CarrierTrackingNumber]	NULL	NULL

Figure 106 – The missing index details

Always be sure to check the existing indexes so that you don't create overlapping indexes. For example, you may have an index in place on Column1. An index hint may suggest an index on

154

Column1 and Column2. It doesn't make sense to have both. You can replace the index with the new definition instead of just adding the second index.

Fellow Data Platform MVP Glenn Berry has a wonderful query that not only lists the missing indexes but also assigns a score to each one. His blog can be found at https://www.sqlskills.com/blogs/glenn/. Look for his latest SQL Server Diagnostic Information Queries post and search the code for the word "missing".

Summary

Indexes can make the difference between a slow application and one that performs great. Tables can be unorganized heaps or clustered indexes organized by a key. Nonclustered indexes can be added to both heaps and clustered indexes. Indexes can be used in one of two ways: seeks and scans. A seek is a very quick search operation while a scan reads every value in the index. If all columns needed in the query are part of the index, then that index is called covering. When the index is not covering, the additional columns must come from the table by using what is called a bookmark lookup.

Figuring out which indexes to add to a database is both an art and a science. I hope that the knowledge gained in this chapter will help you on your way.

Chapter 5
Data Visualization in Power BI

By: Meagan Longoria

Power BI can be used to make impressive and engaging visual designs that deliver insights and a great user experience. If you are not a data viz geek, you might be surprised how much cognitive science is involved in making a good data visualization. This chapter includes platform agnostic data visualization concepts as well as practical tips for creating Power BI reports.

The Only Thing Constant is Change

I felt I needed to place a warning that Power BI (web service and desktop application) gets updated every month. This makes it tough to create content that stays accurate and relevant for a long period of time. Many aspects of the product are fairly stable, but Power BI has such momentum and a great community around it that I'm sure some great features will be released even before these words get published. That is the risk I took in writing about this topic, and I have accepted my fate. For reference, I wrote this chapter using Power BI Desktop version 2.47.4766.801, which was published in June 2017. Please be aware that features and menus in the Power BI products will change. You can make sure you are aware of newly released features by reading the Power BI blog[21].

Sample Data

I use two sample datasets throughout this chapter. The first contains sales data that shows sales revenue by product and month. I used this because it is a very common dataset that most people can understand. The second dataset contains blood glucose (blood sugar) readings for a patient who is suffering from chronic hyperglycemia. The values in both datasets are made up to protect the innocent (and the guilty), but they are inspired by real data that I recently encountered. I needed two different datasets to show good example uses of various Power BI features. I show an example report concerning visiting BBQ restaurants in Kansas City. The data for that report is real (although out of date), but used with permission.

What Is Data Visualization?

When we talk about building reports in Power BI, it's best to start conceptually to understand our actions and goals. Data visualization is a collection of methods that use visual representations to explore, make sense of, and communicate data.[22] Rather than looking at tables of data and holding them in our memory, it's easier for us to use a picture that summarizes or highlights specific

---

[21] Microsoft, Power BI Blog, https://powerbi.microsoft.com/en-us/blog/
[22] Stephen Few. Visual Business Intelligence. https://www.perceptualedge.com/blog/?p=2636

trends and relationships. We as humans have limited short-term memory and are very visual people. When we need to understand the revenue trend for the last 12 months, we could look at the table and check each number and evaluate it relative to the previous month's number.

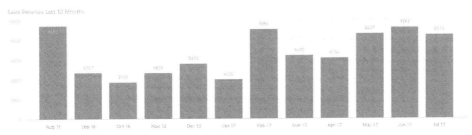

Sales Revenue Last 12 Months

Aug 16	Sep 16	Oct 16	Nov 16	Dec 16	Jan 17	Feb 17	Mar 17	Apr 17	May 17	Jun 17	Jul 17
9,452	4,707	3,727	4,670	5,603	4,002	9,086	6,432	6,154	8,637	9,243	8,512

Figure 107 – Example Table

Or we could use a bar chart.

Figure 108 – Example Bar Chart

Take a minute and compare your experience answering the following questions with the table and then with the bar chart.

1) Which month had the lowest revenue?
2) Which month had the highest revenue?
3) Is July 2017 revenue greater or less than revenue for each of the previous two months?
4) Is revenue steadily increasing over time?

Unless your mind works differently than most other humans, you were probably able to answer those questions more quickly and easily using the bar chart.

To answer the first two questions with the table, you had to read the revenue value for each month and hold in your mind the maximum or minimum value until you read each number. That is a lot of effort.

When you looked at the bar chart, your eyes were probably immediately drawn to the color. Then you easily compared the heights of the bars with a quick scan to answer the questions.

It's easy to make this argument while comparing a table to a chart. But let's compare two different charts. Try using the tree map to answer the four questions.

Chapter 5 Data Visualization in Power BI

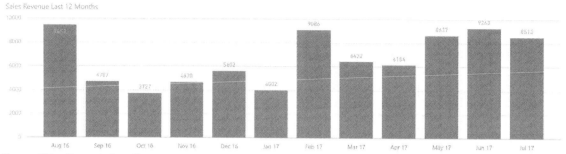

Figure 109 – Example Bar Chart

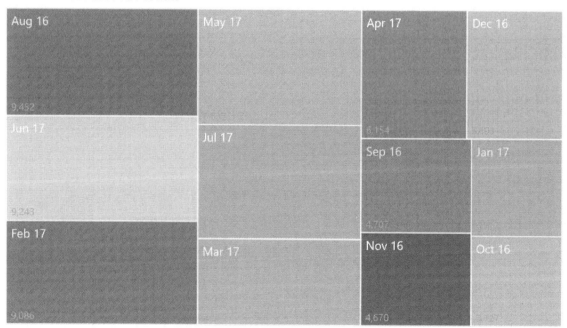

Figure 110 - Example Tree Map

Because of the way the rectangles were ordered (with the largest value in the top left corner and the smallest value in the bottom right corner), you might be able to quickly answer the first two questions. But the third and fourth questions require entirely too much effort using the tree map – they may actually be harder to answer with the tree map than with the table. You have to go back to searching for individual values. But this time, the values aren't in chronological order, and some of the data labels are difficult to read.

Now imagine that you are at work and you need to communicate the information in the revenue numbers to your boss. You must cut through the noise of coworkers and email notifications to get and keep their attention long enough to deliver the highlights before their mind jumps to the next

Chapter 5   **Data Visualization** in Power BI

item on their to-do list. They have just a few minutes before their meeting for which they need the revenue info, and you send them the tree map.

Ain't nobody got time for that!

A lot of detailed technical work goes into data acquisition, integration, and modeling. But data visualization is the last mile. It is often the only part of BI/analytics efforts that business users see. The designer of the Power BI report has the responsibility to decide what insights are important and how to display the information to make that clear to users while presenting a user interface that keeps them engaged and makes them want to explore their data. Tools such as Power BI make data visualization seem as easy as dragging a chart onto the page and populating the required fields in the fields list. But there is so much more to it. You can have the best data warehouse in the world as the data source for your Power BI report, and you can render it useless with poor data visualization design.

When we talk about consuming data visualization in Power BI or any other tool, we can categorize our analysis into one of two types: exploratory or explanatory. In exploratory visual analysis, we are looking for insights (patterns, trends, max and min values, counts). We interact with our visualization tool to switch dimensions, attributes, and measures and then drill down to find specific points of interest. When we do this, we usually start with a few bar charts or line charts to get a general summary or trend. Exploratory analysis is commonly performed with pivot tables in Excel or conditional formatting added. The main point of exploratory data visualization is that we are using visuals to perform analysis, for which we don't know the answer. We are getting to know our data.

Once we have found information which we would like to communicate with others, we may then engage in explanatory data visualization. In explanatory visualization (or explanatory analysis), we have already analyzed the data and identified a message we are trying to share with someone else. When we share a Power BI report, we are using explanatory data visualization to:

- Clarify information
- Provide memorable insights
- Helps users make a decision or take action

In operational analytics, there is often a kind of in-between type of analysis and visualization. We have recurring reports for which a data refresh is set up. We know the relationships in the data and have analyzed the data before, but the message and highlights may change at any time based upon the new data points. While the data may change, users do the same types of analysis (same thought process and questions) each time they visit the report.

In this chapter, I will focus on explanatory analysis and the hybrid analysis in recurring reports. While there are certain chart types and color schemes that may help in explanatory analysis, I think the rules are quite different when you are exploring. There are some guidelines you can follow, but at the end of the day I think you can use whatever works best for you to make sense of the data. When it comes to sharing what you have found with others, we have research and some common sense to guide us in providing insights to users. Although it can be argued that not all explanatory data visualization is about communicating information efficiently at a glance, many Power BI reports in professional settings do have this requirement.

We can combine cognitive psychology, computer science, and Power BI to make efficient and effective data visualizations that help our users accomplish all kinds of things ranging from clarifying important points in a meeting to getting home to their families an hour earlier to saving their company millions of dollars or curing a chronic illness.

Preparation Before We Put Anything on the Report Page

I would venture to say that at least half of our success in using data visualizations for explanatory analysis is determined before we ever put a chart on the report page. My experience working in business intelligence has taught me that most data visualization failures in a professional setting can be categorized into four main issues:

- Lack of appropriate data
- Reports as intermediate steps
- Poor presentation that makes it difficult to gain insight and take action
- Poor presentation that discourages engagement

Lack of Appropriate Data

You may have been inspired while building your last department metrics report, and you followed all the latest data viz guidelines. But if you are missing the most important data, you have set yourself up to fail. Sometimes we are limited to using data only from a certain system (e.g., data warehouse or main CRM system). But the data that shows us what we really need to know lives in another system. We could attempt to continue to build, but if there is a gap in what we have and what we need, how can we ensure that we are creating something that delivers great insights or is even useful to our audience? In addition to lacking some data altogether, using data that isn't from a trusted source can also lead to failure. Many times, companies have client data in their CRM system, sales system, finance system, and ERP system, but the data doesn't match across all those systems. Without a good master data management system, many times a system of record is chosen as the authoritative system with the most correct data. If the CRM system is the system of record, but you built a report with client data from the ERP system, your information might be considered wrong. We only get a few chances to recover from having wrong data before users stop trusting our report and find some other way to get the information they need.

Reports as Intermediate Steps

I can't count the number of times users have asked if a report can be exported to Excel. Often, a bit of questioning reveals that they are really asking for a data dump because the report in question is an intermediate step in a process. The financial analyst doesn't want my cost report in which I have labored over creating stunning visuals. This is not because my design is bad, but because he really just takes the data and plugs it into a Power Pivot model of his own. In this situation, the report is not the end goal and is not the interface between users and the data. It's just a way to obtain the data that was needed. It is someone else's way of overcoming their lack of access to appropriate data. Another way a report can be an intermediate step is from not understanding the decision-making process that goes on after using the report. We can overcome this issue by talking to our intended audience before we design the report to ensure we thoroughly understand their needs. Maybe that analyst uses the report just to pass information to their department manager, and the manager looks at the report and calls the operations manager when a certain metric hits a defined threshold. This could be an opportunity to skip the middle men and set a data alert for the operations manager. And if monitoring that metric is important, we might consider predictive (and later prescriptive capabilities). Perhaps we could use R with Power BI to predict the value of the metric so that we can proactively address the situation instead of reacting after the fact.

Poor Presentation That Prohibits Insight

When I create data visualizations, I have two goals:
1) Clearly communicate my intended message/insight
2) Provide a positive user experience

Studies have shown that having a positive experience through good aesthetic design contributes to the perceived effectiveness of data visualization, so we can't just focus on efficiency.[23] But there are boundless examples where overdecoration leads to obfuscation of the intended message. Sights such as Viz.WTF and others have thousands of examples of design failures. Some of this comes from adding heavy formatting to the visual and to the page. Some of it comes from us wanting to share all we have learned and cover our bases for any further questions (hint: you cannot answer all the questions with one Power BI report). There is a sweet spot in balancing communication and user experience. There is no single right way to visualize a dataset, but there are definitely several wrong ways.

Poor Presentation That Discourages Engagement

Sometimes we create a data visualization that clearly communicates the intended information, but it's rather unpleasant to use. This could be due to design choices (poor color choices), but it could also be about other aspects of usability. Sometimes a Power BI report built on a DirectQuery model isn't responsive enough. A user clicks a slicer or changes a filter and is forced to wait several seconds each time. Or a user really needs to view a report on the go, but doesn't have the Power BI mobile app and is forced to print out a copy of a dashboard and each report page, which greatly degrades the user experience. Although some of these issues are not strictly related to data visualization, they are related to how your users interact with your visual design, and they contribute to the overall user experience.

Preparation Checklist

---

[23] Cole Knussbaumer Knaflic, Storytelling With Data, pg 145

The first two issues (lack of data and reports as intermediate steps) occur due to lack of preparation, or due to organizational constraints that must be changed before we can achieve success. The second two issues can largely be avoided by preparation in understanding our audience and our message, and then making the requisite design choices in the Power BI model and reports to meet our users' needs.

You do not need loads of documentation before you can create a Power BI report. But there are steps you should take in preparation, whether they are quick mental checkpoints or a quick document you create for your team at work. The questions below will help you to design your report, and they can be left behind as documentation should ownership of your report be transferred to someone else.

Before you put anything on a page, you should consider the following questions:
- Who is your audience?
- What do you want them to know or do?
- How can the data be visualized to help make the point?

Once you know your general message, you should then ask:
- What specific items of information should be displayed?
- What does each of these items tell you, and why is that important?
- At what level of detail should the information be shown?

This is slightly more difficult if you are using dynamic, ever changing data, but you can do it. In this case, you want to focus on the main questions your users would ask. If you are building a sales revenue report for sales region managers, you want to think like them and try to answer their top 3 – 5 questions they would commonly have of the data. Although you won't know which region had the highest sales this quarter, or whether sales are up month over month, you can know that those are the questions your users will ask.

Once you can answer the above questions about audience and message, then you can move on to visual design.

In addition to mental preparation, there are a few things we can do in our Power BI models to prepare them for report creation.

1. Make sure all fields have the correct data type and default formatting. Your temperature data may have come in with two decimal points, but does your audience need that level of precision? Do you have fields such as phone numbers or zip codes that have a numeric data type when they should be text? Choosing the best data type in Power BI can help ensure the data is used correctly in the visuals and keep you from getting hung up fixing it later.
2. Set the appropriate default aggregation. By default, numerical fields in Power BI have a default summarization set to Sum. It may be more appropriate to count or average them. This will help your report development go smoothly. You don't want to use an implicit measure in a visual, have it aggregate inappropriately, and not catch it in testing.

3. Make sure the sort order is set correctly for all fields. By default, fields are sorted alphabetically or numerically ascending by their value, depending on data type. But you can select another field by which to sort a field. For instance, fields in your date table such as Month Name will need to be sorted by the Month Number so they are listed chronologically in a visual rather than alphabetically.

Choosing the Right Chart Type

Now that you have completed your preparation, you may start adding visuals to your report page.

We saw from the table, bar chart, and tree map earlier in the chapter that chart type can have a significant impact on our ability to quickly interpret data and gain insights. The biggest factor in determining the appropriate chart type is your intended message. If your data is static, you can create a detailed message such as "Sales have fluctuated over the last year, but the last three months have been high". If you are making a report that will be routinely refreshed with new data, your message might just be that your intended audience needs to see the data a certain way: "Sales analysts want to see the sales by month for a rolling 12-month period".

Your report should tell a story, and even if you don't know exactly how it ends, you can create an outline. You choose the important metrics and categories that should be shown in each visual, the type of visual to use, and the placement of the visual on the report page to provide your audience the right information in the right order to gain insight and decide.

Once you have chosen the data points you want to show, you must choose a chart type. As of the time of writing, Power BI has about 28 chart types available by default. You can add more chart types by importing custom visuals from the Office Store.[24]

---

[24] Microsoft, Office Store, Custom Visuals For Power BI, https://store.office.com/en-us/appshome.aspx?productgroup=PowerBI

Chapter 5   Data Visualization in Power BI

Figure 111 – Available Visual Types in Power BI

Example Report and Chart Type Selection

Below is a page from a Power BI Report I built for a person with hyperglycemia who is trying to manage their blood glucose levels. Keeping blood glucose at healthy levels is important because chronic hyperglycemia can lead to kidney disease, heart disease, nerve damage, gum disease, and more. The purpose of this report is to help the user identify and understand patterns in their glucose levels over time, so they can try changing medications, diet, or exercise to keep glucose levels better in range. Other pages within the report show exercise and food information, but this page focuses just on the blood glucose readings.

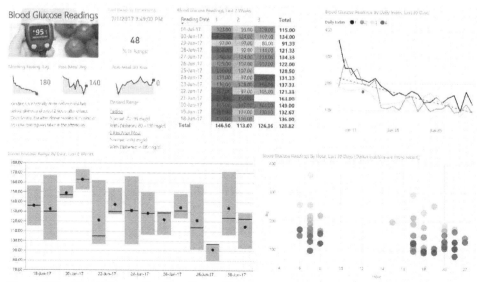

Figure 112 – Blood Glucose Readings Power BI Report

Since the data is periodically updated, I planned the outline of the data story without knowing the exact results. The user goes to the Blood Glucose Readings report page, checks that the data is complete by reviewing the Last Reading Timestamp, then checks the key metrics such as Morning Fasting Avg, which are visualized as KPIs with the data label showing the average over time.

The next chart is a matrix showing the detailed values for each blood glucose reading. If something is out of range, in the KPIs, the user can see the readings that pushed it out of range in the matrix. Higher readings are easy to spot because of the conditional formatting.

Next, the user can check the readings by Daily Index over time. Daily index is the order of the glucose test within the day. This user typically performs three glucose tests per day (before breakfast, before dinner, and after dinner), so the Daily Index number is meaningful to them (1 is before breakfast). The line chart shows the trend over time by Daily Index and provides a general trend over time for all readings.

Next the readings are shown in a box-and-whisker plot to emphasize the range of blood glucose levels throughout each day. And finally, the readings are split by hour of the day, in case there is an hour that seems to have more out of range readings.

Each chart type emphasizes a different important aspect of these blood sugar levels.

Chart Choosing Guidance

If you need help choosing your chart type, there are several helpful guides available. Stephen Few has published a graph selection matrix.[25] Stephanie Evergreen has Chart Chooser cards.[26] My favorite resource is Andy Kirk's book *Data Visualisation: A Handbook for Data Driven Design*. You will hear a lot of guidelines about chart types. For example, Stephen Few is against the use of pie charts except in rare circumstances.[27] Andy Kirk's philosophy is "No chart is evil: They play different roles and all have limitations."[28] His book enumerates several chart types and provides, examples, explanations of how to read the chart type, and presentation tips. He will tell you that pie charts can be used to show a part-to-whole relationship when there are 2 – 3 categories. I like to use them to visualize yes/no answers to survey questions.

If you have reviewed the resources in the previous paragraph and are still unsure which chart type to use, go with the great advice from Storytelling with Data:

> *"Once you've answered the question of what you want to show and determined the right suite of charts that might be appropriate, the right answer to the*

---

[25] Stephen Few, Graph Selection Matrix,
http://www.perceptualedge.com/articles/misc/Graph_Selection_Matrix.pdf
[26] Stephanie Evergreen, Chart Chooser Cards, http://chartchoosercards.com/
[27] Stephen Few, Save the Pies For Desert,
https://www.perceptualedge.com/articles/visual_business_intelligence/save_the_pies_for_dessert.pdf
[28] Andy Kirk, Separating Myth From Truth in Data Visualization, slide 15,
https://www.slideshare.net/visualisingdata/separating-myth-from-truth-in-data-visualisation-64910711

question what is the right chart for my situation? will always be the same: whatever will be easiest for your audience to read."[29]

You can simply pick a chart, share it with a coworker/neighbor/mom/child, and see if they get your intended message. I discuss later in the chapter how data visualization should be iterative. If you don't get it right the first time, don't worry. It's all part of the process.

A Note on Big Data

I would like to note that your big data often isn't that different from small data when it comes to visualization. The majority of the time, users want to see a summary or a subset of the data, not every single data point. Once you have summarized it or chosen your subset, you can use the same chart types as you would for anything else. In other words, big data fits in a bar chart just fine. You will want to make sure you have a way to drill down to reach different subsets of data so your users can explore a bit. Occasionally you will see a visual that shows every data point from a big data source, but about the only thing you can communicate is the count and cardinality of values in your data. The chord diagram is an example where lots of data points can be shown. I have used it to visualize data for a transportation company to show number of shipments between various sources and destinations. At some point, you don't really see each individual arc, you just notice the predominant colors and the number of colors present.

Visual Interactions Inform Chart Selection

In Power BI, there is another concept that may inform your chart selection. Visualizations on a report page can be used to cross-filter or cross-highlight the other visualizations on the page. Chart types that have area (bar charts, pie charts, etc.) can be cross-highlighted, while other charts, such as line charts and cards can only be filtered. In addition, some charts can be cross-highlighted, but the results are not usually very useful. This is often the case with tree maps. If you know that a sales analyst is going to look at the sales trends by month and then immediately want to know which products sold the most that month, you will want to have a visual that can be cross-filtered by the original sales by month chart. Most charts can be filtered. And most charts can filter other charts. But you will want to test interactivity to understand how they work. For instance, a line chart with a single line cannot filter or highlight other charts on a page. But a line chart with multiple lines can filter a bar chart on the same page. The bar chart is filtered by the value of the field in the legend of the line chart. As you are planning the visual path your users should take through your Power BI report, make sure the interactions work as expected. If they do not, you may want to consider switching to a different chart type to achieve your goals.

Custom Visuals

Discussing chart types and features requires discussion of custom visuals. Custom visuals are visuals created and supported by the community. You can find many of them in the Office Store, although there is no requirement to submit them there. In the Office Store, Power BI custom visuals can be Office Store Approved or Power BI Certified. Office Store Approved visuals can be

---

[29] Cole Knussbaumer Knaflic, Storytelling With Data, Chart Chooser, http://www.storytellingwithdata.com/blog/2013/04/chart-chooser

run in browsers, reports, and dashboards. Power BI Certified visuals have passed rigorous testing, and are supported in additional scenarios, such as email subscriptions, and export to PowerPoint.[30]

Custom visuals can be very useful in creating a report that is visually engaging for your audience while communicating the right message. But they come with risks of which you should be aware.

- The visual may not work in all the situations in which you want to use it. The chord diagram is Office Store Approved but not Power BI Certified (as of this writing), so it might not work as intended if you set up email subscriptions for the report in which it is used.
- If a Power BI update breaks the custom visual, you may have to wait a while for it to be updated. The Power BI team does test some of the custom visuals against new releases of Power BI Desktop and Power BI Web Service. But occasionally a change comes through that causes a custom visual to behave differently. If the developer who made the visual is busy with work or on vacation on a remote island, you might be waiting a while for a fix. That probably doesn't happen too often, but it might happen at the most inconvenient time for you.
- Some custom visuals do not offer the same interactions as the default visuals. Occasionally the cross-highlighting or cross-filtering isn't available as expected.
- If you upgrade Power BI Desktop and upgrade a report to use the newer version, you may need to retrieve a newer version of your custom visuals to ensure they work properly. Once you have done that, you will need to test the data, formatting, and interactions again to ensure it still behaves as expected.
- Custom visuals often don't offer all the formatting options of regular visuals. For instance, currently the preview matrix visual is not correctly formatting the values. When a whole number is placed in Values, it shows it as a decimal with 2 places after the decimal point.

Once you are aware of the risks, you must decide if it is beneficial to use custom visuals. If you are designing a report just for you, the risks are low. But if you are using Power BI for corporate reporting with a large audience and a team of report developers, you may find that you would prefer not to use them. Depending on your organization's security requirements, your IT department may prohibit their use. There have been times where I decided that a custom visual was the only thing that could deliver the necessary visual message. If you cannot use custom visuals, you can still get creative with the default visuals. See the Get Creative section later in the chapter for ideas.

In the Power BI Store, there are custom visuals made with NodeJS and some made using various R packages. If you use the R visuals, you need to install R and the required R package(s) on the machine where you are developing the report. You may also need to enable R visuals in the options in Power BI Desktop. R visuals have some limitations:

- Data used by the R visual for plotting is limited to 150,000 rows.

---

[30] Microsoft, Custom Visualizations in Power BI, https://powerbi.microsoft.com/en-us/documentation/powerbi-custom-visuals/

- If an R visual calculation exceeds 5 minutes the execution times out.
- R visuals cannot be the source of cross-filtering.

R visuals can be extremely useful as they enable advanced calculations and advanced visualizations that are not otherwise possible in Power BI. They offer an array of chart types with a level of formatting and detail that isn't possible with the built-in charts in Power BI. In the first half of this year, capabilities were added to allow R custom visuals to be interactive, by generating the visual as HTML instead of a static image. This means these R visuals can support tooltips and selections.

In addition to using the R visuals found in the Office Store, you can make your own R visuals.

Adding Calculations to Support a Visual

Once you have chosen a chart type, you may find that you need to switch the measure to more clearly communicate your message. For example, I work at a consulting company. We are constantly analyzing revenue vs capacity or hours billed vs capacity. I could show the total revenue and the total expected capacity for any month on a chart. Or we could show the variance (Revenue – Capacity). If we want to emphasize the variance rather than just report the numbers, we may create a calculated measure in our Power BI model and plot the variance by month instead. You might decide that you want to see sales by product as a percent of total instead of absolute amounts. Don't be afraid to add extra calculations to your model to support your intended message.

Smart Use of Color

Color is one of the most powerful and most misused attributes we have in report design. Color has three basic properties: hue, value, and intensity. Hue is the color as we might label it on the color wheel (red, blue, green, etc.). Value is the darkness or lightness of a color, created by adding black or white to the pure hue. Intensity refers to the brightness or saturation of a color. Intensity, or saturation, is adjusted by adding additional colors to the pure hue.

Hue and intensity are both preattentive attributes. Preattentive attributes are visual properties that we notice without using conscious effort to do so. When you look at the sales by month chart below, what is the first thing you notice?

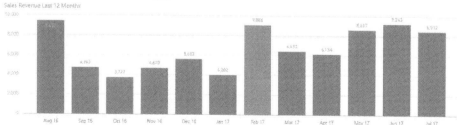

Figure 113 – Preattentive Attributes Color Example Chart

It was probably the bar for February 2017 because it has a different hue from the other bars. This demonstrates that we can use color to draw attention to a chart or element within a chart. This also means that we need to be careful that our color choices don't distract our audience. When we use lots of different colors (hues) that are all very intense, the users don't know where to look. I tell people that using all bright colors is the data visualization equivalent to TYPING IN ALL CAPS. Doing so without purpose makes you look old fashioned or ill-informed. It is acceptable to use bright colors, but use them judiciously and purposefully to direct attention or highlight an important data point.

Color Palettes and Report Themes

Using too many colors can also become distracting. Although you can, you don't need to use every color on the color wheel. I tend to choose two main colors and either two analogous (adjacent on the color wheel) or two complementary (across from each other on the color wheel) colors to use as my color palette.

Often one or both of the main colors come from (or are inspired by) the organization's logo or corporate colors, if they have them defined. While each palette I create is slightly different based upon the scenario, I generally know I will need two colors to use in charts and each of those colors could potentially need an easily distinguished color to show a comparison value. Add in another color for highlighting/drawing attention and a few shades of gray for text, borders, and background shading. That gives you a great start on a color palette. Creating a color palette can take a bit of time. Once you have a color palette you like, you should reuse it (where appropriate) and not re-make those color decisions all over again.

Power BI now has report themes, which allow you to define colors and import them into a report.[31] A report theme may contain a name, data colors, a table/matrix background color, a table/matrix foreground color, and a table/matrix accent color. As of July 2017, you must create and import a JSON file to Power BI Desktop in order to use a report theme. But there may eventually be a graphical user interface. Here is an example of a theme file and the theme that was created in Power BI Desktop.

```
{
"name":"CoolAnalogousWithHighlight",
"dataColors":["#004a72", "#007fc3", "#12aafb", "#4dad33", "#a4d49c", "#9d84fd", "#898586","#ff971a"],
"background":"#f6f6f6",
"foreground":"#494747",
"tableAccent":"#b2e6ff"
}
```

Figure 114 – Example Report Theme JSON

---

[31] Microsoft, Use Report Themes In Power BI Desktop, https://powerbi.microsoft.com/en-us/documentation/powerbi-desktop-report-themes/

Chapter 5   Data Visualization in Power BI

Figure 115 – Example Report Theme

If you need a little inspiration or just want to see what themes others have created, you can check out the Power BI Theme Gallery[32].

When we talk about using color, we need to be aware of color vision deficiency (also known as colorblindness). If you are designing a Power BI report to be shared with the general public or a large audience, you should keep color vision deficiency in mind. Color vision deficiency affects 1 in 12 men and 1 in 200 women.[33] Red-green deficiency is the most common. You don't always know when someone is colorblind. Sometimes they have found ways to cope, but sometimes our color choices can be confusing or even misleading. Since many people have trouble distinguishing between red and green, those may not be good choices to indicate good and bad statuses of a KPI if you know you have a colorblind user. Storytelling With Data recommends switching to blue and orange instead of using green and red.[34] There are several free tools that allow you to see what your Power BI Report looks like for a colorblind person. Some of the OKViz branded custom visuals have a colorblind-friendly color option in the Formatting Pane for the visual that allows you to customize colors for a specific type of color vision deficiency.

---

[32] Microsoft, Power BI Report Themes Gallery, https://community.powerbi.com/t5/Themes-Gallery/bd-p/ThemesGallery
[33] Colourblind Awareness, http://www.colourblindawareness.org/colour-blindness/
[34] Cole Nussbaumer Knaflic, Storytelling With Data, pg 121.

Chapter 5 **Data Visualization** in Power BI

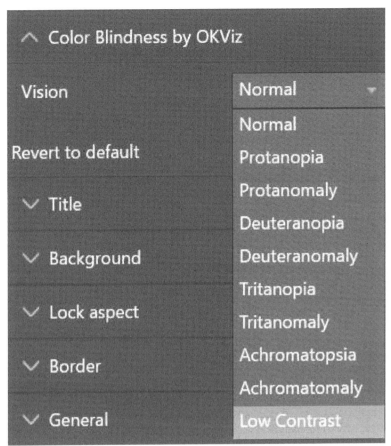

Figure 116 – OKViz Colorblindness Settings

Alternatives to the Standard Power BI Report

Sometimes a Power BI report is just not the right visualization tool for your data. Luckily, you are not limited to the Power BI reporting engine if your data is in a Power BI model. You can use the Analyze in Excel functionality in Power BI to open a connection to your data model in Excel. Many people like to explore data with pivot tables. When I am getting to know a data set, I look at important metrics and categories in a pivot table and add conditional formatting such as data bars or shading. At this time, Power BI reports don't offer all the capabilities of Excel PivotTables (e.g. measures on rows, advanced sorting, etc.). If a pivot table is what your audience needs, there may not be a reason to fight it.

Another Excel-based option is cube functions. Cube functions are Excel formulas that can execute MDX against your Power BI model to return a specific value in the specified cell. They are great when you have a lot of data that is very tabular in nature because you can just copy formulas across. They are also great when you need to use Excel's more detailed formatting options.

Another option is to use Q&A to create your visuals for you. You or your users can ask natural language questions of your data model, and Power BI will retrieve the data and display it in the visual it has determined is most appropriate (card, bar chart, map, etc.). Setting this up to work well requires a bit of tweaking with synonyms. Synonyms help Power BI to know that when someone says sales, that means the same thing as revenue in the data set. If you don't like the visual that Power BI creates, you can edit it. If the question you asked has become a recurring theme, you can pin the visual from your question to a dashboard.

Considerations for Users' Preferred Consumption Methods

Although most people consume Power BI reports through a web browser, there are several other options. It's important to consider how your users want to interact with your reports.

Dashboards

Do the users want to have dashboards for summary or navigation purposes? If so, you'll want to test how your visuals look in a dashboard. If your users intend to look at the dashboard first and only look at the report if they see something that requires attention or action, you'll need to make sure the charts in your dashboard are easy to read. It can be tempting to try to fit everything in a dashboard within the screen so you have no need to scroll. But make sure you don't make the chart so small that your scale is tiny or you can't read the labels. Allow your charts to take up some space in your dashboard. If you need quick at-a-glance metrics, consider using cards or KPIs in your report which can then be pinned to the dashboard.

Mobile Apps

Will your users consume your report via the Power BI mobile app? If so, make sure that you have created a mobile view or at least tested that the default view works well on a phone and/or tablet. If you do not create a phone report, users will see the original report in landscape mode. This can make some of your visuals rather small and difficult to select for cross-filtering/highlighting purposes. A phone report is a vertical or portrait layout. You can choose whether to include all items from the master report or only a subset. For example, if you used an image in the master report, do you need it taking up space on the phone report? Keep in mind that if someone is looking at a report on their phone, there is a good chance that they are referencing it to answer a specific question while on the go or to prep for a meeting. You want high usability and low clutter so they can get the information they need. Feel free to resize and rearrange the visuals as you need. Make sure the flow of information makes sense for your mobile users. Do they need to choose an item in a slicer before reviewing the information? That should be the object you put first. If you have a report with multiple pages, you can choose which pages should get a mobile report layout. You don't have to create a mobile layout for all pages, but if you optimize only some of the pages in the report, users will have to rotate their phone to go between the optimized portrait and unoptimized landscape pages.

Print

Chapter 5 **Data Visualization** in Power BI

Do your users print their reports? Power BI makes interactive web reports, but they aren't always very printer friendly. While I would recommend encouraging your users to access reports in a web browser or mobile app, sometimes you need to accommodate users who need to print. This means you need to test to see how your report pages print. If you don't have a printer, at least print to PDF (usually a built-in printer option) so you can get an idea of how it would look. Testing printability may lead you to simplify your report. I often make reports with text boxes layered over images, which looks great in a web browser, but doesn't print so well. Another thing to check is colors. Make sure your colors are easily distinguishable from each other (e.g. you easily can tell the lines in a line chart apart). When you print a report, you lose the interactivity and contextual navigation you get from a Power BI report on the web. You can use Power BI to make a flat or static report. Just remember to look at it the way your user does.

Exporting and Viewing Underlying Data

Do your users want to access data from the visuals in your report? There are three ways that users can access data that supports a visual. Each visual has an Export option that downloads the data points used in the visual to an Excel or CSV file. Users can choose to download the summary data that make up the data points in the visuals, or the underlying data for the table in the model. The option to download an Excel file and to choose to download underlying (detail) data are only available through PowerBI.com, not in Power BI Desktop. There are a couple of caveats with this functionality:

- There is a limit to how much data is exported (30,000 rows for a CSV or 150,000 rows for XLSX).
- Not all custom visuals and R visuals support this functionality.
- Report measures (measures built in Power BI on top of an SSAS model or another Power BI model) cannot be used.

If users need a lot of data exported to Excel, it might be best for them to use the Analyze in Excel functionality. When discussions of exporting data arise, it is worth considering if the report is not fulfilling users' needs. This goes back to the common reasons for data viz failure. Is your Power BI report being used as an intermediate step in a data gathering process rather than an end result visualization? Is the design not allowing users to easily get the information they need in a pleasant user environment? Sometimes people adopt a report that was built for an entirely different audience or purpose and then use it to export data. Perhaps this audience who wishes to export, needs their own report page or report.

If users just need to see the data that makes up a visual rather than export it, they can use the See Data functionality. It will show the data that makes up a visual as a table. One nice feature of this function that you can use to your advantage is that it shows all the data points that are part of the visual, even if they are not visible. Anything you include in tooltips will be included in the table generated by See Data. Also, if you add multiple fields to a visual to enable drilldown, you will get the drilldown fields as well as the visible field. This is sometimes helpful in visuals that don't have data labels turned on. It helps users validate the data and see all data points at one time without losing the cognitive benefits of pattern recognition they get from the chart you created.

There is another feature called See Records that allows you to see the row-level data from the table in the Power BI model. You must click See Records and then choose a specific data point on your chart (e.g. a bar in your bar chart). Power BI will show the detail records for that data point only. This is helpful again for data validation. See Records only works with implicit measures rather than calculated (explicit) or user created measures.

Export to PowerPoint

There is also an option to export a report to Power Point. If you know your users are taking screenshots of your report to put into presentations, you can help them skip a step with Export to PowerPoint. Export to PowerPoint creates a slide for each page in your report, with each visual turned into an image and a link to your report on PowerBI.com. This feature is still in preview as of this writing, and there are a handful of limitations.

- R visuals and non-certified custom visuals are not supported.
- Reports with more than 15 pages can't be exported to PowerPoint.
- Background images are cropped with the chart's bounding areas during export.

Exporting to PowerPoint removes the interactivity of your report and places static objects in a PowerPoint file. But sometimes that is necessary to integrate the information with other meeting content or for the rare times when you know there will be no internet access during your meeting.

As mentioned earlier, data visualization design is iterative. You may need to change your report to get the information to the users in the manner that works best for them. And that is ok, perhaps even encouraged.

Cortana

Power BI has integration with the Cortana digital assistant such that Cortana can display special answer cards when searching. Answer cards are special report pages designed specifically to answer Cortana questions.[35] Cortana answer cards allow selection of individual data points in charts for visual interactions and setting page filters through a verbal command. The design canvas is smaller, so you must prioritize and consolidate visuals to keep your answer card clutter free.

Use What You Got

According to the award-winning musical The Life, "You gotta use what you got to get what you want". This is true in Power BI. If our goal is to communicate a data message and engage your users, we need to know what it is we "got" as far as helpful Power BI features for report design. Power BI desktop is updated monthly, so the array of features is (quickly) ever expanding. I have listed resources to help you keep up with changes at the end of this chapter. You can reference

---

[35] Microsoft. Use Power BI to Create a Custom Answer Page for Cortana, https://powerbi.microsoft.com/en-us/documentation/powerbi-service-cortana-desktop-entity-cards/#create-an-answer-card-designed-specifically-for-cortana

them to find out about new features as they arrive. In the current product, there are a handful of features that can be useful in enhancing your data visualization designs.

Filters and Slicers

Filters and slicers are both used to narrow down the data in a report to the subset that is important to the user. I've noticed that those who come from an Excel background tend to use slicers more often because they were already familiar with them in Excel. There are times when slicers are a good choice, but consider that slicers take up valuable screen real estate. You can make a filter quite compact by changing the orientation or switching the format to a dropdown box. If it is important to show what items are selected on a page, it might be worth the use of the space on the page, although you could also do this with filters and a card or table to show selected values. Filters remain off to the side in their own pane, and they can be set via query string parameters in a URL. If your users like to explore the data in your reports and look at different slices, you might consider placing a handful of filters in your page or report filter.

Read-only users of a report can change the values of existing filters in a report, but they can't add new filters. If there are attributes that you know your users will need to filter, make sure to add them to the filters pane. There is such a thing as filter overload, so try to find a balance between adding all the fields to the filters and adding only the important or highly used fields.

One thing to note is that you cannot use visual level filters on slicers. A slicer will show all the available values for the attribute by which you are slicing. There is a workaround for this: Create a calculated table and use the values in the calculated table to populate a slicer. If I have a need to have users select a product to see the monthly sales for that product and I make a slicer based upon Product Name, I will see all products listed.

Product Name
- ☐ Product A
- ☐ Product B
- ☐ Product C
- ☐ Product D
- ☐ Product E
- ☐ Product F
- ☐ Product G
- ☐ Product H
- ☐ Product I
- ☐ Product J
- ☐ Product K
- ☐ Product L
- ☐ Product M
- ☐ Product N

Figure 117 – Slicer with All Values

If I need to remove some products from selection, perhaps remove all the products that do not have sales, I cannot use a visual filter to accomplish this task, but I can write a quick DAX calculation to make a calculated table:

```
Product Selection =
SELECTCOLUMNS (
    FILTER (
        CROSSJOIN ( 'Product', 'Monthly Sales' ),
        'Product'[Product Code] = 'Monthly Sales'[Product]
    ),
    "Product Name", 'Product'[Product Name]
)
```

Figure 118 – DAX Calculated Table Formula to Reduce Slicer Values

If only products A, B, and C have sales, this DAX formula produces a calculated table from which I can create a slicer that shows only those three products.

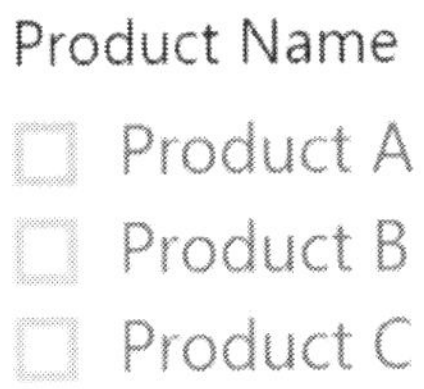

Chapter 5 Data Visualization in Power BI

Product Name
☐ Product A
☐ Product B
☐ Product C

Figure 119 – Resulting Filtered Slicer Values

Make sure that a relationship is built between the new calculated table and the fact table, so the slicer works as intended. The example DAX limits the table to the Product Name field for the purpose of the slicer, but if the extra products are not needed anywhere in the report, the original Product table can be hidden and all columns from the product table can be left in the Product Selection table.

Visual Interactions

We often overuse filters and slicers, when we could rely on the interactivity between visuals to allow users to filter rather than adding another element to the report. For instance, if I need to see my sales by month chart sliced by product, I could add a slicer for product, or I could add a chart and have users select the bar for the desired product. That allows me to show the sales numbers by product and month without taking up room for a slicer or adding another filter to the report.

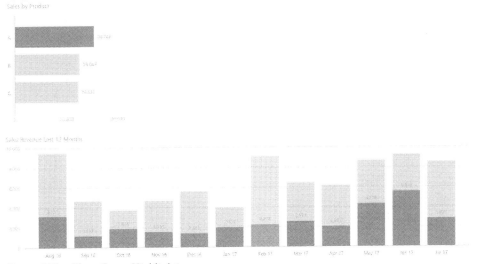

Figure 120 – Chart Cross-Highlighting

Again, we have control over how visuals interact with other visuals. When we click on a data point in a chart, we can choose to have other charts cross-highlight, cross-filter, or ignore that data point selection.

The KPIs near the top left of the Blood Glucose Management report (Figure 112) ignore interactions from the line chart near the top right. When I click a point on the line chart, I am selecting a Daily Index Number (the order of the glucose test within the day). The Morning Fasting Average KPI is referring to daily index 1 (the first reading done in the day). Filtering on any daily index other than 1 would yield an empty result set. The Post-Meal average is usually the third reading of the day, so filtering on anything other than daily index 3 will yield an empty or incomplete result set. The Post-Meal BG Rise compares two readings in a day that will have different daily indexes (usually 2 and 3), so selecting a single index will yield an empty result set. Rather than make them empty, I would like to have them continue to show the 30-day average while I explore other data points.

The information value we get from cross-highlighting depends on the chart type. Remember that pie charts and tree maps allow cross-highlighting but are often difficult to read, so it is more useful to change them to be filtered by interactions with other charts.

Grouping & Binning

Another good set of Power BI features is grouping and binning. How many times have you wanted to build a visual that showed your top 5 customers/products/projects with the rest grouped into Other? You can do this with grouping.

If I run a small business that sells three main products and a bunch of ancillary products, when I look at my sales, they may look like the chart below.

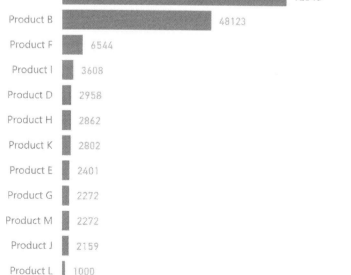

Figure 121 – Sales by Product Before Grouping

It may be more informative for me to see this:

Figure 122 – Sales by Product with Grouping

My chart still includes all sales, but all the ancillary products are grouped, removing some of the clutter from the visual. I can leave the original products underneath the Product Name group in the axis to allow drilldown to see the individual products that make up the Other group, so that information is still available.

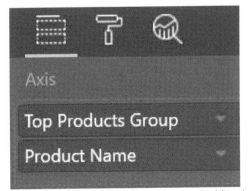

Figure 123 – Group and Product Name Field in Axis

This is achieved by creating a group where my top 3 (previously identified) products each have their own group, and I leave all other values ungrouped to be put into the Other bucket.

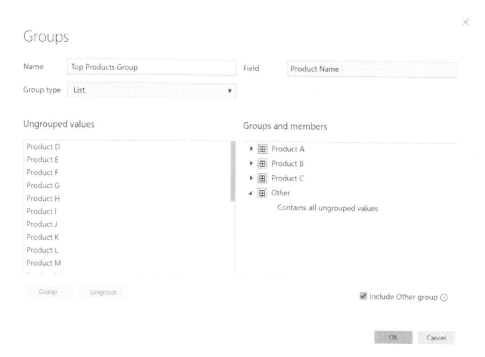

Figure 124 – Grouping Menu in Power BI

Binning is like grouping, except it uses a numeric or date field. You choose whether you want a certain number of bins or bins of equal sizes. If I go back to my blood glucose data, I may want to see how many readings fell into various bins.

Chapter 5 **Data Visualization** in Power BI

Groups

Name	Bg (bins)	Field	Bg
Group type	Bin	Min value	97
Bin Type	Size of bins	Max value	361

Binning splits numeric or date/time data into equally sized groups. The default bin size is calculated based on your data.

Bin size   25

Reset to default

OK   Cancel

Figure 125 – Binning Menu in Power BI

Creating bins of 25 mg/dL can help show how well the patient stays in the recommended healthy range.

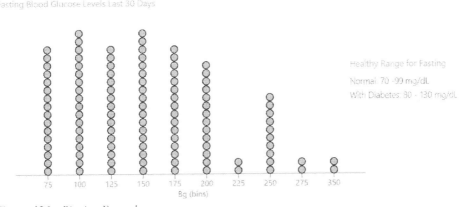

Figure 126 – Binning Example

Analytics Pane

In case you haven't noticed, there is an Analytics Pane next to the Format Pane. It first appeared in the product around August 2016. It enables us to add trend lines and references lines

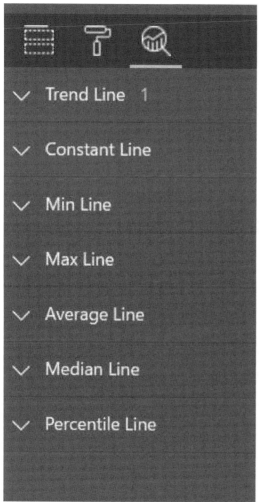

Figure 127 – Analytics Pane in Power BI

I used a trend line on the Blood Glucose Readings report page.

Chapter 5 **Data Visualization** in Power BI

Figure 128 – Trend Line Example

It shows the trend across all Daily Index values. Since I'm showing each daily index in a day as a line, this trend line shows the daily average. It is helpful to see that the daily average is trending down, even if some individual readings bounce back up. In addition to trend lines, you can add lines for min, max, average, mean, and percentile, as well as a constant value. Reference lines can be quite helpful when the reference is meaningful, but don't add them just to add them.

Data Visualization is Iterative

Once you have understood your audience, identified the important data, created visuals, placed them on the page, and employed extra features to enhance the user experience, you are…
Not done.
Data visualization design is iterative. If you work with databases or web design, this should sound familiar. We don't often get it perfect the first time so we work to fulfill our requirements, and then re-evaluate, gather user feedback, and make changes. Then we re-evaluate and gather user feedback again.

Before we can consider our work complete, we need to validate that we are achieving our intended goals of communicating the message and providing a pleasant and engaging user interface.

Squint Test

The first and easiest test is the Squint Test. To perform the Squint Test, shrink things down and/or half close your eyes and look at your report page to see what items on the page are most prominent. If you first notice the shape of your data on a chart, and that chart is clearly supporting your intended message, you have passed the squint test. If the first thing you notice is a background color or borders, or a non-data-related image or shape, you will want to tweak your design a bit.

Layout and Priority

Next check your layout to ensure your visuals are placed appropriately on the page. In western cultures, we tend to read in a Z-pattern starting from top left to bottom right. For a Power BI report, this means you can break your report into quadrants. You want to make sure that any intro information that is needed to understand or interact with your report is placed in the top left quadrant so it is read first. You also want your most important information (usually the answer to the initial question your users would ask of your report) in the top left quadrant. Any slicers that need to be set before reviewing the report should be in or close to the top left quadrant.
You can also apply this check at the individual chart level. How many times have you read a chart like this?

Chapter 5 **Data Visualization** in Power BI

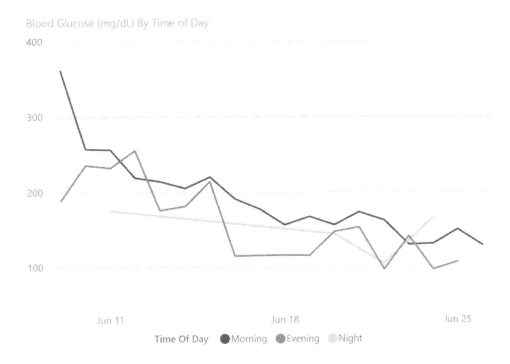

Figure 129 – Chart with Legend at Bottom

When you looked at this chart, you probably looked at the title, then looked at the lines, then wondered what you were looking at and referenced the legend at the bottom. Then you had to look at the lines all over again because you now had the information you needed to read the chart. We can fix this by moving the legend to the top left so it is read before the lines.

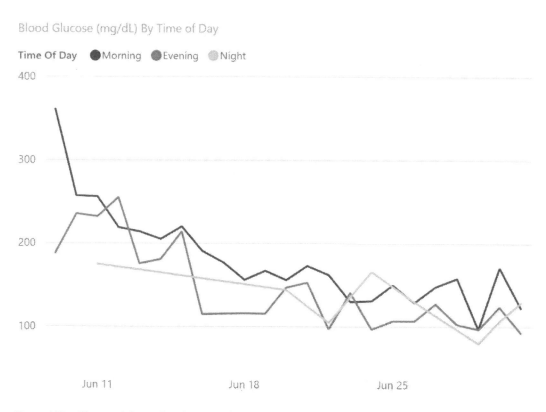

Figure 130 – Chart with Legend at the Top Left

Gestalt Principles of Proximity and Enclosure

Check that visuals that are related are placed near each other. Humans interpret proximity as the items being related. This is a Gestalt Principle.[36] If you need to group some visuals together and separate them from others, you might put a shape around them such as a rectangle. This relates to the principle of common region. Elements tend to be logically grouped together if they are within the same closed region.

Reduce Clutter and Cognitive Load
Cognitive load refers to the amount of mental effort being used in working memory to take in information. Extraneous cognitive load is the mental effort that is required due to the way information is presented that doesn't help the user understand the information. This is usually due to poor design. There are several concepts related to the idea of reducing or eliminating

---

[36] Scholarpedia. Gestalt principles. http://www.scholarpedia.org/article/Gestalt_principles

extraneous cognitive load. Edward Tufte refers to maximizing the data-ink ratio such that of all the ink (pixels) on your page, the majority go to communicating data rather than formatting or decoration.[37] Nancy Duarte has a similar concept called signal-to-noise ratio, where signal is the information we want to communicate (our data and message) and noise is anything that detracts or doesn't add to our message.[38] Andy Kirk takes a more nuanced view by saying that we should maximize the reward to effort ratio.[39] In this case, effort refers to the act of trying to understand the information presented in our report and reward is achieving understanding. This makes it less about every pixel on the page and more about accessibility and the user experience. But part of accessibility is removing clutter. There is no exact metric to identify what aspects of a report or visual should be considered clutter. Great minds can and do disagree. But if you look at your report and find that something is distracting from the message and important data points, you should consider it clutter. Kirk's version of the equation weights the user experience more heavily than strictly adhering to design principles, which I think is advisable for more advanced data viz designers. If you are just getting started with report design and need something more tangible, maximizing the data-ink ratio is a great place to start.

Storytelling with Data has taught us that cognitive load is important, but perceived cognitive load is even more important.[40] If your users think they will have a low reward to effort ratio, they will not use your report to the fullest extent, if at all. It's important to remember the level of technical and subject matter expertise of your intended audience. It may seem like reasonable cognitive load to you, but you must assess it based upon your users' experience and knowledge rather than your own.

A lot of what creates clutter (and therefore cognitive load) can be attributed to inadequate mastery of preattentive attributes. Preattentive attributes include:

- Length
- Width
- Orientation
- Size
- Shape
- Curvature
- Enclosure
- Blur
- Hue
- Intensity

---

[37] Edward Tufte, The Visual Display of Quantitative Information, pg 93
[38] Nancy Duarte, Clear Presentation Slides: Glance Media, http://www.duarte.com/clear-presentation-slides-glance-media/
[39] Andy Kirk, Data Visualisation: A Handbook for Data Driven Design, pg 38
[40] Cole Nussbaumer Knaflic, Storytelling With Data, pg 73

- 2-D position
- Spatial Grouping
- Direction of Motion[41]

Common issues in report design that cause distraction or clutter include:

- Lack of alignment – When we don't align visuals, the 2-D position catches our eye, and we start to wonder why things are not aligned rather than paying attention to the information.
- Diagonal chart labels – How many times have you looked at a chart and tilted your head sideways to read the labels? It is both annoying to read and distracting because usually these labels are the only thing with a diagonal orientation.
- Bold chart title backgrounds – When the chart title background is the thing that stands out most on the page, we have failed the squint test. We spend more time with our eyes drawn to the chart title rather than the important data points. We want to use color intensity to strategically draw attention to information rather than simply decorate a chart title. If we were highlighting a chart title to have users look at it first, or to make sure someone notices it, that is different. But if all chart titles are the same intense color, we need to adjust them.
- Too many data labels – It is understandable that users want to see both the visual trend or comparison and the precise values, but sometimes data labels clutter up a visual more than they help. If the data labels are difficult to read or you had to change the font size to be very small in order to fit them in, you probably need to remove them. If the data labels distract from the chart, you need to remove them. The data points will still be available through tooltips, See Data, and Export Data.
- Non-strategic use of color contrast – When we use many high-intensity colors, we cause our users' eyes to dart back and forth. They don't know where to look because every color on the page is screaming at them. We should not be using different colors just because they exist. We want to use it to highlight important data points and relate categories or measures across charts (e.g., use the same color for revenue in a bar chart showing sales by product and in the adjacent line chart showing sales by month).
- Overuse of chart borders – chart borders are usually unnecessary. We can instead use white space to differentiate one visual from another on the report page. If you need something more than whitespace to differentiate a chart or group of charts, consider using a shape with no border and a light fill color.
- Using bar charts with a truncated axis that does not start at zero – We use the preattentive attribute of length to help us compare values and find trends. When you truncate the axis, it changes the scale of the differences between values.

---

[41] Stephen Few, Tapping the Power of Visual Perception, https://www.perceptualedge.com/articles/ie/visual_perception.pdf

Chapter 5 **Data Visualization** in Power BI

- Too many charts on a page – Sometimes report designers try to cram too many charts on a page to try to anticipate all the data questions a user might ask. At some point, this degrades the user experience because the report is too busy. Although you may have painstakingly designed and formatted that certain visual, if it doesn't support your message and removing it would help clarify the report, it needs to go. You can strategically use links, drilldown, and visual interactions to provide additional related data.

Stephanie Evergreen has a great Data Visualization Checklist that you can use to evaluate individual charts.[42]

Once you have evaluated your report to ensure you have optimized cognitive load and effectively communicated your message, make any necessary changes and evaluate once more. If possible, show it to your intended users and get their feedback.

Get Creative

While it may seem like there are a lot of Power BI features and design guidelines to remember, data visualization can be fun! Remembering guidelines and spotting clutter gets easier with practice. Once you have basic report design down, it's time to get creative.

Power BI can do more than just a basic four-quadrant sales report. If you need some inspiration, check out the Power BI Data Stories Gallery[43]. While not all the reports in the gallery display good visual design, they can spark ideas for new ways to visualize your data.
Here are a few tips to enhance your visual design repertoire:

- Don't be afraid to add text. Sometimes we need some text to help tell the story or explain the intended insight. I demonstrated this by listing acceptable ranges in the Blood Glucose Measurement report.
- Use images to help communicate your message. Images don't have to be purely decoration. A common data-centric way to use images is to put them in a slicer. There they serve a purpose in your report. The below report was used to show how many BBQ restaurants in Kansas City my friend Bill and I had visited, both individually and in total. I used a picture of a plate full of BBQ in a Chiclet Slicer custom visual to indicate restaurants we had yet to visit and an empty plate to indicate restaurants we had visited. I also used my picture underneath the chart that showed my restaurant visit stats and Bill's

---

[42] Stephanie Evergreen, Updated Data Visualization Checklist, http://stephanieevergreen.com/updated-data-visualization-checklist/
[43] Microsoft. Data Stories Gallery. https://community.powerbi.com/t5/Data-Stories-Gallery/bd-p/DataStoriesGallery

picture underneath his chart. These images add to the data story rather than just serving as decoration.

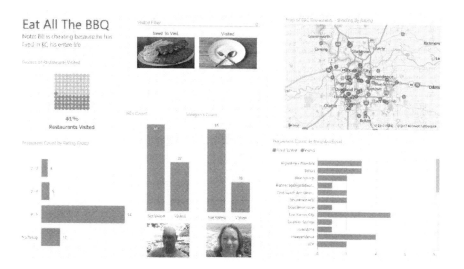

Figure 131 – Slicers with Image Example

- Check out new custom visuals to see if they can enhance your report. For instance, a preview of the Visio custom visual was released during the 2017 Data Insights Summit. Being able to create flow charts and org diagrams and retain interactivity with other charts could be a great enhancement to a report. Picture a report about department success metrics with an org chart where you can click on the department manager's picture. Since custom visuals come from both Microsoft and the community, be sure to check the custom visual gallery to see what's new at least quarterly.
- Make use of microcharts. The newer version of the table and matrix visuals support data bars. You can also use line charts to make sparklines or use the custom visual from the gallery.
- Don't just look at example Power BI reports. Look at data visualizations from other tools and see if you can make Power BI mimic them. For example, there is currently no slopegraph in the Power BI product or custom visual gallery, but David Eldersveld has shown on his blog how to use Power BI to create a slopegraph.[44] Check out sites like

---

[44] David Eldersveld, DataVeld, Creating Slopegraphs in Power BI, https://dataveld.wordpress.com/2017/05/18/creating-slopegraphs-in-power-bi/

Makeover Monday[45] to see how people improved upon published data visualizations. There are indeed some amazing Power BI entries in Makeover Monday!
- Try visualizing non-work-related data to help yourself get out of a data viz rut. Pick a dataset that is interesting or helpful to you and be your own target user. This will help you build to accommodate user needs and encourage you to use different chart types.

I hope you'll join me in learning Power BI and experimenting to find new and powerful ways to visualize your data. And I hope reading this chapter has moved you a little further along on the knowledge curve.

---

[45] Makeover Monday, http://www.makeovermonday.co.uk/

Chapter 6
Creating a Disaster Recovery Plan

By: Rie Irish

Your boss asked for a copy of your Disaster Recovery plan. Once you've wiped that deer-in-the-headlights look off your face, you realize "We've got database backups." isn't exactly a plan. From Wikipedia, a **disaster recovery plan** (DRP) is a documented process or set of procedures to recover and protect a business IT infrastructure in the event of a disaster. Such a plan, ordinarily documented in written form, specifies procedures an organization is to follow in the event of a disaster. You'll need to define what a disaster could be, document the business impact and identify your limitations.

So where do you start? Well, that's the easy part. You start at the beginning. This chapter will walk you through how to identify what's important, who owns it and how to put all that information in one place. Create a check list, fill in some contact points, follow up for business needs and you're well on your way to a working Disaster Recovery Plan.

You'll frequently hear a DR plan referred to interchangeably as a Business Continuity Plan. That may be more accurate a term for a business wide strategy & not just an infrastructure or data centric DR plan. The focus shouldn't be solely about coming back from a cataclysmic event or keeping the lights on. Plan for what your company needs to do to be a functioning, revenue generating business. You'll need to do some basic business impact analysis. Define what a disaster could cost you in lost revenue & sales, customer dissatisfaction and regulatory fines.

According to ISO/IEC 27031, the global standard for IT disaster recovery, "Strategies should define the approaches to implement the required resilience so that the principles of incident prevention, detection, response, recovery and restoration are put in place." Your strategy defines WHAT you will do while the plans describes the HOW.

Define what's important... before a disaster.

"Remember, when disaster strikes, the time to prepare has passed." — *Steven Cyros*

There are lots of questions to ask before you have a disaster. They're even more important before you build your disaster recovery plan. It's essentially the WHO, WHAT & WHEN of your plan. How long can you be down & how much data you can lose. Define what data is important. Who is responsible for declaring a disaster? Who is responsible for doing the actual recovery work? Even knowing where you store your plan and who is allowed access to it is something to think about now. It should contain a structured approach and response to any incident that affects your hardware, software, network, facilities or processes.

As you move through answering all the questions posed in the upcoming pages, keep track of what is identified as important by each team and department. Ultimately, that team may not get to say what goes into immediate business recovery plans. You'll need this information to submit to those in the company that do make those decisions. You'll need a clear definition of who thinks a system or process is vital, how it will impact their team and the level of effort it will take to maintain an appropriate level of backup & estimated recovery. The homework you do now, will directly affect how decisions on the final plan are made.

Who are my stakeholders?

"There's nothing like a jolly good disaster to make people start doing something." — *Prince Charles*

In a single statement, they're the people that can answer all the questions we're asking here. This starts with C-level execs, since they'll be the ones that have to answer to the board after a disaster. They're also the ones that pay for it. Next, identify the people that will be affected by any data loss or a system outage. Who can't do their job? Are they critical to the business function? Go through each application and ask yourself "Who cares?" and then follow up with them. For example, if the billing department database is corrupted, then your company can't bring in money. That's a disaster to them, so you should probably speak to them before things go South.

Who is the primary person to fulfill each need? That's your contact. Who does that job when person 1 is on vacation? You'll want them on the list too, they're your secondary contact.

Finally, talk to the people that will have to implement the DR plan: system admins, networking & security, Operations, Storage & Infrastructure, DBA team, etc.

It may surprise you when I tell you that you should talk to your marketing department as well. They'll be the ones that handle communications with the outside world. They'll handle the messaging your company decides to wrap around this disaster. They'll want an established, documented protocol for handling information. Remember this when we cover creating your contact list.

What are my critical systems?

You'll need to define what systems are critical to business continuity. Sometimes, these things define themselves. Think back to the last time you saw people either scrambling around your office to fix something or sitting around with nothing to do because some system was inoperable. Wikipedia defines mission critical factor of a system as any factor (component, equipment, personnel, process, procedure, software, etc.) that is essential to business operation or to an organization. Failure or disruption of mission critical factors will result in serious impact on business operations or upon an organization, and even can cause social turmoil and catastrophes.

For some industries, these are easily defined. If you run a body shop, but your paint sprayers stop working, then you might as well be at a full production line shut down. If you run a mining operation and drills, fans, elevators, etc. aren't going at 100% then you've got a problem. For other industries, it's less tangible. They'll probably be able to easily identify the big things; the main work output for the company. There will be more ethereal, less specific needs that will be harder to define, more difficult to get on paper. It's important that you seek out those easily missed and less definable things. For most IT companies, your critical systems include databases, back end storage, web & application servers and even email/phone systems. It's easier to miss things like notification servers, certificates, IP mappings or sftp configuration settings.

Each team or department in your company should have their own processes documented. If they don't already, encourage them to do so. Each team and maybe each job function should have a manual on how things work. As you're meeting with different department stakeholders, have them define what's most critical and what's slightly less important. You'll want to put processes into different categories as you go: critical, vital, important, sensitive, etc. Tell them how your company has decided to define "critical". Then ask them a series of questions to help them define what's important to the business versus making their job easier.

- If this data was lost, could your department or the company function without it? Long-term or short-term?

- If this system (application) were down, could your department or the company continue to operate?

- How long of an outage of system A, B or C is acceptable, before the customer is impacted? Before the company stops making money? Before the company starts losing money?

- Would loss of this data or functionality affect clients and/or sales?

- Would loss of this data or functionality have financial or regulatory repercussions?

- Is there any short term alternative for this particular functionality?

RPO & RTO

These are terms you see thrown around in sessions, in meetings, in blogs and on twitter. They're specific values tied closely to disaster preparation and recovery. They are the most important pieces of information in your Disaster Recovery Plan because they'll be a key decision maker in every piece of the plan as you move forward. The official definitions are little wordy and not as helpful as you might think. The difference in these values is sometimes scale. RTO is a wide cast net that is likely to refer more business wide, while RPO is a narrower focus, on data.

Recovery Time Objective (RTO) is the targeted duration of time and a service level within which a business process must be restored after a disaster (or disruption) in order to avoid unacceptable consequences associated with a break in business continuity.

Your Recovery Time Objective is a way of defining how long can you be down. Or put another way, how long until you have, to come back up. So find out how your business defines RTO and then build toward that. Of course, this can vary based on the nature of your disaster. Did you lose a database or an instance? Is there corruption in a file system or did someone kick the storage out from under everything? Did you have to fail over to your DR site? Were you the victim of a DDOS attack, either directly or indirectly?

Take a look at the infrastructure that you have currently. If you're running a mission critical app on a 3TB database and all of your backups are stored off-site, then you should consider how long a copy and restore will take. If that time is unacceptable to the business, then look at changing your strategy. That strategy could change to storing most recent backups locally to a pre-determined point in time.

Recovery Point Objective (RPO) is the previous point in time to which data must be restored, and defines an amount of data loss which is acceptable to the business.

Your Recovery Point Objective is easily summed up by asking "How much data can you afford to lose?" For some systems, like payments and healthcare systems, that answer will be zero. The approach and expense for those systems is vastly different than others. The infrastructure, build and design will vary by a large degree when you're allowed to lose milliseconds of data versus up to 15 minutes. For slow changing systems, could you restore on Tuesday from a Sunday full backup and Monday's differential? In some instances, rebuilding is faster and easier than restoring, so be sure to explore that as an option.

While Execs can help you define RTO & RPO, they aren't the ones who have to make it happen. If you can't meet their requirements, be honest. You also need to be aware of contractual obligations to external clients. While these are out of your direct control, you should encourage sales & legal to work with you while you prep a contract. If they're promising 5 9's in uptime but you can only deliver 3 9's, they need to know. Use phrases like "claw back", "refund of fees" or "violation of terms". That should get their attention.

You'll also want to consider your company's Maximum Tolerable Period of Disruption (MTPD). According to Wikipedia, this is the maximum amount of time that an enterprise's key products or services can be unavailable or undeliverable after an event that causes disruption to operations, before its stakeholders perceive unacceptable consequences. Simply put, this is when you're down so long the business viability is irreparably harmed. MTPD is going to be greater than your RTO & RPO and is considered the end of the road, resumé-generating, maximum acceptable outage point on the timeline.

Document your Physical Structure/Facilities

"Every step gets him closer to greatness...or disaster." — *Jody Feldman*

If I asked you right now to describe your company's hardware set up, could you do it? Probably not from memory. Even if you could spout off everything, I'm going to guess you'd be working on rebuilding things during a disaster instead of dictating set up to your co-workers. This knowledge should be captured in documentation that's stored securely but accessible to the people who will need it, when they'll need it. You'll need a structured, up-to-date document that lays out every server in your primary & secondary data centers, locally hosted servers and anything in a Co-Lo facility. This document should be a detailed list of OS version, any software installed along with versions, any accounts that have access, drive layout & space allocated. Make sure

Chapter 6 **Creating a** Disaster Recovery Plan

your infrastructure or SysAdmin team has captured a mapping of where all hardware is located and properly labeled connections from servers to storage.

For database servers, this section of the document should contain a full description of each server and instance. For each server, create a matrix that maps install drive, database names, all files and their corresponding drive. To save time during a recovery event, make sure you describe database backup locations here, both original and secondary location for DR purposes. Make note of each database backup schedule (i.e., Sunday 11 PM – Full, Mon-Sat 11PM Diff., 15 minute T-logs).

Office locations also fall under facilities. If you lose power or internet capabilities in an office location, do you have an alternate plan? Can employees do their job remotely? Do you have a secondary internet option you could switch to? Does your company have a list of each employee that works at any given site, any company owned technology they have, their contact information and emergency contact info? While the odds are low you'll need their emergency contact information, it's better to be safe than sorry, right? Site security can fall under the scope of your DR plan. Do your employees have badges that gain them access or control locks? Would those continue to work if there were a power outage or the database server holding credentials goes down?

This documentation is vital to the business during a disaster, but can be especially useful during day to day functioning. Server set up documentation could be easily referenced as you create environment change tickets, create deployment scripts with variables or when you need to build out a new server matching existing specifications. However, this information is only valuable if it's well maintained. When you build out a new server, a requirement for the build should be documentation. As you hire new employees or as they leave the company, you'll want an up to date inventory of any assets they had in their possession. This is important whether the employee left voluntarily, with well wishes to all or were escorted out the door. Add a step to the above processes that involves updating documentation. Don't consider the task finished until you have a full accounting or description in place.

Define & Document Technology

Documenting the software installed on every server is vital to the recovery process if you could be required to rebuild something from the ground up. While a bulk of that load could be streamlined with clones of existing VMs, that won't solve every problem. Just as you would fully document your physical layout, you'll need to do the same with installed software, permissions and interconnectivity between servers. This documentation process could be used to create new and cloned VMs to enter your environment, a check list of sorts, to help the Ops team identify any new server for an existing purpose should match these specs. All the more reason to do it now, you'll reap double the benefits.

You'll want to include the fields shown below at a bare minimum: Server name, OS, IP Address, general overall system purpose (web server, application server, load balancer, etc.), installed software and version, as well as anything else deemed important to the rebuild process. If domain, data center, subnet, etc are something that vary widely in your environment, then you need to be sure to include this information as well. Permissions (to server, software, etc) could also be included in this document.

Server Documentation, WIT Software, LLC

Server Specs		
Server Name	Prod-DB-258-Acct	
Operating System	Windows Server 2013	
IP Address	192.168.1.1	
Purpose	Accounting System	
Software Installed	Name	Version
SAGE	SAGE 50	50.1.56
Microsoft	SQL Server	12.1.4100.1

Define Suppliers, Delivery Services, Contract Technicians

"Eighteen years since the Chernobyl disaster. Is it just me surprised? Still no superheroes!"
— *Jimmy Carr*

This might be the section of a great disaster recovery plan that's most often overlooked. Why would you need suppliers or contract technicians identified as part of a failure? What happens when a server goes belly up and you must purchase new? How about if the server or storage that crashed is where all your back up software or monitoring agents were installed? Are you going to have time to go through your normal procurement process? Will you have time to shop around for the best price? If the answer to that is yes, then you're either not having a disaster or you aren't taking things seriously. You're going to call your supplier that's on this list and tell him exactly what replacement hardware you need delivered to your data center immediately. You're going to want the number of the support desk with your software company ready to go, so a quick phone call results in a new license key being issued. If your data center is in another state you'll need to have that contract technician on the access list to start install the minute it arrives. Make sure you note any contact information you need to grant someone physical access to your data center. Do you know who can grant access to a technician when you need a blade replaced?

Chapter 6 **Creating a** Disaster Recovery Plan

Systems by Vendor, WIT Software, LLC 2017

System	Product	Vendor	Contact Name	Contact #	Contact Email
Monitoring Server	SQL dm	Idera	Georgia O'Keefe		GOkeefe@Idera
Monitoring Server		Sentry One	Mary Cassatt		MaryC@Sentry
Database Server	SQL Server 2014	Microsoft/ CDW	Grace Hopper		GHopper@EDB
Database Server	PostGRESQL	EDB	Ada Lovelace	—	
Web Server			Marie Curie		
Application Server			Sally Ride		

Source: Fictitious data, for illustration purposes only

Building a Backup Strategy

"Disaster mitigation… increases the self-reliance of people who are at risk – in other words, it is empowering." — *Ian Davis*

I'm sure you've heard someone in the industry say that any DBA is only as good as their last backup. If that's the case, then start with the basics. Now that you know how much data you can lose and how long you've got to get things back up and running, set about making that happen. Step one: document the backup process for every system. Step two: put them into place across the enterprise. Make sure all of your servers are following the rules you've established. If you can lose 15 minutes' worth of data and take 2 hours to come back online, then set the schedule. Establish full, differential and log back ups at a frequency that supports your timeline to restore. Document backup locations & script out a skeleton restore code where possible.

Learn how to restore the tail end of a log. Practice that skill on a non-production server/database. Know that the same backup strategy may not be applicable (or even practical) for the entire business. If you work for a financial institution, it's likely your production transaction database can tolerate less data loss than your system that delivers files via sftp once an evening. A slow changing database might have a greater fault tolerance as well.

Chapter 6   Creating a Disaster Recovery Plan

We're not just talking about database backups. If you use it, you'll need it. Defining items to backup other than databases means an end to end examination of your business. In some cases, scripting things out ahead of time and maintaining those scripts monthly would be a great idea. You can regularly scripts DB users & roles, SQL Agent jobs, database restore scripts, etc.

Backup Checklist

- Active Directory
- Application configs
- Development source code
- External files
- Encryption Keys
- Passwords
- SQL Agent Jobs
- Create Database User/Role Scripts
- Database Restore scripts (full, diff, logs)
- Service Accounts

Define a schedule for when you'll back those things up. Publish that schedule and stick to it. Make a copy of configuration documentation and keep it updated regularly. You can build jobs to routinely script SQL Agent jobs & restore them on a remote disaster recovery system. The same can be said for database roles, etc. There are plenty of vendors out there with products that do all of this and more. It's worth looking into if your company has the budget for it. It's especially important if you're company doesn't have the staff to maintain this regularly.

Building a Recovery Strategy

> "A good plan violently executed today is better than a perfect plan next week." – George Patton

That whole "only as good as their last backup" line? It's not entirely accurate. Database professionals who have been through a week of little to no sleep restoring & rebuilding might disagree. I think it's more helpful to think about it this way: Any DBA is only as good as their last restore. That means you should be doing that regularly. As you create your backup strategy, it's important to do so with the recovery strategy in mind. Once a disaster has been declared, your clock is ticking. You'll want this part of the process to be as streamlined as possible.

Chapter 6 **Creating a** Disaster Recovery Plan

You'll need to establish recovery baselines. During a disaster, the longer something takes, the more likely you are to panic. Make sure you know ahead of time everything you'll need: backup file locations, drive mappings, data file locations, a timeline for a full restore of every database, etc. Make sure you have copies of database backups locally and a copy at your DR site. You should know how long it's going to take to restore. Of course, the biggest pay off to practicing restores is knowing that your backups work. This isn't just for long term disaster recovery planning. This is for every day peace of mind. No one should discover their backups have been failing or contained corruption for the last 3 months when you begin recovery efforts.

In some cases, you'll discover that it's easier to rebuild a database or application than it is to restore one. If the data is slow changing or building out the database is an automatable process, then document the process. Set it up ahead of time. Can you clone a VM and have that ready to go? If so, do it. Freeing up time to recovery works for other segment of the business as well, not just database restores. The less time Operations spends rebuilding servers, the more time they'll have for re-establishing connectivity or setting configurations.

Recovery Checklist

- Backup file locations
- Offsite backup storage locations
- Encrypted backup passwords
- Expected time to copy from offsite
- Expected restore time
- Server drive mapping & space needed
- Database logical and physical file names, layout, & location
- Pre-staged restore scripts
- Database users, logins & service accounts

Establishing Responsibilities

"Procrastination is the foundation of all disasters." — *Pandora Poikilos*

How do you know who is responsible for all the work that needs to be done after a disaster? It should be documented in the plan. You've already made note of the stakeholder or data/application user, make sure to note what team or even specific personnel who are responsible for recovery. Most shops have people who specialize or are experts in part of their job. It's why you hired them in the first place.

For example, you've got a person who is the in-house expert on everything to do with your virtual platform. Not only do they need to be involved with the DR planning related to all things VM, but they'll be the person that's going to do the work. Everyone on the team should know what tasks they'll be responsible for when things go off the rails. While Laura is working on the storage side of things, John is getting ready to rebuild VMs. Once the VMs are built with the appropriate storage layout, the DBA team can begin working on database tasks.

Another one of those overlooked tasks is your communication plan. This means both internal communications and external contact with the client, the media or any other interested parties. Establish early how different types of contact gets handled. If it's internal, you'll want to create an incident response plan that includes a dial-in bridge number. Publish that number internally so that anyone assigned to a responsibility during a disaster can be on a call and speaking with the team immediately.

Responsibility & Contact List, WIT Software LLC, 2017

Critical Incident Bridge	ALL CALL	1-877-555-2322;439765
Team/Task Owner	**Team Member**	**Contact**
Operations		
Web Servers	Jean Grey	770-555-1000
Application Connectivity	Diana Prince	770-555-2300
Storage	Carol Danvers	404-555-1278
Client Services		
Client Failure/Connectivity	Natasha Romanova	404-555-2123
Database Administration		
SQL Server Availability Groups	Wanda Maximoff	678-555-6161
Application Deployment Issues	Harleen Quinzel	404-555-9087
Source: Fictitious data, for illustration purposes only		

Build your plan

Now that you've defined your critical systems, RTO/RPO, stakeholders and possible outage scenarios, start tracking them in an organized fashion. Begin creating a risk matrix. This table should contain all systems vital to your business, how long you have to fix it, who it matters to and even what could go wrong, what you're going to do to fix it. This can be a 50,000-foot view. You're just getting started on the 10,000-foot view.

Risk Matrix, WIT Software LLC

System	RTO/RPO	Stakeholder	Threat	Response	Recovery
Accounts Payable	6 hr/2 hrs	Katherine Johnson, Comptroller	Data Corruption	DBA team notified, begin disk checks to identify where corruption located	Availability Groups, repair data Recover w/o data loss
Client Web Access	2 hr/ N/A	Kathryn Peddrew, Operations	DDOS attack, either direct or indirect	Request data center reroute	
Payment Transaction System	4 hr/15 min	Mary Jackson, DevOps Mgr.	Deploy of bad code, application server crash	Rollback deploy, take app server out of load balancer	
Office Email Access	4 hr/ 1 hr	Dorothy Vaughan, Operations			
Site Search Functionality	2 hr/ NA	Miriam Daniel Mann, Client Support Mgr.			
Database Back End	4 hr/15 min	Sojourner Truth, Database Mgr.			

Source: modified from original at techtarget.com

Test your plan

"Next week there can't be any crisis. My schedule is already full." — *Henry Kissinger*

An important part of the streamlining effort is practice and repetition. Some sage advice from Allan Hirt, "If you don't test your D/R plan, you don't have a plan. You have a document." It's important to put your DR plan down on paper. Have every team involved review it and approve it. They're also going to want to change it a little along the way. And that's how it should be. Any disaster recovery plan worth its weight in salt is a living document.

Document. Publish. Practice. Automate. Adjust. Document. Practice again. It's the only way to really be sure. A disaster recovery plan only has value if it works, so you'll need to test. A full disaster recovery test can be time consuming and costly. Consider smaller, segmented testing on a quarterly basis. In January, test a database corruption issue. In April, test a failure on the SAN. Of course, you don't tell the DBA team or Storage team what specifically you'll be "breaking" because you'll want to test how they respond and when.

If your business can't support a full-scale failover test, consider a tabletop test instead. Once your plan is documented, have a meeting with all the people responsible for recovery. Go through each and every step of your DR plan. Make sure everyone agrees this should work. Make sure everyone understands their role. Make sure they have all the pieces they need to put this plan into action. Record who attended the meeting and when. Document any weaknesses identified and the steps you took to correct them. Save this information for your PCI-DSS auditor.

Disaster Recovery Testing Checklist

- Schedule a time with all players to test/review your plan
- Review each player their responsibilities
- Simulate the failure
- Recover from failure
- Examine results, what worked & what didn't work, then adjust your plan accordingly

Define disaster

> *"If there are two or more ways to do something, and one of those ways can result in a catastrophe, then someone will do it."* — *Edward A. Murphy Jr*

Most people paraphrase Murphy's law as "Whatever can go wrong, will go wrong." While it might not be true, it certainly benefits you to believe it. There are many different things your business might consider a disaster. There are also a lot of things that would be better described as disruptions. There are big "D" Disasters and little "d" disasters. Don't just practice for the big ones. Practice for those smaller disasters & disruptions. Things like DDOS, ISP going down, a

Chapter 6 **Creating a** Disaster Recovery Plan

data center power outage, natural and unnatural disasters. While these aren't directly a DBA problem, if they cause you to fail to your secondary data center, it just became your problem.

In the first quarter of 2013, Quorum.net published the results of a survey of IT professionals. In a surprise to no one in the business, hardware failure is the number one cause of downtime for small to mid-sized businesses. Fifty-five percent of IT professionals indicated this had caused a disaster for them. Even when you think you've built in layers of protections, like power supplies, network controllers and hard drives — it's where things break the most. However, exactly what piece will fail in your Rube Goldberg machine that makes up your complicated system of application, web and database servers is anyone's guess. Most common among hardware failures, is an issue with the Storage Area Network (SAN).

Second on the list of disaster causes was human error at 22 percent. Don't assume these are rookie mistakes. Having experience doesn't protect you. Ask any DBA if they've ever run a delete statement on production and failed to highlight the where clause. If they tell you "no", they don't have production rights or they're lying. Human beings are fallible. They get tired and they get careless. As my grandmother used to say, they get a little too big for their britches. It happens, so prepare for it.

Coming in third, at 18 percent, was software failure. Often legacy software runs and runs for years, successfully. You don't have to touch it, babysit it or modify it. Then something in the environment changes. This can also be caused by something as important as Windows patches. If you aren't fully testing updates in your lower environments, you should take extra care when prepping this part of your disaster recovery plan. Now, not patching shouldn't be an option. Software fails if you don't routinely run updates as well. Think malware, viruses & ransomware.

There are also the smaller but potentially devastating events that you should prepare for whenever possible. When a DBA executes delete or update code but forgets a where clause in production, it could be catastrophic. In this case, you should be prepared to do an object level restore, restore the database to an alternate server to pull the data across or rebuild the table in its entirety. What if you have a drive failure? Depending on what was stored on that drive, your plan for recovery could vary greatly. In some cases, storage or file corruption might render only a few records unusable. Was the corruption on the clustered index or just some regular old data? Would you be willing to repair with data loss? Do you have availability groups so SQL Server can repair itself?

How about a damage caused by a malicious insider? A pissed off employee can wreak havoc by deleting or modifying data that is vital to your company. As mentioned previously, with an accidental deletion, be prepared to do an object level restore or a side-by-side restore to recover data that may have been compromised. If they merely modified data, would you know when they did it and have the ability to correct it? We won't cover auditing here, but it's something to consider as a security measure. A malicious insider can exist in all levels of the company, in all departments. You don't need database write permissions to cause problems. Often times, employees have read/write capabilities to all kinds of data, just as a necessary part of their job function. They can misuse this with devastating results.

Fourth on the list, at only five percent was a natural disaster. There isn't a state in the union where your data center or office facility would be completely safe. Tornadoes, earthquakes, hurricanes, Sharknado, etc. can wreak havoc on the best laid plans. Keep in mind that a natural disaster will likely also affect your work force. It's possible they'll be without power and/or internet, they could be unable to get into the office or be dealing with the effects of the natural disaster on a personal level.

Possible Disaster Causes

- Hardware Failure
- DDOS
- ISP outage
- Data center power outage
- Natural disasters (tornado, earthquake, hurricane, etc.)
- Storage failure
- Malicious Insider
- Human Error
- [Your Answer Here]
- [The unbelievable story your coworker told you here]

Publish your plan

Congratulations! You've built your plan, scheduled testing and started building out hardware to put it into action should disaster strike. Now what do you do with it? Your plan needs to be readily available to team members for reference, implementation and regular updates. It also needs to be stored securely. Some of the information you've collected could be an instruction manual on how to hack your system. It's vital that this not fall into the wrong hands. Where you store this plan is likely a decision made above your pay grade. First, make sure management understands the risks associated with publishing your DR plan. Second, come up with a list of only those people in the company that will need access. People on this list would include IT management and anyone on the team tasked with keeping it maintained and up to date. At this point, it doesn't have to be every single person on the list with a job to do in case of a disaster. Hopefully, that time never comes. When it does, you'll be ready.

Store your disaster recovery plan on someone's computer. I'd recommend having a copy saved on the laptop belonging to your VP of IT or CTO/CIO and any IT directors with team members listed in the responsibility matrix. You may choose to have a file widely disseminated among the IT staff, so it's easily referenced should the need arise. Having the file encrypted may not be necessary if your company has the proper protocols in place to prevent sending sensitive information via email. If they don't have these protocols in place, require that the file, at minimum, be password protected.

Store your disaster recovery plan securely on both a local & remote server. Again, it's important that the appropriate team members have access to the file. Protect access to it via Active Directory permissions at a minimum. You should consider having it password protected there as well. Make sure any team member on the responsibility matrix knows the full file path and has the necessary permissions to access the file.

Publish your disaster recovery plan via SharePoint, cloud storage or your company's intranet. Using SharePoint, you can control who can view, edit and download any given document. You should grant different levels of permissions to the file based on business need. SharePoint allows you to publish both minor & major versions of a document, making it very easy to track or revert changes as your document continues to reflect changes in the environment. The biggest advantage to storing your plan in this manner, is ease of access from almost anywhere (local or remote).

Print your disaster recovery plan and put it in a binder. Place that binder on a shelf in some IT persons office that has a lock & key. Sounds like an old school way to handle it, but a paper copy of your disaster recovery plan will work when every previously mentioned storage method has failed you. The downside to this is how quickly the print version will become outdated. The thing to remember is to re-print any sections that were modified during your quarterly review.

Building it out

"The future belongs to those who prepare for it today." — Malcolm X

Let's be honest. Most companies can't afford to build & maintain a hot standby environment equal to your current production. If yours can, good for you. Feel free to skip this section. But if they're like many companies, DR is currently sharing real estate with staging, QA or UAT. It's not a hot site or it barely has the processing power you'd need to run your business. How much will it cost you to build? Probably less than it will cost in lost revenue, client trust and public relations.

Begin by describing your gold standard set up. Then break that list down so you can more easily identify your wants versus your needs. Lay out what you WANT your DR site to look like and how you need for it to function. Identify how you're going to keep it up to date. Then lay out what you NEED to have for your disaster recovery site. I suspect the final product will fall somewhere in the middle. Still, aim high. This is one instance where reaching for the top shelf has a great business need driving it: sustainability!

Don't forget hardware, licensing and maintenance. Plan for enough storage space for the live databases and backups. You'll need enough web servers to run your applications. Don't forget to factor in enough time, and the people required to build this out and maintain it on a monthly basis. You'll have to patch all those servers and keep versions aligned.

Based on cost, many companies are considering utilizing the cloud for their DR site. Sometimes referred to as Disaster Recovery as a Service (DRaaS). Smaller companies have found that utilizing a usage-based cost of cloud services is a great fit for their DR needs. In this model, the secondary infrastructure is idling most of the time. The cost savings is most noticeable by reducing the need for data center space, IT infrastructure and on-site resources. Migrating your DR site to the cloud enables smaller companies to develop disaster recovery solutions that look more like those of larger, enterprise software companies.

It's important to note that migrating to the cloud is far from perfect. It raises additional questions, particularly with security. Are data files stored & transmitted securely? Does your cloud provider meet specific regulatory requirements for security that are required for your industry? How is access to the data controlled? Password protected? Is there two-factor authentication? Maybe just as important as access and security, it accessibility. Can your cloud provider guarantee a certain level of availability? Are they allowed to go "offline" for up to 8 hours & call it "planned maintenance"? Do they have the option to fail over to other regional cloud servers quickly so that you're protected with 4 9's? What about 5 9's?

Chapter 6 **Creating a** Disaster Recovery Plan

Plan complete. Get yourself a drink.

If only it were that simple. Any disaster recovery plan is complete for only a moment. It's a living, breathing document. Businesses change, so your disaster recovery plan should too. It's constantly changing as your environment modifies, contracts and expands. Set aside time quarterly for your team to review the document. Encourage your company to build time into a project plan for DR planning every time they build out new systems or develop new products.

Our goal for this chapter was to establish the building blocks you'd need to create a disaster recovery plan for your company. Our goal wasn't to build your plan for you. Every company is different. Every division of the same company is different. What stays the same is the process. Any company, big or small, takes the same path to get to a functional recovery plan. As you go through building your plan, check off each box along the way. It's amazingly satisfying.

Disaster Recovery Plan checklist.

- Define what's important.
- Define your stakeholders for each part of the business.
- Define your critical systems.
- Define your company's RTO & RPO.
- Document your infrastructure.
- Document your Technology.
- Document your contractors, suppliers & service providers.
- Build a backup strategy.
- Build a recovery strategy.
- Establish responsibilities.
- Compile your plan from what you've learned.
- Test you plan in part, in full or in theory.
- Build it out.
- Publish your plan.
- Maintain your plan.

Chapter 7
Using Extended Events to figure out why an Application is slow

By: Mindy Curnutt - Microsoft MVP Data Platform

It's been my experience, and the experience of every DBA I've commiserated with over the last 20+ years, that the database is automatically assumed guilty if performance issues arise. As a means of survival, I've come up with a homegrown method that more often than not is able to identify the root cause(s) of application slowness. I initially developed this methodology using SQL Server Profiler, but have adapted it to Extended Events. The concepts work equally well with either, the event classes are the same. Actually, this used to be easier to do in Profiler than it is now in Extended Events, but that's water under the bridge. My approach has three components:

Method	Source of Issue
Long Running Queries Find a single/few large queries that are using resources or blocking others.	Database
Thousands of Paper Cuts Identify a very chatty application that is sending thousands of small queries.	Application or Database
Application Pauses / Latency Diagnose repetitive pauses between SQL statements coming from an application or pinpoint a large pause that is happening on the application side.	Application

In this chapter, I will go over each of these three approaches in detail.

Extended Event Session Setup

I'm not going to spend time explaining what Extended Events are and how they work, that itself could be an entire chapter. I'm going to assume that you have a basic understanding of SQL Server Extended Events and/or Tracing using the Profiler tool.

To get started with any of the three methods above requires the setup of an Extended Event Session. For each of the methods we are going to capture the same three basic events:

1. **sqlserver.rpc_completed**
   Captures Stored Procedure calls or Transact-SQL executed using sp_executeSQL.

2. **sqlserver.sql_batch_completed**
   Captures ad-hoc SQL batches or groupings of ad-hoc SQL Statements run as a group. Most of the time this event will return only a single statement.

3. **sqlserver.sp_statement_completed**
   Captures individual statements within a stored procedure. Also captures triggers and scalar function calls. This is used in conjunction with rpc_completed as a mechanism for "drilling down" to find out which SQL statement within a procedure is responsible for a long duration.

> **Note:** Although it is tempting (especially for those of use with OCE tendencies) to fix "everything" and to make code as perfect as can be, it is not the best use of time. There's only so much time in a workday. Try to focus on only fixing the things that are causing the problem and just let the other stuff go. "Let it go, let it go…"

Within SQL Server Management Studio (SSMS) the Extended Events Wizard can be used to setup a session that captures the three events we are concerned with. I personally find the Wizard clunky and time consuming. Click, drill down, click, click, back up, did I forget something, click over here. Ugh! I much prefer using Transact-SQL scripting over the wizard. Below is an example of code that will automatically setup an Extended Events Session for you that's "ready to go".

```
CREATE EVENT SESSION CompletedEventswithDurationFilter
ON SERVER

ADD EVENT sqlserver.rpc_completed
        (
        ACTION
            (
            sqlserver.database_id,
            sqlserver.transaction_id,
            sqlserver.nt_username,
            sqlserver.client_hostname,
            sqlserver.client_app_name,
            sqlserver.server_principal_name,
            sqlserver.session_id,
            sqlserver.server_instance_name,
            sqlserver.database_name
```

Chapter 7 Using Extended Events to figure out why an Application is slow

```
                )
                WHERE
                (
                duration >= 5000 --5 seconds / 5000 milliseconds
                )
            ),
ADD EVENT sqlserver.sp_statement_completed
            (
            ACTION
                (
                sqlserver.transaction_id,
                sqlserver.nt_username,
                sqlserver.client_hostname,
                sqlserver.client_app_name,
                sqlserver.server_principal_name,
                sqlserver.session_id,
                sqlserver.server_instance_name,
                sqlserver.database_name
                )
                WHERE
                (
                duration >= 1000 --1 second. Note this one is different!
                )
            ),
ADD EVENT sqlserver.sql_batch_completed
            (
            ACTION
                (
                        sqlserver.database_id,
                        sqlserver.transaction_id,
                        sqlserver.nt_username,
                        sqlserver.client_hostname,
                        sqlserver.client_app_name,
                        sqlserver.server_principal_name,
                        sqlserver.session_id,
                        sqlserver.server_instance_name,
                        sqlserver.database_name
                )
                WHERE
                (
                duration >= 5000000 --5 seconds / 5000 microseconds
                )
            )
ADD TARGET package0.asynchronous_file_target
    (
    SET filename=N'C:\temp\xevents~lrq.xel',
            metadatafile =N'C:\temp\xevents~lrq.xem',
            max_file_size=(50000), --close to 50mb
            max_rollover_files=5
    )
WITH (MAX_MEMORY = 4MB, EVENT_RETENTION_MODE = NO_EVENT_LOSS)
go
```

I'd like to point out a few things about the script above.

1. It is creating a SESSION called CompletedEventswithDurationFilter.

2. Within that SESSION it adds three EVENTS, one for each of the types of completed events to be investigated.

3. Each of the EVENTS comes with a small set of default columns (ACTIONS) that are captured (you don't see those mentioned). These are included automatically. There are additional columns that I find necessary, the script explicitly adds these extra columns for each EVENT to provide more detail.

4. Each of the events has a WHERE clause (a FILTER). In this case, the script is specifically filtering on DURATION. For the two high-level EVENTS (rpc_completed and sql_batch_completed) it specifies to only include items that take longer than 5 seconds to complete. For the more granular EVENT (sqlserver.sp_statement_completed) I have set the "trap" to capture anything longer than 1 second. I've set the FILTERS this way because we are looking for Long Running Queries.

5. The script includes a TARGET, which is located on the SQL Server itself, not on the machine where SSMS happens to be running. The folder and path must be valid (in this case, a C:\temp folder must exist on the SQL Server).

Note: Filters are Critical. It is extremely important that you use filters when using extended events to capture completed events (the same holds true for profiler traces). Starting up a "wide open" session without any filters is likely to severely impact the performance of your SQL Server. It's one of the reasons that people tell you that both profiler and extended events are dangerous tools. Think of them like a machine gun. It's a tool that should only be used by someone who knows what they are doing and who has a good understanding of the power of the tool. You wouldn't want a total gun noob to pick up a machine gun and pull down on the trigger – All kinds of unintended consequences could happen as a result.

This script above creates an Extended Event Session that can be started or stopped either by right clicking on it in SSMS or via transact-SQL like this:

To start:

```
ALTER EVENT SESSION CompletedEventswithDurationFilter
ON SERVER
STATE=START;
GO
```

To stop:

```
ALTER EVENT SESSION CompletedEventswithDurationFilter
ON SERVER
STATE=STOP;
GO
```

Chapter 7   Using Extended Events to figure out why an Application is slow

Long Running Queries

Finding a single Long Running Query that is blocking everyone, or that is running repetitively and using up resources is the "Holy Grail" of performance tuning. This is what you are hoping to find. Basically, whenever I go into one of these investigations I cross my fingers and toes, bite my bottom lip and hope that THIS is what the trace is going to expose. One of my favorite things to do is to find one of these beasts, tune it, and then watch the SQL Server take a deep sigh of relief. Your co-workers or clients will think you're a miracle worker. Win-Win.

There are two scenarios where this approach is helpful – Occasional Slowness or Specific Application Area Slowness. The script for both is essentially the same, it is how and when the script is used that is different. Because heavy filtering is applied in both approaches, the performance impacts are negligible.

Occasional Slowness

For Occasional Slowness that comes and goes without a pattern or means of reproducing I recommend creating a SESSION that you start (and stop) once a day automatically via a job. Since the trace will be running all the time, you may want to increase the duration filter on all three EVENTS to a higher amount (say 10 seconds), and then adjust downward as you see how large the daily file(s) are. You'll also need a way of purging or archiving the files that are created so you do not eventually fill up a hard drive with years of traces. A SQL job that executes Transact-SQL using the xp_delete_file system stored procedure or a windows scheduled task that calls a batch file, either of which deletes trace files older than X days will do the trick. Below is an example of Transact-SQL code along these lines:

```
declare @dt nvarchar(19)
select @dt = CONVERT(nvarchar(19), dateadd(dd,-(180), getdate()))
exec master.dbo.xp_delete_file 0,'c:\temp', 'XEL',@dt
exec master.dbo.xp_delete_file 0,'c:\temp', 'XEM',@dt
```

Even if you are not having any performance issues, proactively setting up a Long Running Query Extended Event capturing system is something that I routinely recommend for any SQL Server implementation. Think of it like a security camera in a 7-11 pointed at the door. You may never go back and look at the tape, but if there's a crime, then you have a recording that you can use to investigate what happened.

- Daily Job to Start / Stop Trace
- 24 x 7 Tracing
- Duration Filter High (~10 seconds to start)
- Mechanism to Clean Up / Archive Trace Files

Specific Application Area Slowness

If the issue you are facing is Specific Application Area Slowness, for instance "it's slow when we try to save an order", you can use the script above to start and stop a trace capture on demand. You'll need to identify something about the user specifically (spid, hostname or login are usually good options). Add those items to the filtering definition of the Extended Event Session. Because you are being specific about who you are tracing, you can lower the duration filter without causing a performance impact.

Ask the user to connect and to get themselves into the application right to the point of hitting the "save" button. Start your trace, tell them to hit "save", ask them to tell you when the process has completed, then stop your trace.

- Requires manual Start / Stop
- Duration Filter Low (~1 second)
- Trace only the single user (filter)
- Capture only the slowly performing application functionality

With either scenario, you will now have a file (or set of files) that you can look at and query to help determine what is going on. The files contain XML, so some parsing is necessary. Don't worry, I've done most of the work for you here, just use this code and you'll be able to treat the trace file like a table and write investigative queries against it:

```sql
WITH XEvents_Trace as
(
SELECT                                                                    reads
        =e.eventdata_XML.value('(//data[@name="logical_reads"]/value)[1]','int') ,
physical_reads=e.eventdata_XML.value('(//data[@name="physical_reads"]/value)[1]','int'),
writes=     e.eventdata_XML.value('(//data[@name="writes"]/value)[1]','int'),
        cpu=e.eventdata_XML.value('(//data[@name="cpu_time"]/value)[1]','int'),
        spid=e.eventdata_XML.value('(//action[@name="session_id"]/value)[1]','int'),
databasename=e.eventdata_XML.value('(//action[@name="database_name"]/value)[1]','nvarchar(255)') ,
duration=e.eventdata_XML.value('(//data[@name="duration"]/value)[1]','int'),
hostname=e.eventdata_XML.value('(//action[@name="client_hostname"]/value)[1]','nvarchar(255)'),
eventclass=e.eventdata_XML.value('(//@name)[1]','nvarchar(50)'),
TIMESTAMP=e.eventdata_XML.value('(//@timestamp)[1]','datetime2(7)'),
objectname=e.eventdata_XML.value('(//data[@name="object_name"]/value)[1]','nvarchar(255)'),
textdata=e.eventdata_XML.value('(//data[@name="statement"]/value)[1]','nvarchar(max)'),
batchSQL=e.eventdata_XML.value('(//data[@name="batch_text"]/value)[1]','nvarchar(max)')
```

Chapter 7 Using Extended Events to figure out why an Application is slow

```
FROM    (
SELECT CAST(eventdata AS XML) AS eventdata_XML
FROM sys.fn_xe_file_target_read_file
('C:\temp\xevents~lrqs.xel', NULL, NULL, NULL)

)e

)
select top 100 * from XEvents_Trace
WHERE eventclass in ('sql_batch_completed','rpc_completed')
order by duration desc
```

Notice in the WHERE clause of the query above I am limiting the results that are being returned to only the high-level events (excluding the sp_statement_completed event). I do this on the first pass-through. If I find something of interest here, I can zoom in to that specific activity or time range by adding constraints to the where clause and including the sp_statement_completed events. Think of it like this – sql_batch_completed and rpc_completed are the summary events. If you want to zoom in (magnifying glass to see the detail going on inside of a stored procedure) then you use sp_statement_completed.

Statements within a Batch

There is one more event you may want to add if your application is grouping together many ad-hoc transact-SQL statements in a single batch. It is extremely rare for this to be necessary. Most of the time the sql_batch_completed event will contain only 1 or at the most 2 statements within it. So, it is already granular by nature. If you find that your sql_batch_completed event is bringing back many transact-SQL statements all bunched together, then adding the sql_statement_completed will get you the same granularity provided by the sp_statement_completed event.

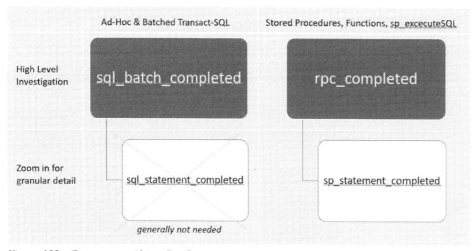

Figure 132 – Statements within a Batch

Chapter 7   **Using Extended** Events to figure out why an Application is slow

I am also sorting by DURATION descending, and returning only the TOP 100 longest running statements that occurred during the duration of the trace capture.

The resulting query results will look something like this (except hopefully you have something on the top row with much higher reads and duration than everything else).

	reads	physical_reads	writes	cpu	spid	databasename	duration	eventclass
1	318	64	5	31000	76	msdb	64036	sql_batch_completed
2	36	0	0	31000	84	master	22549	rpc_completed
3	316	40	0	0	76	msdb	12385	rpc_completed
4	48	0	0	16000	76	master	9127	rpc_completed
5	24	0	0	0	84	master	5934	rpc_completed
6	13	0	0	16000	76	msdb	5457	sql_batch_completed

Figure 133 – SQL Query Sorting by DURATION

If, using this process, I find something that looks suspiciously like a grape clogging a straw (one big fat query either blocking processes or using tons of resources), I then focus in on that and adjust my XML parsing query. I note the timestamp, spid and other identifying columns (hostname, objectname, transaction ID, etc) and instead of looking at the high-level EVENTS I drill into the statements themselves. For instance, below is a script that would allow me to look at a specific spid and objectname (stored procedure or function) and to see the statements within it that were captured by the trace.

```
WITH XEvents_Trace as
(
SELECT                                                                       reads
        =e.eventdata_XML.value('(//data[@name="logical_reads"]/value)[1]','i
nt') ,
physical_reads=e.eventdata_XML.value('(//data[@name="physical_reads"]/value)[1]'
,'int'),
writes=      e.eventdata_XML.value('(//data[@name="writes"]/value)[1]','int'),

        cpu=e.eventdata_XML.value('(//data[@name="cpu_time"]/value)[1]','int
'),
        spid=e.eventdata_XML.value('(//action[@name="session_id"]/value)[1]'
,'int'),
databasename=e.eventdata_XML.value('(//action[@name="database_name"]/value)[1]',
'nvarchar(255)')              ,
duration=e.eventdata_XML.value('(//data[@name="duration"]/value)[1]','int'),
hostname=e.eventdata_XML.value('(//action[@name="client_hostname"]/value)[1]','n
varchar(255)'),
eventclass=e.eventdata_XML.value('(//@name)[1]','nvarchar(50)'),
TIMESTAMP=e.eventdata_XML.value('(//@timestamp)[1]','datetime2(7)'),
objectname=e.eventdata_XML.value('(//data[@name="object_name"]/value)[1]','nvarc
```

```
har(255)'),
textdata=e.eventdata_XML.value('(//data[@name="statement"]/value)[1]','nvarchar(
max)'),
batchSQL=e.eventdata_XML.value('(//data[@name="batch_text"]/value)[1]','nvarchar
(max)')

FROM    (
SELECT CAST(eventdata AS XML) AS eventdata_XML
FROM sys.fn_xe_file_target_read_file
('C:\temp\xevents~lrqs.xel', NULL, NULL, NULL)

)e
)
select top 100 * from XEvents_Trace
WHERE eventclass = ('sp_statement_completed') and spid = 76 and objectname =
'saveorder'
order by duration desc
```

Thousands of Paper Cuts

If you're not so fortunate as to strike the Holy Grail by finding a big, fat, juicy (and hopefully easily fixable) query, well then things get a little more difficult. It is not uncommon for applications that are written by ORM Frameworks (Object Relational Mapping) like Entity Framework, LINQ or NHibernate for example to forego joins for a parent-child style transact-SQL approach that results in many subqueries. Of course, a human coding by hand can do the same thing by coding using loops, subqueries or scalar functions! Spotting this type of behavior can be challenging because it requires the duration filter on a trace be lowered to 0 to expose that the issue is thousands of small queries and not a few large queries.

Sometimes I use the analogy of using a wheelbarrow to move a boulder versus a load of gravel to describe the issue. Think of trying to move 1 gigantic boulder using a wheelbarrow. It's hard. It's heavy. You may hurt your back. The boulder is easy to see and it's obvious what the problem is. What I you had a load of a million pebbles of gravel that all together weighed as much as the boulder? You still might hurt your back. In fact, you may hurt your back worse, because the gravel would have more of a tendency to slosh this way or that and shift its weight on you. It's not only heavy, it's unwieldy.

Your general Long Running Query trace is designed to spot the large Boulders. Lowering the duration filter down, you may be able to spot some decent sized rocks. To see the wheelbarrow full of gravel and understand the impact clearly requires lowering the duration all the way down to 0 and then getting out and then looking for loops and/or aggregating like statements.

Chapter 7 Using Extended Events to figure out why an Application is slow

Common Causes of "Thousands of Paper Cuts" Syndrome

- ORM Frameworks
- Looping Style Coding (Cursors, For/Next, While Loops)
- Subqueries
- Scalar Functions
- Trigger Storms (Triggers firing triggers firing triggers)

I often tell folks that this trace type is kind of like taking a "core sample" because the duration of the trace is usually very short (1 minute). You're hoping that you will take the sample in the right area (at just the right time) and come up with something interesting / important that helps you to decipher what's causing the application slowness. If you don't time your "core sample" just right, you may miss the problem causing behavior. Sometimes it is necessary to take many core samples to catch the behavior in action. If there is any filter item you can find that lessens the impact of the tracing, you may be able to take a trace with a longer duration. For instance, if you can filter on a single user and action, lowering the duration filter down to 0 will most likely not impact server performance.

A few things about this approach:

- High likelihood it will cause a noticeable performance impact
- Even a very short trace can create huge / many files
- Aggregation of statements is challenging if parameterization is not used
- Extended Event captures only contain an ENDTIME and not a STARTTIME like Profiler Traces do. This makes it necessary to reverse engineer what the STARTTIME must have been by using the ENDTIME and the DURATION and backing into the STARTTIME. It's a bit inconvenient, but it works.

Chapter 7 Using Extended Events to figure out why an Application is slow

To create an Extended Event Session for this type of trace capture simply remove the duration filter and run the trace for a very short period of time. If possible, add in a filter that contains something that will reduce the amount of statements coming in (just not duration, you want EVERY statement). Examples of good filter choices may be client_app_name, session_id (spid), client_hostname or nt_username. An example of the transact-SQL code that creates a session like this is below. Be sure to use the code that starts and stops the session (especially the stop!).

```
CREATE EVENT SESSION CompletedEventsPaperCuts
ON SERVER

ADD EVENT sqlserver.rpc_completed
        (
            ACTION
                (
                sqlserver.database_id,
                sqlserver.transaction_id,
                sqlserver.nt_username,
                sqlserver.client_hostname,
                sqlserver.client_app_name,
                sqlserver.server_principal_name,
                sqlserver.session_id,
                sqlserver.server_instance_name,
                sqlserver.database_name
                )
    /* --optional, filter on a user. Notice NO duration filter anymore.
            WHERE
                (
                session_id = 98 --user's spid goes here
                )
    */
            ),
ADD EVENT sqlserver.sp_statement_completed
        (
            ACTION
                (
                sqlserver.transaction_id,
                sqlserver.nt_username,
                sqlserver.client_hostname,
                sqlserver.client_app_name,
                sqlserver.server_principal_name,
                sqlserver.session_id,
                sqlserver.server_instance_name,
                sqlserver.database_name
                )
    /*
            WHERE
                (
                session_id = 98 --user's spid goes here
                )
    */
            ),
ADD EVENT sqlserver.sql_batch_completed
        (
```

Chapter 7 Using Extended Events to figure out why an Application is slow

```
            ACTION
                (
                        sqlserver.database_id,
                        sqlserver.transaction_id,
                        sqlserver.nt_username,
                        sqlserver.client_hostname,
                        sqlserver.client_app_name,
                        sqlserver.server_principal_name,
                        sqlserver.session_id,
                        sqlserver.server_instance_name,
                        sqlserver.database_name
                )
   /*
                WHERE
                (
                session_id = 98  --user's spid goes here
                )
   */
                )
ADD TARGET package0.asynchronous_file_target
    (
      SET filename=N'C:\temp\xevents~papercuts.xel',
          metadatafile =N'C:\temp\xevents~papercuts.xem',
          max_file_size=(50000),  --close to 50mb
          max_rollover_files=5
    )
WITH (MAX_MEMORY = 4MB, EVENT_RETENTION_MODE = NO_EVENT_LOSS)
go
```

Once you have your trace captured, you'll want to take a different approach to looking at it. I have some snippets below taken from the full script at the end of this section to point out where / how this information is being retrieved.

A. First of all, how long was the total duration of the trace?

Remember there is no STARTTIME in Extended Events, so I am using the ENDTIME and subtracting the DURATION to back into the STARTTIME.

```
datediff(s,min(dateadd(mcs,-duration,endtime)),max(endtime)) as
total_duration
```

B. How much of that duration took place on the SQL Server?

```
sum(duration) as time_on_sql,
```

C. Did most of the time that the process took to complete consist of queries running on SQL Server (B) or is (B) only a small portion of the total duration (A)? This is an important question, as it tells you whether tuning statements on the SQL Server is going to be a viable strategy. For instance, if the entire process took 20 seconds, but only 1 second of

Chapter 7 Using Extended Events to figure out why an Application is slow

time was the SQL Server running queries, then tuning the SQL code or adding indexes is only going to be improving that 1 second of time, the 19 seconds will not be affected. The 19 seconds of time can be found in-between the calls (difference between the end time of one statement and the start time of then next).

D. How many total high-level statements happened? Is the application doing a reasonable amount of round trips in order to populate a screen, or is it doing literally thousands of round trips?

```
count(*) as stmt_qty,
```

E. Is there any one statement that took a long time?
F. How about total reads and cpu for the longest occurring grouped statements?

These questions and more can be answered by running the following statement against the trace file created. The great thing about this approach is that you can freely slice and dice the trace results, spotting patterns and behaviors.

```
WITH XEvents_Trace as
(
SELECT
reads=e.eventdata_XML.value('(//data[@name="logical_reads"]/value)[1]','int'),
physical_reads
            =e.eventdata_XML.value('(//data[@name="physical_reads"]/value)[1]','int'),
            writes=
    e.eventdata_XML.value('(//data[@name="writes"]/value)[1]','int'),

            cpu=e.eventdata_XML.value('(//data[@name="cpu_time"]/value)[1]','int'),
spid=e.eventdata_XML.value('(//action[@name="session_id"]/value)[1]','int'),
databasename=e.eventdata_XML.value('(//action[@name="database_name"]/value)[1]','nvarchar(255)'),
duration=e.eventdata_XML.value('(//data[@name="duration"]/value)[1]','int') ,
hostname=e.eventdata_XML.value('(//action[@name="client_hostname"]/value)[1]','nvarchar(255)'),
eventclass=e.eventdata_XML.value('(//@name)[1]','nvarchar(50)'),
endtime=e.eventdata_XML.value('(//@timestamp)[1]','datetime2(7)'),
objectname=e.eventdata_XML.value('(//data[@name="object_name"]/value)[1]','nvarchar(255)'),
textdata=e.eventdata_XML.value('(//data[@name="statement"]/value)[1]','nvarchar(max)'),
batchSQL=e.eventdata_XML.value('(//data[@name="batch_text"]/value)[1]','nvarchar(max)')
FROM

(
SELECT CAST(eventdata AS XML) AS eventdata_XML
```

Chapter 7 Using Extended Events to figure out why an Application is slow

```
FROM sys.fn_xe_file_target_read_file('C:\temp\xevents~papercuts.xel', NULL,
NULL, NULL)
) e

)
select sum(reads) as sum_reads,
sum(writes) as sum_writes,
sum(cpu) as sum_cpu,
count(*) as stmt_qty, --(C)
min(dateadd(mcs,-duration,endtime)) as starttime,
max(endtime) as endtime,
sum(duration) as time_on_sql,--(B)
datediff(s,min(dateadd(mcs,-duration,endtime)),max(endtime)) as total_duration -
-(A)
from XEvents_Trace
WHERE eventclass in ('sql_batch_completed','rpc_completed')
order by endtime
```

Some Looping Discovery Questions to Ask

- Does it appear that there is looping?
- Can you see each loop? What is the pattern? How many statements comprise a single loop?
- Are there loops and subloops?
- What if you look at only a particular spid between X and Y times?
- Does it look like the statement before is being used to provide the predicate for the next statement?
- Are the statements specifically requesting only the columns needed, or does it look like many more columns are being requested than ever used?
- Look at the user's screen (good to have them give you a screen shot). What do you see on the screen that corresponds to the queries you see happening from the SQL side?
- Does it look like set based SQL is happening most of the time, but perhaps just not in one place?

And most importantly:

- Is there any way that the work could have been done using Set Based SQL? Can you write up an example and share with development?

Sometimes it helps to take the statements and drop them into an excel workbook, sort alphabetically and number them by group, then do a Pivot table on the groups. This is especially helpful if parameterizing wasn't used (which allows easy grouping). This is a budget-friendly grouping exercise, but it works. I often do something along these lines (see below), which makes it very clear that although Query Group 7 (on average) doesn't do an abnormally high amount of reads for any one execution, it ran much more often than the other queries. If this was what your results looked like, whatever the query pattern was behind Group 7, that would be a good place to focus your attention. You can do similar exploration playing with CPU time and writes.

Chapter 7   Using Extended Events to figure out why an Application is slow

Query Group	Total Reads	Avg Reads	Qty	Percent Reads	Percent Qty
7	304,492,285	338,325	900	82% Yikes!	67%
8	20,962,118	232,912	90	6%	7%
3	9,028,618	273,594	33	2%	2%
1	8,269,626	551,308	15	2%	1%
15	6,243,061	74,322	84	2%	6%
14	4,732,960	262,942	18	1%	1%
9	3,342,424	278,535	12	1%	1%
6	3,341,893	371,321	9	1%	1%
13	1,733,530	173,353	10	0%	1%
12	1,531,563	63,815	24	0%	2%
11	1,470,006	63,913	23	0%	2%
2	1,352,702	676,351	2	0%	0%
5	1,300,859	14,454	90	0%	7%
10	1,139,517	67,030	17	0%	1%
4	1,577,318	105,155	15	0%	1%
	370,518,480	276,094	1342		

Application Pauses / Latency

Well, you've looked for the Long Running Query and found nothing. Took a few "core samples" and don't particularly see a lot of chattiness. The user's experience is just flat out slow and there doesn't seem to be any logical reason why. This next method of looking at trace data uses the trace itself to clearly show the time between statements; the time when SQL Server isn't being asked to do anything (but is being accused of being the problem). This is a non-traditional somewhat "hack" way of using SQL Server's trace data to point out that the problem is not actually SQL.

There are two scenarios where Application Pauses or Latency can be a problem.

1. One is universal, relatively even slowness in turnaround time (the application is slow to ask for the next SQL statement almost all the time).

Chapter 7   Using Extended Events to figure out why an Application is slow

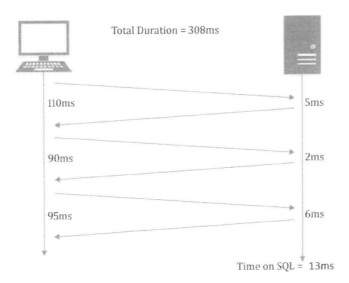

2. The other is that things are moving along just fine, and then there is a long pause, almost like the application taking a big breath of air, nothing happens, then things resume. In this case, the application could be calling out to a webpage, trying to do difficult custom formatting, or many other things.

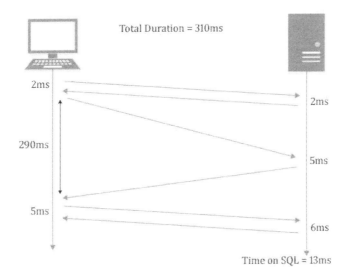

In both scenarios, SQL Server is not involved other than it is waiting for the application.

225

Chapter 7 Using Extended Events to figure out why an Application is slow

> **Note: Waitstats No Help Here**
>
> The WaitStat of async_io_completion is normally what folks go to when they are looking for the application or network being responsible for waits. While this is very useful, it doesn't work in the case where the application has received the data, and the problem is that it is simply not asking for the next query right away. SQL Server knows nothing about this type of slowness, in fact, SQL itself is completely uninvolved and idle if the this is happening. Durations involved in async_io_completion show up in a SQL query's duration. An application pausing and not interacting with SQL at all shows up nowhere from the SQL Server's perspective. UNLESS – you read between the lines!

The Extended Event Capture Session is the same one we used for attempting to diagnose the Paper Cuts. How the trace file is analyzed is a bit different. The script below uses recursive SQL and CTEs to number each row and to take the difference between the STARTTIME of a statement with the ENDTIME of the statement immediately before.

- A. Application pause is calculated by using the datediff Transact-SQL function. The STARTTIME is backed into in the CTE by using the ENDTIME and subtracting DURATION.
- B. This works best if you limit your selection to a single spid or something user / process specific
- C. A where clause can be added to only display those intervals where the pause was larger than X amount of time (1 second for example).

```
WITH XEvents_Trace as
(
SELECT
reads=e.eventdata_XML.value('(//data[@name="logical_reads"]/value)[1]','int'),
physical_reads=e.eventdata_XML.value('(//data[@name="physical_reads"]/value)[1]','int'),
writes=e.eventdata_XML.value('(//data[@name="writes"]/value)[1]','int'),

cpu=e.eventdata_XML.value('(//data[@name="cpu_time"]/value)[1]','int'),

spid=e.eventdata_XML.value('(//action[@name="session_id"]/value)[1]','int'),
databasename=e.eventdata_XML.value('(//action[@name="database_name"]/value)[1]','nvarchar(255)'),
duration=e.eventdata_XML.value('(//data[@name="duration"]/value)[1]','int'),
hostname=e.eventdata_XML.value('(//action[@name="client_hostname"]/value)[1]','nvarchar(255)'),
eventclass=e.eventdata_XML.value('(//@name)[1]','nvarchar(50)'),
endtime=e.eventdata_XML.value('(//@timestamp)[1]','datetime2(7)'),
objectname=e.eventdata_XML.value('(//data[@name="object_name"]/value)[1]','nvarchar(255)'),
textdata=e.eventdata_XML.value('(//data[@name="statement"]/value)[1]','nv
```

Chapter 7 Using Extended Events to figure out why an Application is slow

```
archar(max)'),
batchSQL=e.eventdata_XML.value('(//data[@name="batch_text"]/value)[1]','n
varchar(max)')
FROM

(
SELECT CAST(eventdata AS XML) AS eventdata_XML
FROM sys.fn_xe_file_target_read_file('C:\temp\xevents~papercuts.xel',
NULL, NULL, NULL)
) e

),
XEventsTraceCTE as
(
select ROW_NUMBER() OVER (ORDER BY endtime) as RowID,
dateadd(mcs,-duration,endtime) as starttime,
endtime,
convert(varchar(max),[textdata]) as sqlstmt
from XEvents_Trace
where eventclass in ('sql_batch_completed','rpc_completed') and spid = 53
-- (B)
)
select
    t1.rowid
   ,t2.endtime as prev_endtime
   ,t1.starttime as next_starttime
   ,datediff(ss, t2.endtime,t1.starttime) as application_pause  --(A)
   ,t2.sqlstmt as prev_stmt
   ,t1.sqlstmt as next_stmt
from XEventsTraceCTE t1
join XEventsTraceCTE t2
     on t2.RowID = (t1.RowID-1)
```

Looking at an Extended Event capture row by row (the traditional method) gives you a viewpoint similar to that below. It doesn't make it immediately clear where the issue lies. The longest running query is only a few milliseconds long.

rowid	Starttime	EndTime	Duration MS
1	7/1/2017 15:50:25.117	7/1/2017 15:50:25.121	4281
2	7/1/2017 15:50:25.130	7/1/2017 15:50:25.130	178
3	7/1/2017 15:50:25.138	7/1/2017 15:50:25.138	168

Chapter 7 Using Extended Events to figure out why an Application is slow

4	7/1/2017 15:50:25.145	7/1/2017 15:50:25.145	185
5	7/1/2017 15:50:25.152	7/1/2017 15:50:25.152	153
6	7/1/2017 15:50:28.159	7/1/2017 15:50:28.159	165
7	7/1/2017 15:50:28.160	7/1/2017 15:50:28.160	64
8	7/1/2017 15:50:28.160	7/1/2017 15:50:28.160	92
9	7/1/2017 15:50:28.160	7/1/2017 15:50:28.160	95
10	7/1/2017 15:50:28.161	7/1/2017 15:50:28.161	57

Using the recursive method and calculating the "missing time" instead provides the same data back in a way that makes it immediately clear that the issue is that the application is pausing to do something and SQL is simply waiting. Those results may look something along these lines:

rowid	prev_endtime	next_starttime	application_pause
1-2	7/1/2017 15:50:25.121	7/1/2017 15:50:25.130	00.009
2-3	7/1/2017 15:50:25.130	7/1/2017 15:50:25.138	00.008
3-4	7/1/2017 15:50:25.138	7/1/2017 15:50:25.145	00.007
4-5	7/1/2017 15:50:25.145	7/1/2017 15:50:25.152	00.007

5-6	7/1/2017 15:50:25.152	7/1/2017 15:50:28.159	**03.007**
6-7	7/1/2017 15:50:28.159	7/1/2017 15:50:28.160	00.001
7-8	7/1/2017 15:50:28.160	7/1/2017 15:50:28.160	00.000
8-9	7/1/2017 15:50:28.160	7/1/2017 15:50:28.160	00.000
9-10	7/1/2017 15:50:28.160	7/1/2017 15:50:28.161	00.001

Summary

I use three methods with both Extended Event and Profile Traces to diagnose the root cause of application slowness.

1. Start with a Long Running Query Trace, look for big, fat queries that are blocking processes and using excessive resources. Go for the easy win.

2. If that doesn't work, depending on if the issue is reproducible or not, do one or more "core sample" traces (duration set to 0). If you can filter a spid or application, do it. If it's reproducible, get a user involved with you, keep the trace defined to just that one activity (nice and clean). Have the user give you a screenshot so that you can look at the date displayed in the application versus what SQL is being asked for. Keep it short, these types of traces can be very hard on the SQL Server.

    a. Look for looping patterns.

    b. Look for repetitive statements by grouping and aggregating.

    c. Focus on eliminating looping or tuning the query that counts, even if you can only tune it a tiny bit. If it's called thousands of times for one user action, a tiny improvement can balloon into something meaningful.

3. If all of the above seems to be leading to a dead end, use the same Papercuts trace combined with recursion and CTEs to look for application pauses.

| Long Running Queries | Death by 1000 Paper Cuts | Application Pauses | **Method of Reviewing** |

| LRQ Trace | Papercuts Trace | | **Extended Event Session Type** |

Analogies and Nuggets

- Try to focus on only fixing the things that are causing the problem and just let the other stuff go.

- Respect the power of Extended Events and Profiler Traces. Machine Guns require careful handling or people get hurt.

- Big, fat, juicy LRQs are the "Holy Grail" of Performance Tuning. Cross your fingers and toes.

- A 24/7 Long Running Query Extended Event Session is like having a security camera in a 7-11 pointed at the door.

- ORMs, scalar functions, subqueries and looping all can cause Thousand Paper Cuts Syndrome.

- A single 1000-pound boulder is as hard to move as 1 million tiny pebbles that weigh the same amount. In fact, they are probably harder to move around because they are unwieldy.

- Diagnosing Paper Cuts or Application Pauses may require performing a wide-open trace with very little filtering. This type of trace may impact your SQL Server's performance while it runs, so keep it short.

- Aggregating statements from a granular trace can be informative, but challenging. Don't be afraid to use Excel.

- Using the times between calls to SQL Server as a "thing" to measure is not the traditional way to use Extended Event or Profiler Traces, but it works!

Chapter 7 **Using Extended** Events to figure out why an Application is slow

- Waitstats can't help you if the application is spending time doing "application stuff" and not talking to SQL.
- Remember to drill down if you find a Long Running Query. Sp_statement_completed is your magnifying glass to see what's going on within a complicated stored procedure.

Sponsors

Sentry One

SentryOne™ enables Microsoft data professionals to monitor, diagnose, and optimize performance across physical, virtual, and cloud environments. Our software provides unparalleled awareness, insight and control over the true source of performance issues.

SentryOne™ is proud to support Microsoft MVP's and professionals by sponsoring books such as this one. It is through amazing community initiatives that are helping to showcase the amazing women in all fields of technology.

About Us

Our highly regarded team, which includes 7 Microsoft MVPs, continually strives to find new and innovative ways to address the toughest performance challenges across the Microsoft Data Platform. Over the years, this has led to multiple ground-breaking capabilities for optimizing SQL Server performance, including our popular free query tuning tool, Plan Explorer.

The team is always working to spread their deep and diverse knowledge through blogging and speaking at conferences around the globe. Be sure to check out our upcoming events, our team blog at blogs.sentryone.com, and our community blog and query plan-sharing site at www.sqlperformance.com.

SentryOne is developed by SQL Sentry, LLC. We are headquartered in the beautiful Lake Norman area just outside of Charlotte, North Carolina. For the past two years we have been nominated as one of the "Best Places to Work" by the Charlotte Business Journal.

Our products are sold and supported directly and through authorized resellers and partners.

Sponsors **Sentry One**

Contact Information

704-895-6241

855-775-7733 toll-free

sales@sentryone.com

Corporate Office

8936 NorthPointe Executive Park Dr

Suite 200

Huntersville, NC 28078

Made in the USA
Lexington, KY
12 October 2017